Fear Itself

Also by Rush W. Dozier, Jr.

Codes of Evolution

Fear   Itself

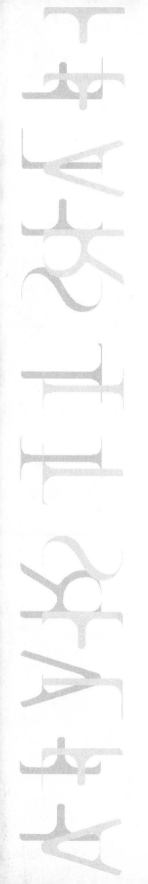

The Origin and Nature
of the Powerful Emotion That
Shapes Our Lives and Our World

{ Rush W. Dozier, Jr. }

St. Martin's Press
New York

THOMAS DUNNE BOOKS.
An imprint of St. Martin's Press.

FEAR ITSELF. Copyright © 1998 by Rush W. Dozier, Jr. All rights reserved. Printed in the United States of America. No part of this book may be used or reproduced in any manner whatsoever without written permission except in the case of brief quotations embodied in critical articles or reviews. For information, address St. Martin's Press, 175 Fifth Avenue, New York, N.Y. 10010.

Design by JUDITH STAGNITTO ABBATE

Library of Congress Cataloging-in-Publication Data

Dozier, Rush W.
    Fear itself : the origin and nature of the powerful emotion that shapes our lives and our world / Rush W. Dozier, Jr. — 1st ed.
        p.   cm.
    Includes bibliographical references and index.
    ISBN 0-312-19412-9 (hardcover)
    1. Fear.   2. Fear—Physiological aspects.
    I. Title.
BF575.F2D65   1998
152.4'6—dc21   98-21122
                                                            CIP

First Edition: November 1998
10 9 8 7 6 5 4 3 2 1

For my wife, Patricia.
This book is as much yours
as it is mine.

{ Contents }

{ Acknowledgments }

Helplessness is a persistent theme in any study of human fear. We dread it. We fight it. We avoid it. We are so much more comfortable without it. Yet like a recurring nightmare it manages to slip, usually without warning, into our lives—sometimes spectacularly, as when something goes terribly wrong on a ship or a plane, but usually in more mundane circumstances, as when some seemingly ordinary event veers alarmingly out of control. When we unexpectedly hit a patch of ice while driving a familiar route, that sickening, sinking feeling in the pit of the stomach is a universal signal of helpless fear.

A writer hits those icy patches all too frequently in the process of research and composition and it is a pleasure to acknowledge the people who help set things back on course, at least temporarily. My wife, Patricia, provided invaluable advice and assistance at every stage of this challenging project. I hope portions of this book convey in some small way the fun I had growing up. For these warm memories, I would like to thank my parents and my brother, Ray. I have had to look no further than my daughter, Beverly, for an inspiring example of phenomenal bravery. At St. Martin's Press my editor, Tom Dunne, associate editor Melissa Jacobs, copy editor Deborah Miller, and production editor Bert Yaeger have been exceptionally helpful.

Of the many people I have consulted on this project, I would like to single out a few for special thanks. Writer-director James Cameron graciously took time out from a busy schedule to help me understand the many dimensions of fear in his extraordinary film *Titanic*. Congressman Randy "Duke" Cunningham, a legendary Navy fighter pilot who now represents the northern section of San Diego County, gave me an exhilarating sense of what air combat was like during the Vietnam War. I have greatly benefited from the advice, comments, and general wisdom of Joseph LeDoux, Henry and Lucy Moses Professor of Science, New York University, Antonio Damasio, M.W. Van Allen Professor and head of the Department of Neurology at the University of Iowa College of Medicine, Thomas Albright, professor and director of the Sloan Center for Theoretical Neurobiology at the Salk Institute in La Jolla, California, James McGaugh, director of the Center for the Neurobiology of Learning and Memory at the University of California at Irvine, Douglas Galesko, associate professor of neuroscience, University of California at San Diego, and reference librarian Martin Hollick of Harvard University's Lamont and Widener libraries. Although I have profited from the insights of many in the writing of this book, responsibility for the contents and conclusions of *Fear Itself* is mine alone.

{ Part I }

The Origin of Fear

What is that thunder that booms within my chest,
That lightning that crashes in my head?
What is that silence so still it cannot be heard,
That darkness I cannot see when I am dead?
It is the unknown, permeating my body and
  stopping my mind.
I know only its looming shadow;
And that shadow is fear.

—Patricia June Dozier

{ Chapter 1 }

What Is Fear?

It is the quintessential human emotion. Some people live lives devoid of joy, happiness, and pleasure but no one escapes the experience of fear and fear's companion, pain. We are born in fear and pain. Our lives are profoundly shaped by them, as well as our efforts to avoid them. We die in fear and pain.

Fear of death, disease, injury, poverty, and countless other fears mold the most mundane aspects of our existence: what we eat, how we drive, where we work. Yet fear also molds our highest nature and the grandest tides of world history. By facing and overcoming our fears, we mature and fulfill our deepest human potential. Fear can make us embrace or deny God, choose good over evil. It can start wars, or end them. Our attitude toward fear dictates how societies are structured. Do we trust people to govern themselves or do we base our social controls on terror, violence, secret police, and hatred of outsiders?

What is fear? Where does it come from? What purpose does it serve? Why are some fears universal? Why do others differ from person to person and culture to culture? Can fear be enjoyed? Can we die of it? Live without it? How can fear be transformed from a destructive to a constructive force in our lives? This book will explore all these questions in a wide-ranging examination of this universal human emotion and its pervasive effects on individuals and societies. For the first time in history, we are in a position to provide scientific insights and concrete answers— revealing the nature of fear itself.

At sixteen I was like every other teenager in America who had just gotten his driver's license. I wanted to joyride with my friends. The feeling of freedom and independence was delicious. The feeling of responsibility was less intense. Frankly, I'm amazed any of us survived to adulthood.

One Saturday night, five of us piled into my best friend's car. I was riding shotgun—sitting on the passenger side of the front seat. The summer night was soft and beautiful as we cruised along a country road through the corn and soybean fields of western Kentucky. Unexpectedly the car of another friend, also packed with teenagers, passed us going the other way. The second car slammed on its brakes and did a quick U-turn. The chase was on.

Our car accelerated down the narrow road, headed toward what seemed to be a gentle curve. At that speed it wasn't. Halfway through the curve we began drifting, out of control, off the road toward a high dirt embankment bordering a cornfield. The experience was terrifying. Time slowed down. As I stared out my window, the embankment seemed to move toward me in slow motion. I was frozen in my seat drenched in a sudden clammy sweat with an awful sinking feeling in the pit of my stomach. My pulse pounded in my ears. I was vividly aware of every blade of grass on that embankment.

With a loud bang, we hit. The car bounced in the air to the other side of the road and came to a stop. Everyone piled out. Miraculously no one was even scratched. I can't say the same for the car. Over the next half hour we milled around in a daze, counting our blessings and waiting for my friend's father to drive out and take us home.

What I experienced was a classic fear reaction. Simply put, fear is the body's way of anticipating and avoiding pain and the danger's pain signals: injury and death. At that moment I thought I was going to die. A series of automatic physical changes designed to maximize my chances of survival took place in my body.

Much of my blood was immediately diverted to the large muscles, particularly my legs, so that I would have the maximum energy necessary for a quick escape. The draining of blood away from the skin produces the characteristic paleness of fear. Perspiration oozing out of my pale, cool skin produced the sensation of a cold sweat. The pounding I heard was my overwrought heart at work and my skyrocketing blood pressure.

Quick-energy hormones like adrenaline were pouring into my blood-stream and muscles. Sometimes this reaction goes awry and so much blood is diverted to the large muscles and away from the brain that a person faints. The odd feeling in my stomach was my digestive system contracting and turning off as all nonessential systems shut down in preparation for the escape.

The momentary feeling of being frozen in place is also a characteristic reaction to fear. Scientists believe this serves a variety of purposes. Most importantly, it forces you to concentrate on every possible avenue of escape. This concentration is accompanied by a dramatic sharpening of perception, stimulated by an instant flood of chemicals into the brain. The eyes widen and the pupils of the eyes expand to take in the maximum amount of information. In my case, every detail of my surroundings came so sharply into focus that it seemed unreal. My very perception of time slowed. This kind of dramatic fear experience produces long-lasting and detailed memories. We remember best what threatens us most. Our survival depends on it. Several decades later I can still recall the event with startling clarity.

Fear is our most primal emotion. Evolution has wired our nervous system in such a way that intense fear takes precedence over everything else in our minds and bodies. When faced with a life-threatening danger, we instantly lose our desire for sex, food, or anything else other than to deal with the peril. Our reproductive system, digestive system, and all other secondary systems shut down almost instantly as the brain mobilizes the body for fight or flight. Fear is fundamental because life is fundamental. If we die, then everything else becomes irrelevant. Fear evolved in the earliest ancestors of all the animals living today. Virtually every type of animal, from fruit fly to monkey, experiences fear.

Charles Darwin was the first scientist to study the evolution of emotions systematically. In his 1872 classic *The Expression of Emotions in Man and Animals* he concluded that "fear was expressed from an extremely remote period in almost the same manner as it now is by man. . . ." The earliest ancestors of human beings dealt with danger and their enemies by "headlong flight, or by violently struggling with them; and such great exertions will have caused the heart to beat rapidly, the breathing to be hurried, the chest to heave, and the nostrils to be dilated." These responses to fear are part of our evolutionary heritage.[1]

Fear is one of our most basic emotions. The word "emotion" comes from the Latin word *motere*, which means "to move." The word "motivation" has the same root. Patients with extensive brain damage that destroys their emotional centers often lose their motivation to carry on everyday activities and become apathetic, even catatonic. "Fear" is derived from the Old English word for danger. The emotion of fear has evolved to move us away from danger.

Because it is found in so many species, fear has become a premier window on the mysteries of the brain. It allows neuroscientists to study the fear circuits of animals with relatively simple brains and use this research to ferret out universal mechanisms, not just of fear but of all forms of memory, emotion, behavior, and learning. Other animals not only feel fear, they learn from it just as we do. In the laboratory, a rat can be taught to associate the sound of a bell with a mild electrical shock to its feet. Thereafter whenever the rat hears the bell it will freeze, fearing what is to follow, even if the shock never comes. The rat has learned to fear the bell. Researchers can study the rat's fear-conditioned brain to see what changes have accompanied this learning.

Through understanding fear we understand ourselves. Fear is something humans have in abundance—more, I believe, than any other species. Science calls human beings *Homo sapiens:* wise man. A better name might be fearful man. Within the animal kingdom, we humans are the connoisseurs of fear. Our big brains harbor vastly more fears than any other animal. Why? Because we are so unspecialized and vulnerable to every change in climate, every predator, every disease. By nature's standards, the individual human being is naked, weak, unprotected, clumsy. We have neither the speed of a jaguar, the strength of a lion, the eye of a hawk, nor the endurance of a camel. We are burdened by children who will quickly die if not given years of careful attention. The young of most other animals need only a few weeks or months of nurturing before becoming independent, if they need any nurturing at all. We must clothe and shelter ourselves without the benefit of fur or feathers or the instincts of a nesting bird. We can eat almost anything, plant or animal, but first we must learn to separate the nutritious from the noxious and deadly. Every large predator—bear, big cat, wolf—is at least as strong as we are, usually much stronger, and comes equipped with better teeth, claws, and keener senses. Even our sex lives reflect this uncommon fearfulness. We are unique among social mammals in having sex almost exclusively in private. All our social cousins among mammals, from rats to monkeys, have sex openly without the slightest embarrassment.

The depth and breadth of our fear is our unique burden as a species, but evolution has also made it our uncommon strength. Every animal learns to fear the things in its environment that cause injury or pain. This learning is centered in its brain, usually modest in size. But human beings have evolved a huge conscious brain, not only for remembering our endless variety of fears, but for analyzing, classifying, unraveling, and neutralizing them. Because we have much to fear, we have much to learn. And this immense store of knowledge that we communicate using another extraordinary evolutionary creation—rich, complex language— has allowed us in less than ten thousand years, a microsecond in geological time, to become the dominant large animal on earth.

By conquering our fears we have conquered the planet. We often think of ourselves as different from other species because we use tools. Yet chimpanzees and other animals are also observed to use crude tools. We have a complex language, but so do honeybees. The truly striking differ- ence between human beings and other species is the ability our big brain gave us to overcome the one fear no other social animal on earth has ever conquered: the fear of fire. Our entire civilization is based on that triumph of early humans. Fire allowed us to conquer the night and intimidate the predators that lurk there. It allowed us to expand out of tropical and subtropical regions and colonize the earth's colder climates. We use it to cook our food and smelt our metals. We studied forms of fire like lightning to discover the secrets of electricity, which powers our electronic age. Fire ignites the fuel for our vehicles. It fuels the chemical reactions that create the materials out of which everything around us is constructed, including the gunpowder we use to kill each other. We ride plumes of fire to other planets. We are, in short, the fire masters.

Being a fear-driven species, however, makes us unstable. We can mold our fear of disease and death into magnificent scientific enterprises that conquer thousands of ailments: smallpox, cholera, polio, and, perhaps someday soon, cancer and AIDS. Yet uncontrolled and primitive fear also breeds hatred and sparks rivalries and bloody conflicts that have killed tens of millions of people in this century alone and threaten the world with nuclear and environmental devastation.

In humans, fear has evolved beyond the traditional animal role of anticipating and avoiding physical pain. In us, it has become the brain's way of anticipating and avoiding mental pain as well—the injuries to our psyche that we call by such names as humiliation, sorrow, regret, guilt, despair. We not only fear for our physical well-being and dread the physical pain of an injury but also the mental anguish we will feel if something happens to us: if we are paralyzed in an automobile accident or develop cancer. Chimpanzees, gorillas, dogs, and some of the other social animals show signs of experiencing psychic pain, particularly grief. In humans, however, this mental realm of fear has blossomed into an elaborate range of emotions, from slight embarrassment to deep depression. Fear of mental pain produces exactly the same physical symptoms as fear of physical pain. If I am unexpectedly asked to stand up and address a large group of people on an unfamiliar topic, my instant apprehension will set off the whole fear response: dry mouth, riveted attention, pounding heart, a surge of adrenaline.

Our capacity for mental suffering tremendously expands the role of fear in our lives. Because of it, we fear not only for ourselves but for others we care about. We worry about the safety of our children not only because of the damage an injury would do to their bodies, but also because of what it would do to our minds. And this exponential expansion of fear does not stop with other people. It includes the things we care about as well. We fear that our house will burn down or that our car will be stolen.

My fascination with fear began in Harvard Yard in the spring of 1969. I was a freshman interested in science and public policy and living in the Yard, the oldest part of Harvard. Yet I found myself endlessly distracted and bemused. The sixties swirled around me, bubbling with hope—and fear: fear of the Vietnam War and of dying in a distant land, fear of the Establishment, fear of anyone over thirty. Radical ideas in culture and politics blossomed everywhere. Among the most seductive of these was revolution, and one day that spring a small group of radical activists decided to start one. Shortly after noon on April 9, they marched into University Hall, the administration building in the center of Harvard Yard, threw out the administrators, and issued a list of non-negotiable demands.

That night was a high-water mark for the counterculture. The Yard pulsed with rock music, a huge psychedelic light show, and psychoactive drugs. It was the strangest party Harvard had seen in its 333 years. I remember wandering through the crowds that swarmed among the stately buildings, thinking how the mighty had fallen. But the Establishment had fears of its own.

Very early the next morning hundreds of riot police marched into the Yard. What followed came to be called the Bust—a classic sixties melee with baton-swinging cops and screaming students and radicals. The radicals were thrown out. I attended a packed protest meeting at Memorial Church in the Yard later that morning. It was my first brush with mob psychology and mass hysteria, two of the most striking manifestations of fear. Speaker after speaker, some with bloody bandages, told of being beaten and dragged off to jail. They shouted their hatred of the police and the university administration. It was hard not to be swept up by these explosive emotions. Harvard would never be quite the same. Fear and defiance had caused the takeover of University Hall. Fear had caused the administration to overreact. Here in America's oldest university, a bastion of reflection and scholarship, fear swept away all hope of compromise and rational discussion.

Two years later I had a chance to study another aspect of fear. My roommate and I won a grant from the Institute of Politics at Harvard to study the pharmaceutical industry for our honors theses. I became intrigued by the tremendous strides medical science has made in developing psychotropic drugs—drugs that affect the mood by altering brain chemistry—and how these drugs play into our national obsession with two common manifestations of fear: stress and anxiety. The enormous demand for some simple solution to stress led to the blatant overprescription of antianxiety drugs like Librium and Valium. This phenomenon continues to this day with the wild popularity of antidepressants like Prozac. It is not by chance that some of the most widely prescribed drugs in the world are used to treat the effects of fear and depression.

Over the years as a writer and government official I have had the opportunity to work with some of the world's top scientists and explore my continuing interest in fear. Neuroscience is making astonishing breakthroughs in understanding the evolution of fear and the detailed mechanisms by which it is produced in the brain. Although this is a young science with many controversies and unanswered questions, we now understand fear better than any other emotion. The implications of these discoveries are stunning, both for our personal lives and for our continued survival on this planet.

Neuroscience has accumulated a growing body of research revealing that the human brain has at least three separate but interconnected systems for reacting to and processing fear. Given the astounding complexity of the brain, finding these fear pathways is one of the great milestones in human history. In the next chapter I will discuss the intricate and surprising anatomical and electrochemical details of these systems. For now, let me just give you a sketch of how they work in action.

system is extremely ancient and is found not only in mammals,
tiles, fish, birds, and most other animals. Let's call it the
fear system. Think of almost any wild animal—a fox, for exam-
t happens if you approach it? It flees into the underbrush. And
what would happen if you managed to catch it? It would struggle wildly,
biting and scratching, fighting desperately to escape. When in danger,
the behavioral repertoire of most animals is simple: fight or flight. This
primal reaction to threats, which evolved hundreds of millions of years
ago, is the foundation of all our reactions to fear.

The primitive fear system, which governs this primal emotional reaction, operates outside direct conscious and rational control. We detect
danger automatically, whether we are paying attention or not, and our
bodies are automatically prepared to respond to it. This fear system is
centered deep within the brain in an extremely old structure called the
limbic system. It was the primitive fear system that galvanized my mind
and body in the automobile accident. Unchecked, however, this primitive
system can lead to phobias, irrational anxieties, panic attacks, obsessive-
compulsive disorder, paranoia, and post-traumatic stress syndrome. The
primitive fear system produces a rapid emotional first impression of
everything we experience—do we like what is happening to us or dislike
it? If the primitive fear system registers an intense enough level of dislike,
it will trigger a massive fear response.

In mammals, and particularly human beings, the primitive fear system
intimately incorporates the complex processing areas of the cerebral cortex, the heavily folded six-layer structure that covers the outside of the
brain like a thin, wrinkled skin. This astonishing organ of thought contains more than half of all the billions of nerve cells in the brain. It is
the seat of our higher cognitive functions, including rationality and planning. The human cerebral cortex has expanded tremendously over the
last million years, which is why we have such large heads—heads so
large that the birth of a human baby is far more dangerous and painful
than that of any other animal. The primitive system has extensive connections with the cortex, which processes the data provided by our senses
to give the brain an image of the outside world. At a very early stage of
cortical processing of sensory data, prior even to our conscious awareness
of it, the cortex flashes the rough image to the primitive fear system,
which then decides whether the image presents a danger. Over the next
brief period—measured in thousandths of a second—the cerebral cortex
refines and sharpens the rough, partially processed sensory information

on which the primitive system has made its initial, rapid decision to fight or flee. It does this by filtering the information through regions of the cortex that pull together the separate streams of incoming data from our eyes, ears, and the other senses, linking them with our memories. As the cortex generates an ever clearer and more comprehensive image from the sensory data, it continually flashes the improved image to the primitive system. Based on this refined information, the primitive fear system can reassess whether its initial decision was correct. If it has already triggered a fight-or-flight response, it can modify it or call it off completely.

The second fear system is slower and even more elaborate. It operates within the massive frontal lobes of the cerebral cortex, particularly the prefrontal cortex, which lies just under the forehead. This complex system applies an extremely sophisticated analysis to the information it monitors from the primitive system and the cortex. It allows us to assess rationally the nature of a specific fear and weigh many different possibilities and options, including responses that are far more intricate than simply fight or flight. Instead of fleeing it might try to bluff. Rather than fighting it might suggest negotiation. I call this second system the *rational fear system.* The rational fear system's decision may be slower in coming, but it is comprehensive and carefully considered compared to the instant analysis of the primitive fear system.

The primitive fear system kicks in around the first tenth of a second after our initial perception, prior to conscious awareness. The rational fear system begins to operate when the sensory data processed by the cortex enter conscious awareness a fraction of a second later. But the rational system does not encompass the entire potential of the brain. There is one final fear system, the most powerful of them all: *consciousness itself,* nature's fantastically advanced evolutionary response to the problem of fear. When we are in a dangerous situation, the primitive fear system stimulates an intense form of alertness to any potential threat. Consciousness, which evolved out of the older limbic fear system in early mammals, is an elaboration of this kind of alertness. Even when many of the brain structures underlying the primitive and rational fear systems are destroyed, consciousness continues to exist.

The primitive fear system is the brain's early warning system and the instigator of our emotional response to every experience. After making its initial decision about whether a fight-or-flight response is necessary, the primitive system works with the cortex to refine the mass of information flowing through our senses into the increasingly sharp perceptions needed to double-check its decision. It can influence the cortex to shift its attention from one aspect of what is going on around us to another. Even if no significant fear response is called for, the primitive fear system conveys into conscious awareness its emotional first impression of what we are experiencing. The rational fear system is the planner, spinning out the possibilities and scenarios we need to consider consciously in order sensibly to counter immediate threats and those we foresee in the future. Consciousness is the supreme decision maker. Although science is still at a loss to explain how the brain creates consciousness, we do have a good idea of its function. Consciousness mediates conflicts between the primitive and rational systems, between emotion and reason. It decides which of the rational system's options to select. It can seek to halt the primitive system's fight-or-flight response. But this isn't easy. The primitive fear system is opinionated, stubborn, and simplistic. It is the source of our phobias, which are notoriously difficult to eliminate consciously. If my primitive system decides it doesn't like heights, then it doesn't like any heights. It ignores my rational fear system's careful distinction between teetering on the edge of a thousand-foot cliff (dangerous) and standing in the glass-enclosed observation deck atop the Sears Tower in Chicago (safe). To the primitive system, heights are heights and it will trigger potent responses at both the cliff and the Sears Tower.

Consciousness must draw on the full power of the cerebral cortex and its interconnections with the rest of the brain to contend with the primitive fear system. Because of the sophistication of its neural network, consciousness can do much more than just quickly analyze and weigh options at the moment of crisis. Over hours, days, weeks, even years, we can consciously employ all our brain's elaborate learning and memory systems to study a threat, learn more about it, share information with others, use our imagination and creativity, and come up with a strategy to avoid or neutralize it next time. Thus consciousness not only decides, it reflects. It is through our conscious awareness as very young children that we first come to know ourselves as independent beings in a challenging world. When we lose consciousness, we seem to cease to exist. We are our consciousness.

Because our species is so vulnerable, we must be exceptionally alert to everything around us so we can defend ourselves. Our brains have increased in size over the course of human evolution, allowing us to comprehend a greater and greater amount of the world in which we live. Consciousness is the supreme defensive system—a pervasive state of alertness that constantly anticipates and analyzes threats from the environment. The key to this system is a model within our minds of the world and its potential dangers. Our enormous brain allows us to create a continuously updated mental model that is far more comprehensive than any other animal's. We are consciously aware of our own existence on a fragile planet that spins around one star in an immense universe. No other animal knows that. We understand that our planet is vulnerable to the kind of stray asteroid that may have driven the dinosaurs to extinction. No other animal knows that asteroids exist, or that dinosaurs ever existed. Our huge range of fears flows from the incredibly complex model of the world that we carry in our heads. The fact that consciousness is an elaboration of the fear mechanism explains much about human nature and human civilization.

Panic is the hallmark of the primitive fear system. This system evolved to meet the primal needs of the savage, brutish, life-or-death environment of one hundred thousand years ago, an environment in which most human beings never reached their thirtieth birthday. The responses of this ancient system are often highly inappropriate in a modern technological society. Whereas a fear of heights warned early man away from cliffs and other high places, modern individuals routinely work in skyscrapers and travel in airplanes six miles above the earth. Most of the problems fear causes— in our personal lives, our societies, and among nations—arise from our failure to use the mental resources of the conscious mind to keep our primitive emotions in check. We now know techniques that enable consciousness and the rational fear system to control these fears effectively. Such scientifically proven techniques allow people literally to rewire their brains and alter their thought patterns. Yet I will also show that fear— even primitive fear—is frequently constructive and, in fact, an essential element of our dynamic nature. Fear brings out the best and the worst in human beings.

Consider an example of how the three fear systems interact. One day not long ago my wife, Pat, and I were taking a morning walk near the Santa Monica Mountains north of Los Angeles. We were enjoying an animated conversation and weren't paying very much attention to our surroundings, though it was a beautiful, sunny day. Suddenly my wife screamed and practically jumped out of her shoes. Instantaneously I glanced down to where she was walking. I saw something—a shape— but before what it was could register in my mind I let out a yelp and sprinted down the path. Side by side, my wife and I dashed about twenty yards before we regained our self-possession and stopped. Only then did I look back and realize that just on the edge of the path was a two-foot-long gopher snake that had been sunning itself. My wife had accidentally stepped on it. We looked at each other and laughed at our overreaction—neither of us has any particular fear of snakes—then went back to see if the snake was all right. Still sluggish in the cool morning air and possibly a little stunned after its encounter with us, the snake stayed where it was for a few minutes, soaking up a little more sunshine as we admired the intricate pattern on its skin. Then it slithered into the underbrush, apparently no worse for the wear.

What went on in my brain when I heard my wife scream and saw her jump? My head automatically jerked down to look where she was walking. I was only barely aware of the twisted shape on the path. "Snake," screamed my primitive fear system and I bolted away from the potential danger before I consciously knew what it was. As I reacted, the visual information from my eyes that the primitive system interpreted as being a snake was being filtered and sharpened through the cerebral cortex. If this enhanced image had indicated to the primitive system that what I had seen was a rattlesnake, my wife and I would probably have run a lot farther. Amid this frenzy of neural and physical activity, my slower, rational system was analyzing the same visual perceptions, applying all the relevant knowledge stored in my brain. I don't remember my exact train of thought but I probably reasoned that nothing I had seen indicated that the snake was poisonous. At that point I was conscious of what was happening and I decided to stop and take another look despite the fact that my primitive system was still pouring adrenaline into my bloodstream.

Joseph LeDoux, a professor of neural science and psychology, and his colleagues at New York University discovered many important mechanisms underlying the primitive fear system by studying the brains of fear-conditioned rats. "Failing to respond to danger," says LeDoux, "is more costly than responding inappropriately to a benign stimulus. . . . We do not need to go through a detailed analysis of whether or not what we are seeing is a snake. Nor do we need to think about the fact that snakes are reptiles and that their skins can be used to make belts and boots. All these details are irrelevant and, in fact, detrimental to an efficient, speedy and potentially lifesaving reaction. The brain simply needs to be able to store primitive cues and detect them. Later, coordination of the basic information with the cortex permits verification (yes, this is a snake) or brings the response (screaming, hyperventilation, sprinting) to a stop."[2]

Even after I stop running, the debate between the rational and primitive fear systems is not over. Should I go back to lo at the snake? Yes or no? Let's say I'm frightened of snakes—absolutely detest them. The rational system might conclude, "Yes, it's a snake, but it's only a gopher snake and they're harmless. Relax." But the primitive system's strongly negative attitude might prompt a fearful thought—"I don't care what kind it is, snakes make my skin crawl"—and result in a conscious decision not to return.

What if I felt guilty or stupid at being afraid of the snake? How might I cope with that feeling? If I went to the library that night and read a book about snakes recounting that most snakes are not poisonous, showing me exactly how to recognize those that are, and telling me that snakes are useful in keeping down populations of rodents and other pests, I would be employing the powers of conscious reflection. I might be able to use this information to modify my behavior consciously, overcoming my fear of harmless snakes and refining my remaining fear to focus only on those that are poisonous. But as we shall see, extinguishing primitive fears can be a very difficult process.

We've all experienced this tension when consciousness must referee between the primitive and rational fear systems in times of stress or danger. The primitive system speaks in strong emotions that we sense immediately and that the brain's language centers translate into words. If you are driving one winter's day and suddenly skid on an icy patch in the road, you might find yourself muttering: "Don't panic. Don't panic." You fight to stay calm and steer the wheels of your car in the direction of the skid, as your rational system struggles with your skittish primitive system.

The three fear systems are an example of parallel processing, an organizing principle frequently found in the brain. When multiple parallel systems do the same or similar things at roughly the same time, each can verify and complement the other. If one system is damaged, the brain's entire ability to perform the overall function is not lost. The brain will still have another one intact. Yet multiple systems can also mean multiple conflicts within the mind. Consciousness and the rational fear system seek to modulate the primitive system's fear response by using a kind of neural volume control, turning the response up or down as necessary. This task can be fairly easy or extremely difficult depending on the strength of the primitive system's reaction, which can range from mild anxiety to stark terror.

Imagine that I am about to begin a hike in the woods. My rational fear system begins churning out options and possibilities. One possibility is that I might see a snake. Since I'm afraid of snakes (let's assume), just the thought of a snake triggers a minor alarm in my primitive fear system, making me breathe a little harder. This is an example of anxiety rather than fear. The usual distinction is that fear is caused by external stimuli (seeing a snake), while anxiety is caused by internal cognitive processes only (thinking about a snake). The distinction is actually somewhat arbitrary since both anxiety and fear produce exactly the same physical reactions. I prefer to view anxiety not as something distinct from fear but as a characteristically human subtype of fear that focuses on the future: what might happen, as opposed to fear of what is happening now.

Mildly upset by my twinge of snake anxiety, I amble along in the woods. Consciously I reassure myself that the chance of encountering a snake is remote. Some way into the woods I hear a noise ahead of me. My heart beats faster as I begin to feel fearful. Again I reassure myself that it's probably nothing and I continue walking, sensitive to every little sound. I catch sight of a large snake in the brush near me. Startled, I jump back, but I realize I've been bitten. If my rational fear system in its analysis of what happened concludes the snake is poisonous, it would signal the primitive system and instantly begin planning a route for me to rush to the nearest hospital. The primitive system would immediately turn up the fear response, increasing my heart rate, blood pressure, sweating, and flow of adrenaline. I would be feeling terrified. Consciously, however, I might remember the effects of snake venom and realize that my intense fear is dangerous because increased heart rate pumps the poison more rapidly through my system. But my primitive system has been highly aroused by the possibly mortal threat and it would take an exceptional exercise of will to calm myself down.

The primitive system's fast reaction to danger is always the same: fight or flight. The only question is how hard you fight or how fast you flee. Whenever you are faced with an unanticipated threat, there is a struggle for control of your behavior. The outcome of the struggle between these two systems, as refereed by consciousness, can sometimes mean the difference between life and death.

As a newspaper editor, I was involved in covering one of the worst nightclub fires in American history—the May 28, 1977, Beverly Hills

Supper Club fire near Cincinnati, Ohio. The club had twenty-one private dining rooms connected by a maze of corridors. The blaze broke out just as singer John Davidson was about to perform. The fire spread quickly through the ventilation system. When people realized what was happening, they swarmed out of the dining rooms into the corridors, trying to find their way out. In the smoke and confusion there was panic. In an instant, common sense and concern for others were obliterated. The primitive flight response took over. In the stampede to find the exits the faster ran over the slower and the stronger tried to shove past the weaker. The result was predictable: chaos and disaster. One hundred sixty-four men and women were crushed, suffocated, and burned to death. Another one hundred thirty were injured. Officials later estimated that if there had been a calm, orderly, and rapid evacuation, many fewer would have died. Sometimes in moments of extreme danger the primitive fear system can overwhelm both the rational system and consciousness itself.

This is not a simple issue, however. Whenever you find an evolutionary feature like the primitive fear system that has been around for millions of years, it is unwise to jump to conclusions and dismiss it as completely outdated. There are plenty of occasions in which action beats knowledge and panic is better than thought. Imagine, for example, that I am waiting at a busy street corner, glancing at the headlines in the newspaper I just bought. Abruptly I jump back as a car swerves out of control up and over the curb, right through the spot I was just standing. Only as I jump back do I consciously realize that, out of the corner of my eye, I had seen something coming toward me. The primitive fear system saved my life. The primitive system works fast, before I am even consciously aware of it, taking just a fraction of a second to interpret sensory data and activate the fight-or-flight response in my body. All I noticed was a dark blob moving toward me. If I had waited even the few extra thousandths of a second for my cerebral cortex to enhance the image and tell me it was a careering car, I might have been run down.

Let's say I'm standing in the middle of a packed Centennial Park during a festival in the center of Atlanta, Georgia, and somehow over the din of the crowd and the blare of the entertainers I hear a nearby security guard say something about a bomb. I have several choices. I can panic and get the hell out of there. I can be a bit more rational and move away quickly, without panicking. Or I might choose to satisfy completely the analytical demands of my rational fear system by asking questions. Did he really say "bomb"? Couldn't it be a hoax? Where is this bomb?

If I had actually been in this situation at the 1996 Atlanta Olympic Games, asking too many questions might have gotten me killed by delaying my flight from the bomb's vicinity. Fleeing was the better choice.

What causes fear to give way to terror, hysteria, and panic? To some extent the reaction varies from person to person. You probably know anxious, excitable people. Their primitive fear systems are strong compared to their rational ones and their conscious control. They panic easily. You probably also know people who are masters of their emotions. Either by nature or through discipline, their rational fear systems consciously dominate the primitive system, keeping their emotions tightly controlled. Despite these differences in temperament, there are general variables that influence the level of fear in any given individual. One obvious variable is the nature of the threat. A sudden life-or-death situation generates intense fear and the tendency to panic. Another important variable is the sense of helplessness or control in a frightening situation.

I have always been amazed by the sensationalized news coverage of airplane crashes. Airline travel is remarkably safe. A year or more may go by with no fatal crash of a commercial airliner in the United States. Yet when there is a crash, the media saturate us with coverage for weeks or even months. Why this horrified fascination with airline crashes? Automobile accidents kill tens of thousands of people a year, far more than the few hundred killed in airline accidents. Of course, more people are killed in an airline disaster than in an automobile accident. And the very rarity of plane crashes makes them noteworthy. But something more is going on.[3]

Why are we uneasy about flying? Why does even the most experienced air traveler sometimes feel a twinge of fear? Because flying involves a terrible sense of vulnerability. You are helpless if anything happens. Your chance of surviving in a crippled plane headed for the ground at five hundred miles an hour is practically nil. And you know that if something goes wrong in a plane at thirty thousand feet, you'll have a long time to think about it before you hit the ground. This kind of helplessness generates the most extreme form of fear reaction: terror. We are petrified at the thought of experiencing it.

Charles Darwin graphically described the phenomenon of abject terror. "The heart beats wildly, or may fail to act and faintness ensue; there is a death-like pallor; the breathing is labored; the wings of the nostrils are widely dilated; there is a gasping and convulsive motion of the lips . . . a gulping and catching of the throat; the uncovered and protruding eyeballs are fixed on the object of terror. . . . As fear rises to an extreme pitch, the dreadful scream of terror is heard. Great beads of sweat stand on the skin. All the muscles of the body are relaxed. Utter prostration soon follows and the mental powers fail. The intestines are affected. The sphincter muscles cease to act, and no longer retain the contents of the body." The tiny muscles surrounding each hair follicle contract and the hair can literally stand on end, just as the fur rises on the back of a frightened cat. The purpose of this reaction in the cat and the human is the same: to make us "appear larger and more terrible" to our "enemies or rivals."[4]

In the Beverly Hills Supper Club case, people felt completely helpless once the shouts of "fire" began. The blaze spread quickly. It was beyond their control. The only thing to do was escape. Their fear swiftly escalated to terror and panic.

Fire victims and airline passengers are helpless and vulnerable. Airplane pilots are another story. Whereas many passengers feel an occasional shudder at the thought of flying, pilots almost never do. Their control over the aircraft compensates for the potential dangers. But what about the pilots of a doomed plane? Their control, again, makes a crucial difference. Transcripts from cockpit voice recorders—one of the "black boxes" that usually survive the crash—indicate that in most cases the attitude of the crew is tense but completely focused on saving the plane. There may be a few curses, but most of the conversation revolves around finding a way out of danger. There is rarely a sign of panic.

Yet even the best pilots can be terrified if they start to feel helpless. Take, for example, legendary test pilot Chuck Yeager, the first man to break the sound barrier. Yeager, a colorful West Virginian, was a World War II fighter ace who once shot down a German Messerschmitt jet while flying a propeller-driven P–51 Mustang. He is famous for his ability to keep his emotions in check, even in ferocious air-to-air combat.

"You fought wide open, full-throttle," Yeager said. "There was no joy in killing someone, but real satisfaction when you outflew a guy and destroyed his machine. . . . The excitement of those dogfights never diminished. For me, combat remains the ultimate flying experience."[5]

One of the themes in this book will be how men and women like Chuck Yeager—the daredevils, the risk takers, the heroes—not only cope with fear, but come to relish being in extremely dangerous situations. Studies have shown that virtually all cultures admire courage. We will try to make the phenomenon of courage—what Tom Wolfe called "the right stuff"—more understandable using the latest insights into the workings of the brain.

Yeager once had serious difficulty handling fear. It happened while he was flying the Bell X–1, the rocket plane now hanging in the Smithsonian Institution that he used to break the sound barrier. It wasn't the danger that bothered him. Or the fact that the X–1's engineers told him he would be cut in half by the thin wings of the thirty-one-foot-long aircraft if he tried to bail out. Or even the belief by many of his colleagues that the X–1 would disintegrate if it ever hit Mach 1—the sound barrier, six-hundred-sixty miles per hour at forty thousand feet. Yeager was confident that with his knowledge of the aircraft he could get himself out of any predicament. But then something came up that he could not understand. He felt helpless, and it drove him crazy.

Testing the X–1 involved dropping the small rocket plane from a B–29 bomber at twenty thousand to thirty thousand feet. Yeager would then turn on the plane's jet engines and begin flying. Starting in late January 1948, three months after Yeager reached Mach 1, the plane began experiencing an unexplained problem. Every time Yeager ignited the rocket engines, his control panel would flash a fire warning light and the cockpit would fill with smoke. He would have to cut the engines, dump his fuel, and glide back to the dry lake bed at Edwards Air Force Base. His ground crew tore the engines apart and put them back together, piece by piece, but nothing helped. Flight after flight the same thing happened. Although Yeager kept his cool exterior, inside he was in turmoil.

"I was scared," he recalled. "I crawled into the X–1 feeling like a condemned man. And I began having real bad nightmares, dreaming I was being burned alive inside the X–1, only to have Glennis [his wife] shake me awake just as I was trying to jump out of our bedroom window that was shaped like the X–1 door."[6]

Finally the problem was found. The wrong gaskets had been installed during an engine overhaul. The fires stopped and so did the nightmares.

Because of the unique structure of our primitive fear system, we sometimes irrationally prefer relatively dangerous situations, in which we have some measure of control, to much safer ones in which we feel completely vulnerable. We find elements of this irrationality in our instinctive emotional assessment of the comparative risks of automobile versus airline travel. Taking a plane from New York to Los Angeles is statistically far safer than driving a few blocks to the local grocery store for a carton of milk. Yet it is hard to feel that truth deep down because of the primitive fear system's abhorrence of any situation that might lead to helpless terror. We feel much calmer behind the wheel of a car, not simply because we are more accustomed to driving than flying. Studies have shown that even people who practically live in airports because of their constant travel fear a plane crash far more than a serious automobile accident.

This instinctive overconfidence when we are in control can lead to irrational, foolish behavior. We often drive too fast and too inattentively. We demand the highest standards of safety for commercial airlines, but our standards for highway and automobile safety are far lower. Though your rational fear system may warn you to be careful when you drive, the wiring of your primitive fear system makes it easy to become lackadaisical. The results of this quirk in the primitive system are painfully obvious: a comparative handful of airline deaths every year, and more than forty thousand lives lost on the highways. Evolution has, nevertheless, provided one method for alerting us, at least temporarily, to dangers we may otherwise take for granted. It is called sensitization.

One December afternoon while writing this book I was finishing some work at the California Institute of Technology (Caltech) in Pasadena. My wife met me near the university and we got into our car for the trip to nearby Los Angeles. We weren't very excited to get on the 210 Freeway. It was pouring rain.

Los Angeles has a monsoon climate. From April to November there may be little or no rain at all. But during the winter the rains come, sometimes for days on end, and with them the floods and mud slides. Every few years, Malibu is nearly washed away. The problem with this kind of climate is that people forget how to drive in the rain. A heavy December rain in Los Angeles is like an ice storm back East—cars and trucks go flying everywhere and there are accidents all over town. Motorists may not have seen rain in months and they refuse to change their aggressive driving habits to compensate for the slick roads.

So there we were heading west in a heavy rain with most of the cars whizzing past us at seventy-five, eighty, or faster. Far ahead, my wife's keen eyes noticed that the heavy traffic seemed to be slowing. We approached a cluster of emergency vehicles parked beside the concrete divider in the center of the highway. A light truck must have just gone out of control on the eastbound side. The badly smashed truck had rolled over and come to rest on its roof atop the concrete divider. As I drove by, I could see the driver hanging upside down in his shoulder harness. Emergency workers were cutting through the door to pull him out. He seemed to be moving.

People invariably slow down to gawk at accidents. As we will see in Part II, not only do we dread fearful situations, we are innately fascinated by them. But something strange happened that day. Once past the accident the traffic didn't speed up as usual but continued driving slowly, as if by magic. All around me were hundreds of cars doing fifty-five, staying in their lanes, not tailgating. I have been to Los Angeles many times but never seen such well-behaved driving—it's rare anywhere. This minor miracle lasted only eight or nine miles, until we crossed Interstate 5. The traffic pouring onto our freeway from I-5 drove in the usual high-speed LA fashion, ignoring the rain.

Unlike the drivers coming off I-5, those of us who had seen the truck accident were almost instantly sensitized to the dangerous condition of the freeway. Scientists have intensively studied the habituation and sensitization process. In humans, sensitization is coordinated by the primitive fear system. It is a form of fear reaction. When you see or experience something warning you that you are in danger—if your car nearly goes out of control on a slick road, for example—the primitive system immediately activates a cascade of automatic changes in the brain and body. You become jumpy, intensely alert to the danger, and vividly aware of your surroundings. Your reactions are on a hair trigger. Muscles tense, heart rate and blood pressure go up. Your rational fear system operates in high gear, analyzing the danger and suggesting courses of action. When you're sensitized you are easily frightened, even panicked.

Some members of Yeager's World War II fighter squadron became excruciatingly sensitive to the risks of combat. In the middle of one dogfight, Yeager said he "heard the most horrifying scream blast into my headphones. 'Oh, God, they got me. My head, my damned head. I'm bleeding to death.' That night at the officers' club, the shrieker showed up wearing a Band-Aid, a goddamned Band-Aid, taped to the back of his neck. He had been nicked by a piece of Plexiglas."[7]

Yeager himself was sensitized when the X–1 developed its repeated fire problem. This explains his constant dread, his unbearable fear every time he had to start the rocket plane's engines, and his nightmares. Yet here was the man who for the previous five months had piloted the X–1 —a plane he admits was little more than a flying bomb—with the supreme confidence necessary to create the first man-made sonic boom in the history of the planet.

Sensitization lowers the threshold of fear. You become afraid of more things, things that never bothered you before you were sensitized. A nick on the neck becomes a terrifying experience. Once again, imagine I am walking in the woods and hear a rustling in the bushes. I freeze, look around, but can't see anything. So I go on my way, maybe walking a little faster. Then I hear the rustling again. My primitive fear system is becoming increasingly sensitized to possible danger. A squirrel noisily darts across my path from the underbrush and I jump back instinctively. My heart rate shoots up, only slowing down after my cortex gives the primitive system and my consciousness a clearer idea of what I saw.

When I jumped, I exhibited the startle response. Humans are not alone in that behavior. Rats, cats, dogs, guinea pigs, monkeys—in fact all mammals—flinch or jump when they are startled, particularly by a loud noise. The response is built in and stereotyped. Your muscles convulse, your face grimaces, your eyes close, you may catch your breath or let out a yell. The tensed muscles, pinched face, and closed eyes are the primitive fear system's way of bracing your body to absorb a possible attack. A series of fears can thus interact to produce different responses. The fear response to the rustling in the bushes made me freeze and sensitized me by lowering my fear threshold. My exaggerated startle response to the squirrel was due to sensitization. Normally a squirrel running across my path might cause me at most to tense slightly, not jump out of my skin.

Sensitization is a powerful process, but so is habituation. Whereas sensitization lowers the threshold of fear, habituation raises it. When you are habituated, things that once caused a fear response don't scare you anymore. Let's go back to the woods. I keep walking along the path and hearing noises in the bushes. A number of squirrels run across the trail. My rational fear system may conclude that it is mating season for squirrels. I quickly become habituated and from then on ignore the squirrels completely when they dart out of the underbrush. My habituated nervous system automatically lowers my heart rate, loosens my muscles, and reduces my heightened state of awareness. I relax and enjoy the walk.

In the summer of 1940 after Hitler had conquered France and most of the rest of continental Europe, the British knew they would be bombed by the Germans. This was the dawn of modern air power. New high-explosive bombs were capable of leveling large parts of a city. The British authorities were apprehensive. One prominent psychologist wrote that "the stimuli presented by a heavy air raid are far more intense and more terrifying than civilized human beings normally experience." He and many other psychologists predicted "widespread panic and hysteria" and huge numbers of psychological casualties.[8]

Once the bombing started, the authorities were completely surprised that the vast majority of people showed amazing resilience. They stayed calm, continued to go to work, and even joked about their nights in the air-raid shelters. There were very few stress-related breakdowns. Studies showed that people living in London, which bore the brunt of the German attacks, were far calmer about the bombing than people in the country-side, who were seldom bombed. This is perfectly consistent with the principles of habituation. For most people, the more frequently they are exposed to a stimulus, even a frightening one like heavy bombing, the higher their threshold of fear becomes and the less afraid they are. When there were long lulls in the bombing, Londoners tended to lose their habituation. After the bombing resumed, they were initially frightened and had to rehabituate.

The great majority of us are capable of habituating to extreme circumstances. Did you ever wonder how doctors, police, fire fighters, coroners, and paramedics deal with grisly accidents and injured or dying people day after day without being emotionally shattered? Or how long-held hostages of terrorists cope with the ever-present threats from their captors? They habituate. How did the people of war-torn Bosnia manage to carry on some semblance of normal life amid the shelling and the snipers? They habituated. The same thing happens to soldiers in combat.[9]

People with serious phobias or other psychological problems suffer terribly because they have often lost the ability to habituate normally. A soldier who jumps and cowers at the slightest noise has developed shell shock. Everyone has occasional aches, pains, sniffles, or other minor symptoms. We don't worry much about them because we know from experience they will go away. We have habituated to minor illness. In hypochondria, however, this normal process goes awry. For a variety of reasons that we will discuss in Chapter 9, a hypochondriac does not easily habituate. To him every trivial symptom may be the beginning of a serious or fatal illness. He lives in perpetual anxiety about his health. Habituation is a form of learning, and the hypochondriac has difficulty learning to ignore minor health problems.

Living in constant fear is exhausting and makes normal functioning impossible. If a danger is short-term, our three fear systems will warn us in unmistakable ways to be careful. But if the danger, even a mild danger, persists for a long time, our brain has evolved a way to let us live relatively normally by habituating, even in stressful environments. If we cannot habituate, then psychological problems—diseases of fear—may cripple our lives.

{ Chapter 2 }

The Science of Fear

The aroma from a musty diary healed Paul Reed of the bitterness and guilt that ruined his life after he returned from Vietnam. Reed had been a sergeant and counterinsurgency fighter in a highly decorated U.S. brigade that saw some of the bloodiest action of that bloody war. During one firefight in Kontum Province he stumbled across the backpack left behind by a North Vietnamese officer. In it was a diary written in Vietnamese with a picture of the man's wife and child. Reed sent the diary to his mother as a memento of the fighting.

His tour of duty ended in 1969 and he was shipped home to Texas. Reed found it impossible to adjust. He went through two divorces, dead-end jobs, and finally became a trucker so he could get away from everyone and nurse his anger.

He showed signs of post-traumatic stress disorder, a crippling disease of fear that sometimes strikes veterans of intense combat and other trauma victims. Their experiences are so frightening that their primitive fear system becomes stuck in the sensitized mode. They lose the ability to habituate to normal life, remaining edgy and wary. If a stranger knocked on the door of Reed's truck, "I'd open it and they'd be looking at a sawed-off shotgun," he said.

In 1989 Reed reached his low point. Months of brooding were punctuated with uncontrollable crying. Hoping to help, his mother brought out the diary from the cabinet where it had been stored for twenty years. "As soon as I unwrapped the plastic, the aromas of the jungle came back," Reed said. He was flooded with terrifying images of war and sat down at his computer to begin writing them down. It was the beginning of a long process of therapy. A few years later Reed's reminiscences became a PBS television documentary and a book.

Reed was determined to return the diary to its owner or his family. With help from the Vietnamese government, he found the author, retired Second Lieutenant Nguyen Van Nghia, living quietly with his wife in the small Vietnamese town of Tien Hai. Reed flew to Vietnam in 1993 and personally delivered the diary to a grateful Nghia. The two immediately liked each other. "Thanks to the diary," Nghia said, "we have a noble friendship." They have remained close. Nghia still suffers the effects of old war wounds. Reed raised the money to fly him to Dallas in November 1996 for medical treatment and a large measure of Texas hospitality.[1]

Fear, anger, bitterness, reconciliation—the human brain is capable of an incredible kaleidoscope of emotions. What is it within the brain's complex circuits that allows such emotional richness? And how is it that a simple smell can bring back a torrent of vibrant memories? The answer begins at the center of the primitive fear system with a pair of structures, like two small clusters of grapes, buried deep within the brain. Collectively they are called the amygdala after the Greek word for "almond" because of their fanciful resemblance to almonds. They are the ancient, ever-watchful eyes of the emotional system of the brain. There is one amygdala grape cluster about the size of a nickel on each side of the brain. If you put your index finger on your temple, one of the amygdala grape clusters will be underneath it, about an inch and a half deep in the brain. That puts each cluster, which consists of a group of smaller specialized knots of nervous tissue, on the inner surface of the right and left cerebral hemispheres that fill the top and sides of the skull. Each hemisphere is covered by the thin, wrinkled cerebral cortex, which wraps around the hemisphere all the way to the inner surface where the amygdala nestles.

Every bit of information that enters your senses also flows through the amygdala and the early warning system of which it is a part. The amygdala continually monitors this huge stream of information, trying to detect any signs of danger. As you read this book your eyes focus on the page. But your amygdala is also scanning those parts of your visual

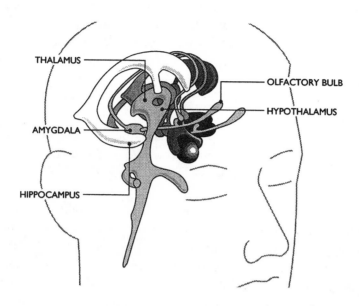

THALAMUS

OLFACTORY BULB

HYPOTHALAMUS

AMYGDALA

HIPPOCAMPUS

FIGURE I

field you are not paying attention to—the edges of your visual field, the corners of your eyes—searching for possible threats: a sudden movement, a looming shadow. It monitors every sound your ears are picking up, including background noises to which you are consciously oblivious. At night you rest, but the amygdala doesn't. It continues monitoring your sensory information for any sign of a threat. If a bedroom bookcase crashes to the floor while you sleep, the amygdala will instantly detect the menacing noise and activate its connections to the startle response so that you leap out of bed, heart racing, ready to protect yourself.

The amygdala is part of the limbic system, a group of ancient structures inside the hemispheres that are interconnected with each other and with the inner portions of the cerebral cortex. Together these structures form the primitive fear system (see Figure 1). This system receives information from virtually every part of the brain and, in turn, from every other part of the brain and body. The amygdala and related structures that constitute this intricate system look for the crude outline of a threat, not the details. The amygdala, in particular, seems to store simple memories of those things we have learned to be fearful of: the shape of a snake, the loudness of a noise. These are cartoon sketches, not full-blown portraits of the threat. Their virtue is that they can be quickly recognized prior even to conscious awareness. The primitive fear system can make you duck, jump, or freeze before you realize what the possible danger is. It was this system that froze me in my seat during the automobile accident when I was sixteen. It was Paul Reed's primitive fear system that scanned the rice paddies and highlands of Vietnam, searching for the shape or sound of peril.

For decades evidence has been accumulating that the limbic system is deeply involved in molding emotional memories and emotional responses, especially fear. When the amygdala of patients having brain surgery is stimulated by a mild electrical current, they often experience exceptionally realistic hallucinations involving memories, thoughts, or perceptions coupled with emotions—almost always fear. If wild, aggressive monkeys that react with screeching terror to any human approach in the laboratory have their amygdalae removed, they completely lose their fear of humans. They can be handled, petted, played with. They show no fear at all. In fact they show little emotion of any kind. This is known as the Klüver-Bucy syndrome, after the researchers who first noticed it in the late 1930s. It was an important clue that led scientists to discover the amygdala's pivotal role in the emotional system. The amygdala appears to be vital in generating all primitive emotions, from ecstasy to terror.

Michael Davis, a psychiatrist at the Yale University School of Medicine, reported that rats with selectively damaged (lesioned) amygdalae seem to lose their fear of cats. In one experiment a sedated cat was placed with such rats. The effect was dramatic. "In fact, some of these lesioned animals crawl all over the cat and even nibble its ear," Davis wrote, "a behavior never shown by non-lesioned animals."[2]

Researchers have found, however, that human beings have a much more elaborate emotional system than monkeys or rats. People whose amygdala has been damaged or destroyed do not completely lose their sense of fear, although they are often more calm and easygoing. In humans the amygdala is part of a larger fear system involving other parts of the limbic system and the cortex. If the amygdala is lost, other parts of the system can compensate to some extent. Researchers are also finding that the primitive fear system in humans is much more than the brain's early warning system. This system is of central importance in an extraordinarily sophisticated system of learning and memory that shapes and motivates our every action. In this system, the amygdala has a unique connection to the sense of smell, which helps explain the powerful effect that the aromas from the diary had on Paul Reed's emotional and mental state. To appreciate this particular role of the amygdala, however, we must delve more deeply into the structure of the three-pound human brain, the most wonderfully complex piece of matter on earth. And before we're through, I will show you how the primitive fear system came to be a secret weapon in the most famous attack in history by the planet Mars on the planet earth.

Our brain evolved over the last half billion years from a small clump of nervous tissue at the end of the spinal cord of our reptilian ancestors into four astonishing structures piled on top of the modern human spinal cord: the brain stem, the cerebellum, the diencephalon, and the cerebral hemispheres. The brain stem was the first of these structures to evolve. It consists of three parts—the medulla, the pons, and the midbrain—and controls automatic functions of the internal organs and muscles. Just behind the brain stem at the lower back of the brain is the cerebellum, which controls voluntary movements. On top of the brain stem is an interlocking structure called the diencephalon, which contains the hypothalamus and thalamus. The diencephalon processes all sensory information flowing into the brain and regulates the flow of hormones in the body. Surrounding the diencephalon and the brain stem are the two cerebral hemispheres, the largest structures in the brain, which generate all higher mental functions including consciousness. The wrinkled outer covering of the right and left cerebral hemispheres is the cerebral cortex. Deep within the cerebral hemispheres is the ancient limbic system, the seat of the primitive fear system. The limbic system contains a number of structures including the amygdala and the hippocampus. To initiate the fight-or-flight response the primitive fear system must communicate directly or indirectly with all parts of the central nervous system, from the spinal cord to the cerebral cortex.

Before I go into more detail about these important structures, let me give you a highly simplified way to conceptualize the rational and primitive fear systems. Think of the cerebral cortex as a kind of wrinkled shower cap that covers the entire top and sides of the brain. And think of the limbic system as a kind of doughnut of structures that fits over the brain stem at the center of the brain. When I discuss the primitive fear system, I am basically talking about this doughnut. The rational fear system is essentially the front third or so of the shower cap. Consciousness is generated in some mysterious way we don't yet understand by the entire shower cap, and includes interconnections with the limbic doughnut and other parts of the brain.

Now let's analyze each of these four structures a bit more closely, since each plays a critical role in fear. The spinal cord is the transatlantic cable of the nervous system, connecting the brain to the far reaches of the body. If that cable is cut, the muscles go limp. Our ability to run or fight when faced with a fearful situation disappears. Nerves from all over the body converge on the spinal cord and ascend into the brain stem, which is a swelling at the top of the spinal cord containing the medulla, the pons, and the midbrain.

The medulla is directly on top of the spinal cord and has centers that control breathing, heart rate, and digestion. When we are afraid, the primitive fear system signals these centers to increase heart rate and stop digestion. Above the medulla is the pons, the communications channel between the cerebral hemispheres and the cerebellum. The cerebellum, about the size of a fist, lies just behind the pons at the base of the rear of the brain. It is the portion of the brain mainly responsible for moving the body—including fleeing from a threat—and learning new physical skills, like swinging a baseball bat or cleanly driving a nail into a two-by-four. As I type these words, the commands to move my fingers go from the front of the cerebral cortex, inside my forehead, through the pons and to the cerebellum, which sends nerve signals down the spinal cord that move my fingers in the proper patterns. If my primitive fear system were to detect an immediate threat (say, the sound of an intruder), the pons would shut down communication with the cerebellum and my fingers would freeze, along with the rest of my body. Recently intriguing evidence has surfaced that the cerebellum not only has a role in coordinating the motion of the muscles, but coordinating the flow of thought in the frontal lobes.

You may remember the television sitcom classic *The Andy Griffith Show* and the character Barney Fife, Sheriff Andy Taylor's high-strung deputy, played to bumbling perfection by actor Don Knotts. Whenever Barney singlehandedly created some new mess, he had a way of turning to Andy and, in a voice rising with barely suppressed panic, pleading, "What are we going to do? What are we going to do?" An area of the pons called the central gray region helps control the muscles of the larynx and vocal cords. When we experience fear, these muscles tighten, producing the characteristic high-pitched fearful voice and, at its most extreme, the scream of terror. Above and slightly in front of the pons is the midbrain, which controls many sensory functions and certain specialized movements. As you read these words the midbrain is choreographing the movement of your eyes.

Above the midbrain are the two tightly linked structures of the diencephalon: the hypothalamus and the thalamus. The hypothalamus regulates automatic body functions, such as the maintenance of the internal organs and the secretion of certain important hormones from the pituitary gland, which hangs from the bottom of the hypothalamus just above the roof of the mouth. These hormones include the key emergency hormone, corticotropin-releasing factor, or CRF, which primes the entire organism for fight or flight by initiating a cascade of hormones and neurochemicals in the body and brain. Researchers have found that by electrically stimulating the hypothalamus of a tame cat, they can instantly turn on the cat's automatic fear response: arched back, hissing, claws unsheathed. The thalamus is the initial processing and switching center for virtually all information from the senses. It also plays a key role, along with the cortex, in maintaining consciousness. Everything in your visual field, including the images you see of these words, is at this moment being transmitted from your eyes through your optic nerves to the thalamus in the center of your brain. The thalamus processes these signals into information the rest of the brain can understand, then routes it to the primary visual cortex in the back of the brain for interpretation and further processing. While being processed by the visual system, this information is scanned by the primitive fear system for possible threats. The thalamus also plays a key role in focusing your attention on the source of a possible threat. The primitive system is extensively connected to the thalamus and hypothalamus.

The brain functions using a complex combination of electrical signals and chemicals called neurotransmitters. Within the brain stem and diencephalon, loose networks of nerve cells organized into knots of tissue (called nuclei) serve as reservoirs of some of the most important neurotransmitters. The two most notable networks are the basal ganglia and the reticular formation. One vital knot of tissue in the reticular formation is called the locus ceruleus. It controls the secretion of an important emergency chemical, noradrenaline (a cousin of adrenaline that is also known as norepinephrine). One effect of noradrenaline is to sensitize key parts of the cerebral cortex, ensuring that our perceptions are vivid and our memories are intense and long lasting. Other neurotransmitter systems found in this region produce serotonin, dopamine, acetylcholine, and adrenaline. (When adrenaline—also known as epinephrine—is secreted by the adrenal glands into the bloodstream, it is considered to be a hormone; when it is secreted by nerve cells in minute quantities at specific sites in the brain, it is considered a neurotransmitter.) Different combinations of these and other neurotransmitters sprayed into specific areas of the brain can produce different states of fear.

Surrounding the thalamus and the entire top of the brain are the enormous cerebral hemispheres. There are two hemispheres, one on each side of the head. They are divided by a deep groove or fissure in the center of the brain that runs from between your eyes to the back of your head. The fissure is bridged by the corpus callosum, a band of fibers about four inches long and half an inch thick that allows the two hemispheres to communicate. For most functions, the left cerebral hemisphere controls the right side of the body and the right hemisphere controls the left side.

Each hemisphere tends to specialize in certain operations, although the exact pattern of specialization can vary from person to person. For most of us (96 percent of right-handed people and 70 percent of left-handers) our primary speech centers are in the left hemisphere. In general, the left hemisphere specializes in language and factual knowledge while the right deals with nonverbal spatial tasks such as recognizing faces. There is also evidence that the left hemisphere is the center for positive emotions while the right specializes in negative emotions, particularly fear. Studies of electrical activity in the facial muscles have shown that the right side of the face, controlled by the left hemisphere, responds more strongly to upbeat thoughts while the left side of the face, controlled by the right hemisphere, responds more strongly to sadness.[3] Epileptic seizures that begin in the left hemisphere can produce uncontrolled laughter. If they begin in the right hemisphere, they may cause uncontrolled crying. This specialization by the hemispheres is both fascinating and exceptionally important in understanding the nature of fear, and we will discuss it in more detail in Chapter 7.

The wrinkled outer covering of the cerebral hemispheres is the cerebral cortex, which is made up of distinct layers of cells, one on top of the other. The color of the living cortex is reddish brown. Only when the brain is dead does the so-called gray matter of the cortex actually look gray. The information-processing cells in the brain are called neurons. A single brain has about 100 billion of them. Half these microscopic neurons are packed into the cortex, which is little more than the thickness of a dime. Underneath the cortex is a thicker layer of white matter made up of billions of microscopic organic "wires" that connect each neuron to a thousand or more other neurons in unbelievably complex electrical and chemical circuits. If all the wires in your brain could be laid end to end, they would stretch several hundred thousand miles. The total number of connections between neurons is on the order of 100 trillion. When mammals evolved 180 million years ago from a group of now-extinct reptiles, the cortex consisted of only a thin blanket of cells covering a rudimentary but promising limbic brain that included the amygdala. About 90 million years ago the outer six layers of the cortex began to evolve. These outer layers are called the neocortex (new cortex). Ninety million years old is new by evolutionary reckoning, when you consider that life has been evolving on earth for about 3.5 billion years. The spectacular expansion in size of this six-layer covering in the human brain has given us our phenomenal mental powers.

The cerebral cortex of each hemisphere is divided into four lobes: occipital, parietal, temporal, and frontal. The occipital lobe is at the back of the head. It contains the primary visual cortex. A blow to the back of the head that damages the occipital lobe can cause blindness. There is a groove in the neocortex that extends across the top of the head from ear to ear. It is called the central sulcus. The parietal lobe extends from the central sulcus back to the boundary of the occipital lobe. The parietal lobe contains the primary area for receiving sensations from the body. The frontal lobe is the portion of the cortex from the central sulcus all the way to the forehead. Many of our highest mental capacities are located there, including the ability to plan for the future and the capacity to feel concern for the consequences of our actions. The frontal lobe is a key structure of consciousness, and the frontmost portion of the lobe—the prefrontal cortex—is the seat of our rational fear system (see Figure 2). The frontal lobes of the two cerebral hemispheres inhibit and shape the primitive fears and other primal urges generated by the underlying limbic system into socially acceptable behaviors. Also located in the frontal lobes is working memory, which is the temporary storage space we use to keep facts or ideas in mind while we make plans or carry out a task. If you ask a telephone operator for a number, working memory is where you store the number until you dial it. Another groove in the cortex is called the Sylvian fissure. It starts in front of each ear and travels diagonally

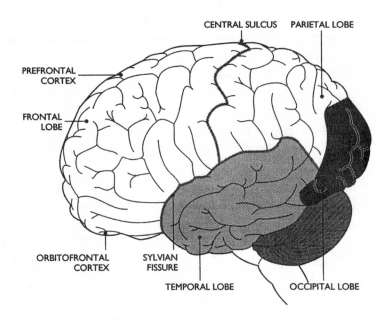

FIGURE 2

and upward around the ear toward the back of the head. The portion of the cortex below this fissure is called the temporal lobe. It is the seat of language and hearing.

Remember, there are four lobes in each cerebral hemisphere. That means for the entire brain (right and left hemispheres) there are two of each lobe: a right and left frontal lobe, a right and left parietal lobe, and so forth. There are also two each of the structures deep inside the two hemispheres, which includes all the structures above the midbrain: a right and left thalamus, a right and left amygdala, a right and left hippocampus.

On the inner surface of the cerebral hemispheres is the limbic system, which contains the group of evolutionarily old structures ringing the brain stem. *Limbus* is Latin for "border." The limbic system plays an important role in memory, motivation, and emotion. Of special importance for the processing of emotions, particularly fear, are the amygdala, the orbitofrontal cortex, and the hippocampus. The orbitofrontal cortex consists of the portion of the underside of the cerebral cortex that wraps around each frontal lobe, resting on top of the eye sockets (the orbitals).

It extends into the deep fissure that separates the two cerebral hemispheres. The orbitofrontal cortex has assumed particular importance in the human primitive fear system, taking on many of the duties that in monkeys and other primates are handled by the amygdala alone. It is the orbitofrontal cortex that allows us to empathize with the fears of others, giving us the understanding necessary to judge their feelings and intentions. If our orbitofrontal cortex is damaged, making decisions becomes almost impossible because we are unable to make an emotional commitment to one course of action instead of another.

Just as there are two amygdalae, one on each side of the head, there are also two hippocampi, each about the size of your little finger. The amygdala is located just at the tip of the hippocampus. Both structures are extensively interconnected and lie on the inner side of the front of the temporal lobe. Neuroscientists believe that the hippocampus is responsible for processing what is called declarative memory—facts and experiences that can be consciously recalled and expressed in words. This includes the context of emotional experiences. The amygdala and related structures seem to be responsible for remembering what I am afraid of, while the hippocampus is responsible for remembering exactly where I am and what I'm doing when the fear occurs. Recall that the cerebellum is responsible for learning skills like swinging a baseball bat or riding a bicycle. This kind of procedural memory is different from declarative memory. If I have never ridden a bicycle, for example, I can read and memorize everything I can find on the subject. I can talk to people about what riding feels like. I can watch movies of the Tour de France. But after all that preparation, what will happen the first time I try to ride? I'll fall over. All the declarative information in the world—facts and words—will not reproduce the sensation of riding a bicycle. You cannot communicate the experience in words. You have to experience it for yourself. Through practice, your body will have to learn what it feels like to balance itself easily while riding. This procedural skill will be stored in the cerebellum. Language is sufficient to convey full meaning only for certain types of factual information: for example, the names of the fifty states. In other words, language can more or less completely reproduce in another person's brain the pattern of neural activity that we call the names of the fifty states. But words alone cannot completely convey the nonverbal sensation of hitting a baseball or running for your life from a mountain lion.

There are at least two other types of memory in the brain besides declarative and procedural: sensory memory and emotional memory. When I think of a blue sky, I am recalling a sensory memory. These memories are stored in the sensory cortices, in this case the visual cortex. I can describe the color blue to someone blind from birth, but that person will never truly understand what I mean unless I can miraculously restore his sight. The sensory experience of blue is a pattern of neural activity in the visual processing areas of the brain, not a pattern of words. Words can refer to blue but they cannot duplicate the sensation of seeing the color. The emotions we attach to our experiences are initially processed by the primitive fear system. Like sensations or skills, words cannot convey the full meaning of emotions. Take jealousy, for example. It is a form of fear—fear of abandonment by someone you are attached to. Until you have experienced jealousy yourself, you cannot truly understand the emotion. It is a feeling that must be personally perceived, not a definition in a dictionary.

These four types of memory illustrate an essential principle of brain organization. Each of the various functional centers of the brain performs a comparatively elementary operation. The four types of memory—facts, skills, sensations, and emotions—combine to give us a comprehensive picture of the world. Yet each type of memory is itself constructed from even more elementary operations. Only when these elementary operations are linked together in systems do we get complex mental functions like vision, hearing, and planning. This principle holds true for the amygdala as well, which consists of a bundle of smaller specialized nuclei. Elementary brain operations are like single words in a language. To make a complicated thought, you must string single words into a sentence. Each word can go in many different sentences meaning many different things. Similarly, each functional brain area can be part of many different systems that do different things.

Memories and perceptual processes are mapped in different ways and a limited brain injury is unlikely to damage them all. For example, our visual system contains separate processing centers for shape, color, movement, and texture among other features. It is not uncommon for someone to have a small stroke in the color processing area of the brain. Thereafter the person is color blind and sees the world in shades of gray, though the rest of his visual system is intact. What neuroscientists have not yet figured out is how all these elementary operations, multiple maps, and parallel processes come together in perfect synchronization to produce the coherent view of the world we call consciousness. This is called the binding problem.

We are now in a position to sketch out the detailed structure of the primitive and rational fear systems. At every moment of our lives information pours into our brains about what we are experiencing: seeing, hearing, smelling, tasting, touching, and thinking. Imagine you are taking a morning walk down a neighborhood street. All the information your senses record goes first to your thalamus, the initial switching hub in the center of the brain. Processing by the thalamus produces a rudimentary representation of the information sorted into different streams of data for each different type of sense, including such esoteric senses as proprioception—the sense of your body's position in space from moment to moment generated by the positions of your joints and muscles. The thalamus routes each stream of data to the proper sensory region of the cortex, where additional processing begins. (Actually, things are a little more complicated since there are two thalamuses, one in each cerebral hemisphere. In general, each receives sensory information from the opposite side of the body, which is processed in the cortex of that cerebral hemisphere. The results of this separate hemispheric processing are shared via the corpus callosum, which interconnects the two hemispheres.)

The processing of information in the cerebral cortex tends to flow from the back and sides of the head forward to the frontal lobes, where the most sophisticated analysis takes place. At each step along the way to the frontal lobes, different brain structures extract more and different information from the raw data and add another layer of richness to your picture of the world. For example, the thalamus first routes visual data to the primary visual cortex in the occipital lobe at the back of the head. Once processed by the primary visual cortex, the information flows forward through at least five other visual processing areas in the occipital lobe, then moves to the parietal lobe. Visual information goes through dozens of different processing areas before it reaches consciousness. At every stage, the brain adds new layers of meaning about the shape, color, movement, and identity of what the eyes are recording. This is far from a simple assembly line, however. Each cortical processing area is connected to others in complex ways we don't fully understand. In addition, information is being processed simultaneously in both the right and left hemispheres. In vision, for example, information from the right side of the visual field of *both* eyes goes to the left occipital lobe, while information from the left side of the visual fields goes to the right occipital lobe. Each hemisphere extracts different qualities from the same basic information as it flows toward the frontal lobes. The left hemisphere is interested in naming what we are seeing, while the right is more concerned in ascertaining its shape. Vision, like all senses, is a dynamic process. The brain does much more than just passively register the scene. It actively tries to classify visual information into categories it understands. Psychologists use this aspect of brain architecture when they ask patients to interpret the random shape of an inkblot ("It looks like a butterfly").

Large areas of the cortex are responsible for seamlessly knitting the data from the different senses into a coherent picture that includes sight, sound, touch, taste, and smell. These are called association areas. One important association area runs roughly from behind each ear to the top of the head. It includes portions of the temporal, parietal, and occipital lobes. It is here, for example, that words are linked to their meanings and faces are recognized. If I have a stroke in this area, I might be unable to identify my wife's face, though I could still recognize her voice. As sensory information moves into this association area, it is simultaneously flashed to the primitive fear system. This is the partially processed sensory information that the primitive system scans for potential threats. The primitive system is made up of the amygdala, hippocampus, and other limbic structures along with the inner portions of the temporal, parietal, and frontal cortex, including the orbitofrontal cortex. The primitive system carries out this scanning by generating an emotional reaction, positive or negative, to everything we perceive. It judges every object and sensation in our perceptual field by how much physical or mental pain or injury it causes or might cause us. If it judges that something might produce great pain (a snake), then it initiates a strong fear response. If the potential pain is slight (a sudden strong gust of wind), the fear response is mild. If it identifies something that will actually reduce our fear and pain— food when we're hungry, for example—then it reacts positively with an emotion we perceive as pleasurable. The primitive system continually monitors and reacts to everything we are experiencing because even an apparently innocuous object or situation may abruptly turn threatening. The twisted shape of a nearby stick may move, signaling the primitive system that it is actually a snake.

As the increasingly refined information moves forward through the cortex toward the frontal lobes, it continues to be relayed to the primitive system so that the system's early response can be double-checked. This emotional processing occurs prior to conscious awareness. It takes about a tenth of a second after we experience something—say, a flash of lightning or the crash of thunder—for its sensory representation to filter through billions of neurons and enter this association area, where the representation is signaled to the primitive fear system over and over as the data are refined. Generally it takes another fraction of a second before the representation enters conscious awareness, although the exact timing is still not known for certain. The moment of consciousness roughly coincides with the moment the sensory information flows forward into the frontal lobes and another key association area—the rational fear circuit centered in the prefrontal cortex, the area of the right and left frontal lobes lying just above the eyes and within the forehead.

Although conscious awareness seems to occur when processed sensory information flows into the frontal lobes, consciousness itself appears to be generated by a system of widely dispersed brain structures that neuroscientists don't yet understand. Damage to areas of the frontal lobes does not destroy consciousness, but seems to selectively delete certain capacities of the conscious mind. If the prefrontal cortex and thus the rational fear system is damaged, for example, a person's ability to make rational decisions is severely reduced. If areas of the limbic system are destroyed, the conscious ability to register emotions diminishes.

The rational fear system is the brain's center for high-level analysis and planning for the future. As you take your morning walk, a stream of thoughts and feelings generated by many different parts of the brain swirls through your consciousness. The centers responsible for drives like hunger, thirst, and sex contribute to this internal thought process. The prefrontal cortex also contributes by generating an inexhaustible flow of possibilities, plans, and scenarios. The primitive fear system adds emotional reactions to this stream. If you're thinking about this afternoon's dental appointment for a root canal, the primitive fear system activates a fear response. This purely internal emotional process is the source of anxiety. Both the prefrontal cortex and the primitive fear system monitor and contribute to your stream of consciousness. The prefrontal cortex uses the contents of these internal musings along with your current circumstances and the sum total of your life experience, as stored in your memory, to update the elaborate mental model you carry in your brain of the world and your place in it, and judge what is and is not important in your life at the moment. It then spins out options and possibilities for you to consider consciously as you plan the rest of your life, from the next second to decades from now. Through the orbitofrontal cortex, the prefrontal cortex is extensively interconnected with the amygdala, hippocampus, and the entire primitive system. It can both influence what we feel and remember, and be influenced by it. This circuit between the prefrontal cortex and the limbic system is what I call the rational fear system.

Some neuroscientists have suggested that there is an even quicker route by which sensory information reaches the amygdala and the primitive fear system. Neuroscientist Joseph LeDoux, a leading investigator of the amygdala, and his colleagues at New York University have discovered a secondary circuit in rats that directly links the thalamus to the amygdala, bypassing the cerebral cortex altogether. He has shown that this is a source of fast reactions by the rat to potentially dangerous stimuli—loud noises, for example. LeDoux believes that a similar direct connection between the thalamus and amygdala underlies fast responses to danger by the human primitive fear system. Yet studies thus far have not uncovered convincing evidence that the the human brain uses such a shortcut to the primitive fear system. I asked LeDoux if we know yet whether thalamus-amygdala pathway exists in humans. "The short answer," he said, "is, no."[4] At this point, there are not enough studies to decide one way or another. Our primitive fear system may be wired similarly to that of the rat. But perhaps not. In humans, the primitive fear system may, instead, receive virtually all its sensory data from the slightly slower but more thoroughly processed cerebral cortex pathway.

Whether this processing shortcut in humans is significant or not, LeDoux and most neuroscientists agree that emotions like fear are processed outside of consciousness. "While the existence of an emotional processing circuit that bypasses the cortex strongly argues for unconscious emotional processing," LeDoux says, "it is likely that even when the amygdala is activated by cortical sensory systems the processing occurs unconsciously. When we are conscious of processing, we are aware of the consequences of processing after the fact rather than being aware of the processing itself."[5]

As you walk through the peaceful neighborhood, the primitive fear system constantly scans the partially processed sensory information for signs of danger. In a sort of running emotional commentary, the amygdala and related structures register an emotional response to everything they perceive and relay this response to the hippocampus. The stronger the emotional response signaled by the amygdala, the more strongly the hippocampus will etch the scene into memory. Note that the primitive fear system is not the only part of the brain signaling the hippocampus about this stream of sensory information. The hypothalamus monitors the state of your body and signals the hippocampus that, for example, you feel hungry and thirsty. In that case, the hippocampus will remember more clearly sensory data involving food and drink. If the stream of sensory information does not evoke any strong feelings from the primitive system, hypothalamus, or other brain area, the hippocampus will record very little of it and it will be forgotten almost immediately. Think of the times you've taken a routine drive to the office or the grocery store and realized when you got there that you remember almost nothing about the trip.

This illustrates a fundamentally important principle of brain architecture: we remember only those things that we feel something about, whether the feeling is fear, hunger, or desire. The stronger our feelings, the more vivid and long lasting our memories. At any moment of your waking life, your senses perceive an enormous amount of information around you, most of which you rapidly forget because it triggers no strong emotional or visceral response. We have evolved to remember those things that our emotions or appetites tell us are important. This applies to learning as well. If you learn something—the Pythagorean theorem, for example—but have no particular feeling about it, you will find it almost impossible to remember. This is what happens to much of what we learn in school. Repetition is not enough. Even if you continually repeat and review textbook knowledge, you will find it very difficult to remember unless the information is associated with an emotion, such as a genuine interest in the subject or a fear that if you don't remember it you will fail a test. Fear is an unfailingly powerful memory aid.

As you continue your walk and turn onto a new street, let's review the sequence of neural processing going on in your brain. About a tenth of a second after your eyes first glimpse the new environs, and before you are consciously aware of the image, your primitive fear system is reviewing the image for signs of a threat through its connections to the early sensory processing regions of the outer portion of the cortex and, perhaps, through a direct connection with the thalamus that bypasses the cortex. If the primitive system detects danger it will immediately shift your body and brain into a fear response, even before you are consciously aware of what is going on. If no danger is detected, the primitive system will simply generate an emotional reaction to the scene based on the totality of your experience, including your current overall emotional state or mood. The cerebral cortex—which consists of increasingly sophisticated processing regions that the information encounters as it flows forward through the occipital, parietal, and temporal lobes—provides the primitive system with a progressively clearer picture on which to make its preconscious emotional judgment. The primitive system might determine that you like this street because some friends live here. Or it might conclude that you dislike the street because the houses are ugly. The information then flows into the frontal lobes and, through some process scientists don't yet understand, you become conscious of the image of the street. At the instant the image registers in your consciousness so too does the emotional reaction—good, bad, or indifferent—that was generated by the primitive system prior to conscious awareness. The image and emotion have been fused into the single perception. After looking carefully at the street, you may consciously decide that the emotional first impression you are experiencing is not how you really feel. But changing that emotional reaction will take an effort of will on your part. Consciousness is perpetually playing catch-up with the primitive fear system, which always has the first word about emotions. At the same time you become aware of the image and its preconscious emotional coloration, you will also be aware of the plans and possibilities being generated by the rational fear system centered in the prefrontal cortex. This image and all subsequent images flow into your mind in an indivisible stream of consciousness that lags a fraction of a second behind the moment your eyes first registered the scene.

As you walk along the tree-lined street, a German shepherd in one of the yards unexpectedly jumps a high fence and begins running toward you. You're not yet consciously aware of this. Yet out of the corner of your eye at the very edge of the visual field your primitive fear system has detected a gray blur moving in your direction. The primitive system uses its interconnections with the hypothalamus and brain stem to prime your hormones and autonomic nervous system immediately—the portion of your nervous system that automatically regulates your muscles and organs—for the fight-or-flight response. Your hypothalamus signals the pituitary gland to secrete the emergency hormones. Your muscles tense, your eyes widen, your blood pressure jumps, and your pupils dilate. The information being filtered through the cerebral cortex clearly shows a German shepherd, now barking furiously. The primitive system signals the hypothalamus to turn up the response. The adrenal glands above the kidneys begin secreting adrenaline into the bloodstream. At the same time, the locus ceruleus in the reticular formation releases stores of noradrenaline directly into the brain, heightening its sensitivity. The hippocampus and amygdala are primed to lay down memories more easily. The chemical balance is delicate. Too much noradrenaline in the brain can overwhelm the system, leading to panic and confusion rather than alertness and attention. Your primitive system signals the pons to shut down the voluntary movement centers in your cerebellum.

You freeze, catch your breath, and turn to face the barking dog as it charges you. Freezing not only gives you a chance to assess your options for fighting or fleeing, it is an ancient response that seeks to make you less conspicuous to a predator. Similarly, catching your breath makes you less noisy and thus less conspicuous. It also allows you to hear things around you more clearly. Your heart races and your face pales as adrenaline-rich blood pours into your muscles. Your mouth goes dry as the primitive fear system shuts down the digestive system, including the salivary glands. You are suddenly covered with sweat as your body channels all available liquid into the perspiration that will be needed to cool you off during a possible flight. The primitive system, through the locus ceruleus, has signaled the prefrontal cortex to be on maximum alert and, as the rational system frantically generates and weighs the options, you consciously try to decide whether to face down the charging dog or run. There is a shout from the yard, "Shep!" The dog stops short. A man runs out, apologizes sheepishly, and drags the dog by its collar back to the house. You sigh. Inside your brain the amygdala, its electrochemical circuits still pulsing from the close call, insistently signals the hippocampus: "Remember that dog."

What would it be like if you lost your primitive fear system? Because of a legendary, long-suffering patient known in the medical literature only by the initials H. M., we have a fairly good idea. As a young man he suffered from disabling seizures due to severe epilepsy. On September 1, 1953, he underwent a brain operation that was supposed to remove portions of his temporal lobes. This was supposed to stop the seizures. It did. But his doctors quickly realized that the operation had severely damaged his memory and emotions. Mistakenly, not only had tissue from H. M.'s temporal lobes been removed, but also the amygdala and the front two-thirds of the hippocampus on each side of his brain.

In the decades since, H. M. has been studied by scientists. The result of this research, when combined with information from other patients with similar brain damage, has been a revolution in the understanding of memory. After the operation, H. M. could still recall all the memories he had formed up until several weeks before. He could no longer form any new long-term declarative memories, however, even though his intelligence was perfectly normal. He forgot every new fact he learned and every new person he met in about twenty minutes. H. M. could not recognize doctors who had been treating him for many years because he had met them after his operation. Shortly after they left his presence, he completely forgot who they were. When he met them again, he acted as if it were for the first time. It seems the only part of his memory that still functions is working memory in the frontal lobes, which we use to remember things like phone numbers for a few minutes, and even that is shaky. H. M. forced neuroscientists to realize that there are different types of memory: declarative and procedural, short-term and long-term. H. M. could learn fresh skills, like using a new tool, because such memories are stored in the cerebellum. Yet he could never remember learning the new skill, although he could use it whenever he wanted.

Since his operation, H. M. appears to be content and placid nearly all the time. Yet he is not completely emotionless. Remember that the human fear circuitry is more complex than that of monkeys or rats and doesn't depend completely on the amygdala. H. M., who is now an elderly man, sometimes expresses strong emotions. On rare occasions he can become angry, but the anger evaporates quickly and he returns to his normal state: even tempered with a quiet sense of humor. H. M. rarely complains, even when he is sick. Without his amygdala and with a damaged hippocampus and temporal lobes, H. M. not only seems virtually unable to generate new emotional memories, his overall emotional responsiveness has significantly diminished.

Suzanne Corkin, a psychologist who has tested H. M. for three decades, made a tape of one of their sessions. The tape begins with pleasantries and banter between Corkin and H. M. "without anything odd or unusual occurring, until Corkin begins asking questions. H. M. does not recall what he did earlier in the day, any of the people who spoke with him, not even Corkin's identity. When she asks if they have met before, H. M. replies in a low, sad voice and ventures that the two of them went to high school together. His voice, tentative and hesitant, suggests that he isn't very convinced about these assertions and, finally, in what sounds like a fatigued resignation, he admits that his memory is severely deficient."[6]

Based on studies of brain-damaged patients like H. M., many neuroscientists have concluded that memories are stored in pieces but retrieved as a whole. Let's say I have just changed jobs and have begun working for a large software company. I am meeting the company president for the first time. I notice her face, listen to the sound of her voice, hear her introduce herself, and feel the firmness of her handshake. I also register an emotional reaction, perhaps a twinge of fear at the thought that her decisions will influence the success or failure of my career here. Each of these perceptions is registered in a separate area of the cortex: visual, auditory, language, somatic, and emotional. The emotional reactions are generated and stored in a circuit that involves the amygdala and other limbic structures. Yet when I think back on this meeting, I will remember it as a whole, not in pieces. Neuroscientists believe that the hippocampus and nearby areas of the cortex create an index of the memory that stores the locations of all the pieces that make it up. The amygdala also appears to retain a link to that index through the emotional response it has stored, although the details of emotional memory storage are less clear. When I think back on the meeting, I am accessing that index, which simultaneously activates all the pieces of the memory, generating an image of the experience as a whole, including its emotional flavor. The hippocampus retains the index for a period of time, assessing its importance. If I continue to access the memory now and then, showing an emotional interest in it, the memory will be reinforced and the hippocampus will move the index out into the cortex for permanent storage. This leaves room in the hippocampus for new memories to be formed. If I don't think about the meeting again, the index will decay and the meeting will be forgotten.

We can now see what happened to H. M. after his operation. By destroying his hippocampus and amygdala, his doctors destroyed the brain structures that create the indexes knitting together new memories and emotions, and storing the important ones. Since H. M.'s hippocampus before the operation had moved the indexes for his memories out into parts of the cortex that were undamaged by his operation, he retained those memories. But he could no longer generate new long-term memories. He was left with only very short-term memory, the kind we use to remember a phone number of no particular importance we are about to dial—a number that once it is dialed will be promptly forgotten forever. Without his amygdala, H. M. has virtually lost the ability to respond emotionally to the events of his life, or experience any emotions at all.

Researchers are also making breakthroughs in understanding how memories are formed at the molecular level. The fundamental information-processing unit in the brain is the neuron, which forms exquisitely complex electrical and chemical connections with other neurons. All the parts of the brain we have discussed are constructed out of intricate circuits of neurons. A neuron consists of three basic parts, a cell body, a single transmitting cable called an axon, which carries an electrical signal called an action potential, and a tangle of receiving antennas called dendrites growing out of the cell body. Axons are the organic wires that connect neurons into complex information-processing circuits. Most neurons use a special kind of connection called a synapse to communicate with other neurons. The axon begins as a single projection from the cell body of the neuron but quickly branches out so it can make multiple connections. At the tip of each axon branch is a tiny bulbous structure called a synaptic terminal. The synaptic terminal of one axon forms a synapse with a second neuron, usually at one of the second neuron's dendrites. The synaptic terminal does not actually touch the dendrite. There is a slight gap called the synaptic cleft through which the synaptic terminal releases chemicals called neurotransmitters. These chemicals are stored in microscopic capsules in the synaptic terminal, which are released when an electrical pulse (action potential) is fired down the axon to the terminal. Common neurotransmitters include serotonin, glutamate, and noradrenaline. There are other chemicals called neuromodulators that influence the efficiency of neurotransmitters.

Neurotransmitters are detected by the dendrites using tiny diverse protein structures called receptors, which are a little like the differently shaped knobs and buttons on a complex control board. The pattern of activity of the receptors determines how the receiving neuron will respond. Learning and memories are stored by changing the strength of synaptic connections, or making new ones. Each neuron may have a thousand or more synaptic connections with other neurons. Since the brain contains 100 billion neurons, the number of synaptic connections is in the trillions. Our mental equipment is so complex that of the hundred thousand genes it takes to create a human being, about a third code for the brain. Most of the cells in your body live only a short time, then die and are replaced. Not neurons. The information in your mind is stored by them through the pattern of synaptic connections they make with other neurons. If one dies, a tiny piece of information is lost. That is why most neurons live as long as you do.

In recent years neuroscientists have discovered a receptor found in abundance in the neurons of both the hippocampus and the amygdala. It is called the NMDA receptor, named after the chemical N-methyl D-aspartate that was used to identify it. Many researchers believe this receptor—along with a handful of others including the recently discovered AMPA receptor—may be the master control for forming declarative, spatial, and fear memories.[7] The NMDA receptor is unusual among known receptors because it requires a two-signal pattern of stimulation before it will respond. First it must receive an electrical signal. This must be immediately followed by a chemical signal in the form of the neurotransmitter glutamate. This two-step pattern is important because it could provide a cellular mechanism for linking separate events together in memory, such as the sight of a German shepherd and the emotion of fear. This type of learning is called fear conditioning and it is a vital part of the way our species uses fear to navigate its way through the world. We've learned to keep our fingers away from a hot stove, for example, for fear of being burned. Through this two-step process—a complex cascade of electrochemical changes involving other receptors and probably the neuron's genetic machinery as well—NMDA receptors have been observed to make lasting changes in the synaptic connections between neurons, a process called long-term potentiation. Studies have shown that blocking NMDA receptors in the rat amygdala prevents rats from being able to form fear memories. Blocking the same receptors in the rat hippocampus, prevents the rats from remembering the circumstances in which they experienced the fear. Pharmaceutical companies are using this newfound understanding of the molecular basis of memory to develop new drugs that not only boost memory, but also suppress the formation of long-term memories. Memory-suppression drugs might be taken after a traumatic event to prevent permanent memories from being stored and possibly head off illnesses like post-traumatic stress disorder.[8]

NMDA receptors may also be implicated in so-called flashbulb memories, in which a shocking event like the death of Princess Diana, the assassination of President Kennedy, or the explosion of the space shuttle *Challenger* stimulate memories so vivid they last a lifetime. Powerful emotions often create exceptionally clear memories. The brain seems to treat shock and surprise as signaling a possible threat to the organism. Shock and surprise are presumed to be fearful until proven otherwise by the analysis of the primitive and rational fear systems. This is why when we are shocked, we often turn pale and display other symptoms of fear (increased heart rate and blood pressure). It is also why, just as in fear, we instantly become alert and lay down vivid memories. The brain quickly decides whether the shock or surprise is truly a threat. If not, it terminates the fear response and often shifts into another emotion—sorrow, sympathy, or pity, for example. This was true for me with the 1986 *Challenger* disaster. Before my fear response was terminated, I had laid down a set of vivid memories. I remember exactly where I was and what was going on around me when I heard about it. This is why people often remember the details about shocking and frightening events, like the World Trade Center bombing or the murder of John Lennon, and exactly what they were doing when they heard the news.

One Saturday night in late August 1997, my wife and I had gone out to see a movie. We were in California at the time. When we returned, I happened to turn on the television to one of the twenty-four-hour news channels while my wife was busy in the other room. I watched the last part of some run-of-the-mill report that ended that half-hour's newscast. Then the anchor came on and said: "In two minutes, more on our top story: the death of Princess Diana." I remember those words and my astonished reaction with crystal clarity. My jaw dropped as I blankly stared at the screen in an agony of suspense during the two minutes of commercials. My mind raced. Impossible, I thought. It must be a mistake. Could there have been some kind of plane crash? My wife and I stayed up half the night listening to the bizarre details of the tragic car crash in the Paris underpass that took the life of Diana and her companions. The dropped jaw and the widened eyes of shock and surprise are preliminaries to a possible fear response. The mouth opens so that, if necessary, we can scream. The eyes widen to allow the brain to take in as much visual information as possible.

The assassination of President Kennedy in 1963 was a particularly intense experience for me. I felt afraid for hours after hearing the news. I was in the eighth grade and I remember the entire afternoon from the moment during lunch when a classmate came running down the driveway of our school, shouting the news that the president had been shot. Everyone was nervous. People feared for the future of the country. I remember going upstairs to my Spanish teacher's classroom where there was a television. The room was packed. Teachers and students were crying. All afternoon we watched the somber coverage. The 1995 bombing of the federal building in Oklahoma City had a similar effect on many people.

Not only do they recall where they were when they heard, they remember much about what was going on around them as they watched the coverage. An important trigger for these vivid memories was the sustained feeling of fear and uncertainty that the bombing generated. If terrorists could strike Oklahoma City, they could strike anywhere.

If the NMDA receptor or some similar one is involved in laying down flashbulb memories, then the process might work something like this. Think of your brain as a thick wax tablet and experience as a sharpened pencil. Experience creates memories by making marks in the wax. But if the wax is cold, it is hard. The tip of the pencil can only make shallow scratches on the surface of the wax, scratches that are easily rubbed off. But when we receive a severe shock, such as the report of an assassination, our brain reacts with a torrent of electrical activity. This is the electrical priming signal needed to begin activating huge numbers of NMDA receptors in our amygdala, hippocampus, cortex, and other memory structures. This priming signal is reinforced chemically, particularly by the release of noradrenaline into the hippocampus and the amygdala.[9] In our wax-tablet analogy, the priming signal heats and softens the wax. Any immediate experience written into the wax with a pencil point (or the neurotransmitter glutamate, in the case of the NMDA receptor) will be deep, easily made, and once the wax cools will last as long as the tablet itself.

In stressful situations, intense and detailed memories are laid down not just of what we see and hear, but of what we might not ordinarily notice: our tastes and smells. The amygdala has a unique and powerful relationship with the sense of smell, which is located in the olfactory bulb. Information from all other senses must be filtered through the thalamus before being passed on to other brain structures. The single exception is the amygdala, with which the olfactory bulb has direct connections, bypassing the thalamus (see Figure 1). And since smell and taste are intimately connected—your sense of taste declines substantially when your nose is congested—this exception opens a rich emotional window. As Marcel Proust wrote in *Remembrance of Things Past:* "When from a long-distant past nothing subsists, after the people are dead, after the things are broken and scattered, still, alone, more fragile, but with more vitality, more unsubstantial, more persistent, more faithful, the smell and taste of things remain poised a long time, like souls, ready to remind us."[10]

My wife, who as a young girl lost her father to an illness, vividly remembers the profusion of flowers at his funeral. Any similar fragrance of flowers causes all the memories of his death to come tumbling out, including the fear she felt when she heard the news. An odor can lay the groundwork for an unusually broad and intense set of memories. If you are in a stressful situation and there is a particular odor, everything you see and do will be associated with that smell, since stress produces a higher state of alertness and more distinct memories. Thereafter, the odor will bring back the entire scene with all its emotions, not just a few details. When Paul Reed opened Nguyen Van Nghia's diary and his primitive system detected the aromas of the jungle, whole episodes of his life surged through his memory, and he was able to begin the process of making peace with himself and his old enemy.

Reed's amygdala helped heal his spirit, yet it was his limbic system that helped make him sick. The terrors of combat can push the amygdala and other limbic structures into hyperactivity. They trigger a major fear response at the slightest sign of stress. In stress illnesses a person has been sensitized and his fear threshold lowered perhaps for years.

Vietnam sensitized a whole generation. What happens if the fear systems of an entire nation are sensitized? Take 1938, for example. Through most of that year, America was in the grip of a war scare. Adolf Hitler had annexed Austria and the German-speaking parts of Czechoslovakia. President Roosevelt sent angry messages to Hitler. Britain and France threatened to go to war against Germany. In the Pacific, tensions were rising with Japan. There were wild rumors of possible invasion and subversion.

October was especially tense. Hitler met with the leaders of Britain and France in Munich. Millions of people listened to their radios, eager for news of the conference. Would there be another war? Would millions more die, as they had in the First World War? Hitler bullied Britain and France into approving his land grab. In exchange he promised he had no further territorial ambitions in Europe. British prime minister Neville Chamberlain waved the Munich agreement in the air and claimed that he had secured "peace in our time." Others shouted "appeasement." They were right. The next year Hitler invaded Poland and World War II began.

On October 30, 1938, Halloween night, Orson Welles and the Mercury Theater began broadcasting an hour-long adaptation of H. G. Wells's classic story *The War of the Worlds*. Orson Welles's opening monologue, describing an interplanetary invasion from Mars, echoed across the nation on the CBS radio network. "Yet across an immense ethereal gulf," Welles said, "minds that are to our minds as ours are to the beasts in the jungle, intellects vast, cool and unsympathetic, regarded this earth with envious eyes and slowly drew their plans against us."[11]

Thus began the most sudden, widespread, and bizarre panic in American history. Later surveys showed over a million people mistakenly believed that the broadcast was an actual account of a Martian invasion. Many fled their homes, fell down on their knees, cried hysterically, or simply froze in terror. Substantial numbers of people reported that their fear of Hitler made them more sensitive to the idea of an invasion—any invasion. The panic offers a case study of the operation of the three fear systems: primitive, rational, and conscious. It also illustrates the incredibly wide array of human fears due to the complex picture of the universe we carry in our minds. Our fears are so extensive as to seem ridiculous sometimes. No other animal could possibly have this kind of fear because no other animal is aware of the planet Mars, much less the hypothetical threat of a Martian invasion.

Alien invasion films have been a Hollywood staple. Major hits in recent years like *Independence Day* and *Mars Attacks* certify that the genre is in no danger of fading away. Yet no movie will ever equal the impact of *War of the Worlds*. The broadcast was exceptionally well done and is still a pleasure to listen to. Just reading Howard Koch's script gives you a flavor of the potent emotions the actors were conveying: fear, panic, desperation, despair, resignation.

The action is set in New Jersey and takes the form of spot coverage of a breaking news event. A musical broadcast is interrupted with a news bulletin that astronomers have detected a series of explosions on Mars. The musical broadcast continues but then is interrupted again for a live interview with Professor Pierson, a Princeton astronomer, played by Welles. There is another bulletin that a meteor has fallen not far from Princeton near the little town of Grovers Mill, New Jersey.

The action shifts to a reporter at Grovers Mill. He describes the scene as the police examine the huge meteor. Suddenly the top of the meteor begins to unscrew. The reporter becomes increasingly excited. "Ladies and gentlemen, this is the most terrifying thing I have ever witnessed. . . . Wait a minute! Someone's crawling out of the hollow top. Someone or . . . something . . . It's large as a bear and it glistens like wet leather. But that face. It . . . it's indescribable. I can hardly force myself to keep looking at it."

Three men approach the meteor holding a white flag. A mirrorlike device rises from the meteor. It fires a heat ray. The reporter panics. "Good Lord, they're turning into flame. . . . Now the whole field's caught fire. . . . It's coming this way. About twenty yards to my right." The reporter's microphone crashes and goes dead.

The program continues with a series of bulletins and reports. State officials put the area around Grovers Mill under martial law. The charred body of the reporter is identified at a nearby hospital. The state militia surrounds the meteor. A giant war machine rises out of the meteor and destroys the militia. A network announcer comes on the air.

"Ladies and gentlemen," he says, "I have a grave announcement to make. Incredible as it may seem, both the observations of science and the evidence of our eyes lead to the inescapable assumption that those strange beings who landed in the Jersey farmlands tonight are the vanguard of an invading army from the planet Mars."

The program goes on to include announcements by national officials, reports of other meteors landing with more Martian war machines, accounts of the army being defeated by the Martians and millions of people fleeing, and finally a poison gas attack by the Martians on New York City. The gas attack is reported by a radio announcer watching from the top of a building in Manhattan.

"No more defenses," the announcer says. "Our army wiped out . . . This may be the last broadcast. We'll stay here to the end. . . . Enemy now in sight above the Palisades. Five great machines . . . Now they're lifting their great hands. This is the end now. Smoke comes out. . . . Now the smoke's spreading faster. It's reached Times Square. People trying to run away . . . They're falling like flies. . . . It's fifty feet." Silence.

The rest of the program is an account by Professor Pierson of wandering through ruined cities as he tries to hide from the Martians. Eventually he comes to New York where he finds the Martians lying dead in Central Park, killed by bacteria, "the humblest thing that God in His wisdom put upon this earth."

During the broadcast, CBS made four announcements that the program was a dramatization. The network made three more after the broadcast had concluded. Many radio stations carrying the program broke in with local announcements. Yet for days afterward, newspapers were full of stories of "the tidal wave of terror that swept the nation."

Princeton University psychologist Hadley Cantril studied the *War of the Worlds* panic not long after it happened. He gathered first-person accounts of people's reaction to the program. "What is most inconceivable and therefore especially interesting psychologically," Cantril wrote, "is why so many people did not do something to verify the information they were receiving from their loudspeakers."[12]

The largest segment of those who became afraid had tuned into the program late. Yet all someone had to do was change to another radio station to see that there was no Martian invasion. Nevertheless tens of thousands did not. The fight-or-flight nature of the primitive fear system provides an explanation. Many of the people who panicked became stuck in it, literally frozen with fear, unable to move. Others immediately began a panicky flight. They were unable to shift to their rational fear system and do some simple checking to see if the story was true. Others did try to check, but when their first efforts failed, they panicked.

Cantril reported the account of a nurse who was having a Halloween party at her house: "Everybody was terribly frightened. . . . Some got down on their knees and prayed. Others were actually trembling. My daughter was terribly frightened and really suffered from shock. A ten-year-old child that was here was petrified. He looked like marble." The fear response was so powerful that some people reported hallucinating: "I stuck my head out of the window and thought I could smell the gas. And it felt as though it was getting hot, like fire was coming."[13]

A senior at large eastern college reported to Cantril that he first tried to call his girlfriend "but the lines were all busy, so that just confirmed my impression that the thing was true. We started driving back to Pough-keepsie. We had heard that Princeton was wiped out and gas was spreading over New Jersey and fire, so I figured there wasn't anything to do—we figured our friends and families were all dead. . . . I drove right through Newburgh and never even knew I went through it. I don't know why we weren't killed. My roommate was crying and praying. . . . I thought the whole human race was going to be wiped out—that seemed more important than the fact we were going to die."[14]

Many initially panicky people were able to shift consciously out of their primitive fear reaction, using the options generated by their rational fear system. They then checked the evidence and realized their mistake. Cantril described the experience of a twenty-nine-year-old physician: "He had missed the first part and did not know the program was a play. For a moment he believed the reports but quickly doubted the reality of the stories because of the rapidity with which things moved. He tuned to a couple of other stations and then turned back to Welles and enjoyed the play."[15]

Cantril's study indicated that those with the least education and limited critical ability were the ones most likely to panic. But even educated people reported panicking, particularly if they were told about the invasion by others gripped by fear. This provides a clue to the reason for the contagiousness of fear and the spread of panic. The primitive fear system appears to be particularly attuned to detecting fear, especially panic, in others. Once it receives a forceful panic signal there is a strong tendency for the primitive system to initiate an automatic panic reaction. The brain becomes stuck in the panic mode of fight or flight, unable to shift to the rational system for confirmation.

One of the better-educated individuals in the survey reported: "When I came out of the telephone booth, the store was filled with people in a rather high state of hysteria. I was already scared but this hysterical group convinced me further that something was wrong." Another said: "I was getting worried when my friend came in and his face was ghastly white. He said, 'We're being invaded,' and his conviction impressed me."[16]

The contagiousness of hysteria has been a major concern of armies throughout history. One study of combat soldiers found that 75 percent of them reported "susceptibility to fear-contagion."[17] As a consequence, in many of the world's major armies, officers engaged in front-line combat are legally authorized to shoot on the spot a soldier who panics and runs in the face of the enemy. Over the centuries, the military has learned the painful lesson that one man's panic on the battlefield can rapidly spread to an entire army.

As Darwin pointed out, all primitive fear system responses are ancient. Our tendency to panic when others do may be an evolutionary carryover from our prehistoric reaction to attacks by predators. Panic is a common response to alarm calls by other social animals, including our closest relatives, chimpanzees (high-pitched scream) and baboons (deep bark). The common feature of most predator attacks is "sudden, fast, direct movement towards the prey, starting either in full view or from cover."[18] Lions, for example, attack from cover, cheetahs and hyenas in full view. For animals, an alarm call must be heeded instantly with panicked flight because the predator is often only a short distance away or moving quickly to the attack. There is no time for thought.

A few years ago my wife and I had a picnic in the picturesque little park in Grovers Mill, New Jersey, that commemorates the *War of the Worlds* broadcast of 1938. There is a bronze plaque on the spot where the infernal Martian spacecraft supposedly landed. At the end of our lunch, we toasted that old mischief-maker Orson Welles.

{ Chapter 3 }

Mind Reading

What if there were a technology that allowed you to read the minds of everyone around you, know the innermost thoughts of your spouse and your friends, instantly realize when someone was lying? What if you could always know the intentions of others, their fears and hopes, their loves and hates? What if we could know with absolute certainty whether someone had committed a crime, and whether a convicted criminal was truly rehabilitated and ready to be returned to society? What if you could objectively read your own mind, including the subconscious processes that regulate your anger and fear, how you learn, and what brings out the best and worst in you? And if your mind broke down and sank into depression or delusions, what if you could use this technology to find out exactly what was wrong and how to fix it? Does the prospect of such a technology sound appealing or terrifying? Would you want someone to use it on you?

Man is a social animal, Aristotle observed, and social animals like humans are obsessed with the emotional and mental states of others. We live in a complex society in which the other people's opinions are vital to whether we survive and thrive. Like our primate cousins, we have evolved many ways to try to intuit what others are thinking. We not only carefully observe and remember what they say and do, we study their body language, expressions, and tone of voice. This insatiable curiosity about what goes on in the minds of others—and our own brains—has led neuroscientists to develop an arsenal of techniques for measuring and monitoring the living brain: X rays, blood flow, electrical activity, stress reactions, electrode implants, oxygen consumption, glucose utilization, and even tiny magnetic changes that take place in brain cells. From these techniques have come a range of technologies, from the police lie detector (polygraph) to the multimillion-dollar positron emission tomography (PET) and magnetic resonance imaging (MRI) machines of major medical and research centers. We can now watch the living brain at work and study how the cortex, limbic system, brain stem, and other areas are activated when we read, write, speak, experience pleasure and fear. Much of this research and technology has been aimed at understanding and treating brain disorders and mental illness. The brain is by far the most complicated structure in our body, and it is vulnerable to more diseases than any other organ. When something goes wrong with the brain, particularly the primitive fear system, the consequences are often devastating not only to the individual and the family, but to society. These cases are frightening because our instincts for understanding what the sufferer is thinking fail us. The disordered mind can become unpredictable and violent, even threaten our lives.

Take the case of C. W., an average, clean-cut young man with a wife, job, and bright prospects. When the severe headaches began he tried stoically to endure them. But with the pain came strange, seemingly uncontrollable fears and violent thoughts. For a while he suffered silently. Finally he broke down and went to a psychiatrist. But the year was 1966 and as Harvard neurosurgeon Vernon H. Mark put it, "In those days nobody thought in terms of a physiological cause. . . . Today we know better than that."[1]

Desperate and frustrated that no one could help him, C. W. wrote a letter describing his anguish: "I don't really understand myself these days. Lately, I have been a victim of many unusual and irrational thoughts. These thoughts constantly recur, and it requires a tremendous mental effort to concentrate. I talked to a doctor once for about two hours and tried to convey to him my fears that I felt overcome by overwhelming violent impulses. After one session I never saw the doctor again, and since then I have been fighting my mental turmoil alone. After my death I wish that an autopsy would be performed to see if there is any physical disorder. I have had tremendous headaches in the past."[2]

A few hours later C. W.—Charles Whitman—killed his wife and mother, drove to the University of Texas campus not far from his Austin home, climbed the stairs to the deck of the tower in the middle of the campus, and with his rifle shot thirty-four people, killing fourteen, before being shot to death himself by terrified police. Whitman was granted his last wish: an autopsy. It revealed a tumor the size of a walnut pressing against his amygdala.

Tragically for Whitman and his victims it has taken science centuries of laborious research to understand the role of the amygdala and limbic system in fear, aggression, and violence. Even now there remains a tremendous amount to learn. As with all great scientific enterprises this one has had its share of mistakes, confusion, missed opportunities, and blind alleys mixed in with an enormous amount of hard work and a fortunate number of dazzling insights. Only with the benefit of hindsight can we look back and see the unbroken threads that led to the breakthroughs. One of the first clues came in 1715 when a physician in Holland, Herman Boerhaave, observed that normal people when bitten by a rabid animal soon begin "gnashing their teeth and snarling like a dog."[3] Autopsies showed that the brains of the victims were swollen and inflamed. Two hundred years later a French neurologist, Henri Gastaut, showed that rabies, by then known to be caused by a virus, infected areas beneath the cerebral cortex.

The great American neuroanatomist, James W. Papez, studied rabies in the 1930s. He, too, was struck by the dramatic transformation of the rabies sufferer. "The prodromal symptoms—insomnia, irritability, and restlessness—usher in the stage of excitement and profound emotional perturbation," he wrote. "Light and sound, and every stimulus situation provokes great apprehension and paroxysms of fear. The patient presents the appearance of intense fright mingled with terror and rage." Papez noted that the rabies lesions were limited to areas deep within the temporal lobes, "an important clue to the probable location of the emotive mechanism."[4] In a brilliant 1937 paper, Papez proposed that a specific system in the brain, centered on the hypothalamus and including many of the limbic structures, provided "a harmonious mechanism which may elaborate the functions of central emotions as well as participate in emotional expressions."[5] A generation of neuroscientists led by neuroanatomist Paul

Maclean built on Papez's research and worked out the structure of the limbic system.

How can the amygdala and the limbic system produce such extreme emotions? Why would an ordinary person be rapidly transformed into savage animal by the rabies virus or into a mass murderer by a tumor? The answer is to be found in the dual nature of fear. When we are faced with a fear-provoking threat, our primitive fear system is programmed to respond in one of two basic patterns. Let's call the first the fear-flight-panic response and the second the fear-fight-anger response. Overwhelming panic was the response of the doomed victims in the Beverly Hills Supper Club fire and of hundreds of thousands of people to the *War of the Worlds* scare. This response does not always mean literally running away. If you perceive yourself to be trapped and helpless, the flight response will tend to keep you frozen in terror.

When your primitive fear system encounters a threat, it makes a split-second determination whether to fight or flee. If the decision is to fight, your fear tends to transform into anger and subtle chemical changes take place in the fear response, so subtle in fact that it is difficult to distinguish between the physiological states of fear and anger.[6] The transformation of fear to anger may be subtle to physiologists but it is obvious to those of us who experience it. Imagine that a government agency announces it is going to build a toxic waste dump next to your house. For most people, the initial fear response—for the health of your family, your neighbors, and the property value of your house—will quickly shift to anger. Rather than sell your house and flee, you probably will aggressively participate in petition drives, angry public meetings, even demonstrations.

The clearest physical difference between fear and anger is that in fear the skin is pale, while in anger it is flushed. This difference goes deeper than the skin, however, as was shown in the unusual case of a New Yorker called Tom in the medical literature. Tom severely damaged his esophagus at the age of nine while drinking hot soup. Doctors had to create a permanent incision in his abdomen that Tom would open to place food directly into his stomach. This incision allowed doctors to observe Tom's stomach when he experienced different emotions. What they found was that Tom's stomach closely mirrored his face. When his face was red with anger so was his stomach. It showed an increased flow of blood, swelling of the mucous membranes, greater flow of hydrochloric acid, and increased activity of the stomach muscles. Prolonged anger produced areas of bleeding that may have been the precursor of ulcers. When his face was pale from anxiety or depression, Tom's stomach became pale as well. The fear response shut down his digestive system and pumped the blood away from his stomach. No matter what Tom's emotion, from terror to outrage, these two patterns were the only ones observed.[7]

What causes anger or panic? One theory is that different combinations of the stress chemicals adrenaline and noradrenaline affect whether we experience the flight state or the fight state. Flight and the related emotions of anxiety and panic may be associated with the predominant secretion of adrenaline, while fighting and anger appear to be associated with noradrenaline. Researchers have pointed out that the adrenal glands of aggressive species like lions have a relatively high concentration of noradrenaline, while timid species like the rabbit have high concentrations of adrenaline. Humans and primates like baboons, who must cooperate in social groups, tend to have more adrenaline than noradrenaline. Studies of astronauts also couple aggression with noradrenaline and anxiety with adrenaline. But other studies show that humans have highly individualistic patterns of responding to the two stress chemicals. Players competing in energy-intensive sports like football and basketball, where emotions tend to fluctuate depending on the course of the game, have high levels of both adrenaline and noradrenaline. The consensus among researchers is that the adrenaline-anxiety and noradrenaline-anger link is not yet conclusive.[8]

Whatever the final outcome of the studies of anxiety and anger, it seems likely that the underlying mechanism will involve a comparatively few physiological variables whose different combinations generate different degrees of the basic fight response or the basic flight response. Such a mechanism might explain how, in changing circumstances, we sometimes feel our emotions shifting back and forth between anger to panic. This oscillation is found in all animals. If a rat is cornered by a cat, it will usually freeze, then try to escape. If its escape fails, the rat will sometimes aggressively attack the cat in a last, desperate attempt to save its life. Its panic shifts immediately into aggression. The history of military conflicts is full of accounts of battles in which an army is initially aggressive, begins to panic when it is beaten back, then after being rallied by its leaders becomes aggressive again. These shifts between anger and panic depend on the mind's perception of the circumstances in which it finds itself, which in turn depend on a complicated interaction between the primitive fear system on the one hand and the rational fear system and consciousness on the other.

The human brain contains a vast potential for both aggression and panic that is drawn upon by the fight-or-flight response, depending on the primitive fear system's assessment of what is necessary to escape injury and survive. For example, if a child is threatened (say, by a vicious dog) in circumstances in which there is no easy escape, most adults will exhibit anger and aggression, even trying to kill the attacker if necessary. It is this capacity for anger, aggression, and violence that is tapped into by malfunctions of the limbic system that result from such causes as the rabies virus and Charles Whitman's tumor. What is so frightening about these malfunctions is that whereas we can easily understand the mental state of someone who is protecting a child, we cannot fathom the mind of someone who for no apparent reason commits an act of extreme violence.

Physicians have a name for the rare condition in which an overactive limbic system causes sudden outbursts of violence. It is called episodic dyscontrol and 75 percent of those who suffer from it are men. In many cases the violent episodes begin after a brain tumor, head injury, brain infection, or because of an epileptic seizure. In other cases, the cause is not so clear and the episodes may have occurred since childhood. There may be a genetic component. The episodes are often completely out of character with the person's normal behavior and they stop just as suddenly as they start. The person is usually utterly shocked, terribly upset, and bitterly remorseful about the behavior although sometimes the episodes are accompanied by partial or complete amnesia. The victims describe their violent impulses as compelling and beyond their control.

When a violent outburst begins, there is a striking transformation in the person who seemed just a few moments before to be perfectly normal. "There is a dramatic change of personality, voice, and manners," according to one neurologist. "The violence often has a primitive quality—gouging, kicking, clawing, biting, spitting—and the attacks are carried out so quickly and with such power that the victim is hard put to escape."[9]

Neurosurgeon Vernon Mark, who specializes in violent patients, described one man "who tried to decapitate his wife and daughter with a meat cleaver. He was so violent the police had to bring him in wrapped in a fishnet. His family explained that his personality had started undergoing a change about six months earlier. And he had been complaining of headaches and blurred vision. A neurological exam showed that he had a tumor underneath the right frontal lobe pressing directly on the limbic system. We removed the tumor, and the patient had a dramatic reversal in behavior."[10]

Another patient of Mark's was Julie, whose physician father, desperate for help, had contacted Mark. Julie had suffered from epilepsy since childhood and began to have unpredictable episodes of violence, an extremely rare occurrence in epileptics. She had attempted suicide four times. "By far the most serious attack," Mark said, "occurred when Julie was eighteen. She was at a movie with her father when she felt a wave of terror pass over her body, 'a knot of fear in the pit of my stomach,' as she termed it. She went to the ladies' room and stared at herself in the mirror while clutching a dinner knife which she always carried to defend herself during those occasions when, after an attack of running away, she would 'come to' in an unsavory part of the city."

While Julie stood before the mirror, another woman brushed her. Julie suddenly became violent and stabbed the woman in the chest. "There was a blood-curdling scream from the restroom. Julie's father rushed in and administered first aid to the stabbing victim and saved her life." Julie was placed under Mark's care. As part of his investigation of her behavior, tiny electrodes were inserted into both her cerebral hemispheres, including her right and left amygdala and right and left hippocampus. These electrodes could be stimulated by remote control to produce electrical impulses.

"On most electrodes we got nothing," said Mark, "no seizures, no attack behavior. But there was one specific pair of electrodes in the amygdala that brought on a dramatic change in her behavior. On the first occasion when we stimulated these electrodes, Julie became unresponsive and stopped answering questions. She began to stare and then took on a facial grimace characteristic of a primitive rage response. All the while seizure activity continued in the amygdala and hippocampus." Suddenly Julie began smashing her fists into the wall.

In order to confirm his observation, Mark later repeated the procedure. "She was playing a guitar and was quite unaware that any stimulation was going to take place. There was a neuropsychiatrist in the room watching her play the guitar. Within five seconds of stimulation, Julie stopped playing and stared blankly ahead. She didn't answer any of the questions that the neuropsychiatrist was now asking her. A cascade of abnormal, spikelike epileptic brain waves from her amygdala was then recorded. This was followed by a sudden and powerful swing of her guitar. She smashed the guitar against the wall, narrowly missing the doctor's head. Obviously that was the last time we have ever stimulated that particular electrode." Mark not only succeeded in reading Julie's mind by discovering how she would behave when a certain part of her brain was activated, he inadvertently demonstrated the human brain's possible vulnerability to an insidious, unthinkable technology: direct mind control.

Based on the data he collected, Mark determined that the focal point of Julie's epileptic seizures was her right amygdala. In a series of operations he destroyed the tissue of that amygdala. Fifteen years after the operation Julie still showed no sign of problems with controlling her fear and anger.[11]

Cases of episodic dyscontrol are not always so spectacular, though they are always tragic to the sufferer. Richard Restak, a physician with a neurology practice, described the case of a fifty-one-year-old middle management executive, the father of three, whose attacks "took the form of sudden facial flushing, heart pounding, 'sparks' before his eyes, and the welling up of rage. He felt totally out of control and would begin smashing windows, breaking up household furniture, punching the walls and doors to the extent of fracturing his hand. On occasion his fury led him to make reckless, impulsive excursions in his car that ended in minor accidents. Finally, as the fury abated, he would return home contrite and embarrassed."[12] An attack of episodic dyscontrol mimics the intense fear and violent anger any of us might feel if a stranger suddenly tried to kill us. But in this illness there is no actual threat, only a misfiring of the primitive fear system.

One of the great dangers of people suffering from episodic dyscontrol is that even when they seem frail they can perform amazing feats of strength during their violent outbursts. One patient tore the door off a refrigerator. He was sixteen years old. Another, a 105-pound woman, in a fit of rage picked up a large upholstered armchair and threw it over a dining room table.[13] This almost superhuman strength is not unique to episodic dyscontrol. Almost anyone is capable of it if they are in the grip of intense fear or anger.

An important part of the body's fear response is the preparation of the muscles for bursts of unusual strength and stamina that are designed by evolution to allow you to escape from danger with the utmost speed, or fight your way out of it. The increased strength is due to a combination of adrenaline, noradrenaline, and the other stress hormones. This burst of hormones enables people in intensely fearful situations—combat or disasters, for example—sometimes to accomplish acts of heroism requiring incredible physical abilities. When threatened, your primitive fear system signals the liver to release its stores of sugar (glucose) into the bloodstream. Stimulated by adrenaline, the liver becomes more efficient in producing new supplies of sugar, which is the fuel used by the muscles. Your breathing deepens and quickens and your lung capacity increases, forcing more oxygen into your bloodstream. Muscles burn sugar for energy by combining it with molecules of oxygen. Your spleen contracts, squirting out more red blood cells, which boost the oxygen-carrying capacity of the blood. More of the oxygen- and sugar-rich blood floods into the large muscles of your arms, chest, and legs as your blood vessels dilate and noradrenaline speeds up your heart rate. Not only does blood reach your muscles more quickly, but the waste products of burning the blood sugar are swiftly carried away from the muscles. Your blood coagulates faster, so bleeding stops sooner.

A teacher friend of mine—a petite, lively woman—once told me about a bizarre incident that happened to her in college. Late one night at her sorority house a bunch of drunken fraternity boys began pounding on the front door, demanding to be let in. When she and several other women refused to open the door, there was momentary silence, then a huge crash against the door. The fraternity boys were back, this time using a telephone pole as a battering ram. A utility company was installing new poles in the area and had left a stack of them nearby. The house mother of the sorority came down to see what was going on just as the boys knocked down the door. Their momentum carried them through the doorway, pole and all. As they stumbled in, they dropped the telephone pole—right on the leg of the house mother. When they realized what they had done, they panicked and ran. My friend said she had never been so frightened in her life. She ran to the house mother, who was pinned with a broken leg under the heavy pole. Desperate, she grabbed the end of the pole and lifted it off the woman. She had no idea how she did it. When the police came, it took six men to carry the pole out the door. She said every muscle in her body was sore for weeks.

This story makes an important point not only about my teacher friend and her ability to respond heroically to a frightening situation, but about the irresponsible behavior of the fraternity boys. Why did they pull such a stupid stunt? They were drunk. Alcohol is one of the oldest psychoactive substances, and it is used in virtually every culture in the world. Alcohol is a central-nervous-system depressant. In moderation it can be relaxing. In excess it can unleash reckless and even deadly behavior, and thousands of drunk-driving deaths every year are an awful reminder of how lethal it can be. It is common knowledge that too much alcohol impairs your judgment. But how? It turns out that alcohol depresses activity in the frontal lobes, particularly the prefrontal cortex, the seat of the rational fear system. By turning off the frontal lobes, excessive drinking shuts down the areas of the brain that control long-term planning and concern for consequences, and inhibit inappropriate and irrelevant impulses. Many victims of episodic dyscontrol also suffer from the symptoms of pathological intoxication. Just one drink can spark a violent outburst. Even among people who don't suffer from episodic dyscontrol, damage to the frontal lobes can be associated with violent behavior. And excessive consumption of alcohol mimics frontal lobe damage. That's why heavy drinking is so often associated with violence: fighting, spouse abuse, even murder.

The human brain has quadrupled in size over the last 2.5 million years, and the area of greatest expansion has been the frontal lobes, particularly the prefrontal cortex under the forehead. Observers as far back as Leonardo da Vinci, an avid anatomist, commented on how overdeveloped our frontal lobes are compared with other animals—more than twice as large as our nearest relative, the chimpanzee. The frontal lobes act as a massive inhibitor and shaper of the potent urges of our limbic system: fearful, aggressive, violent, sexual. Why are our frontal lobes so huge? Perhaps because our fears and other primitive urges are so powerful.

There is a constant struggle between our frontal lobes and limbic system to control our behavior, and when the frontal lobes lose, we often find ourselves in the midst of a burst of anger or fear. In episodic dyscontrol the exceptional intensity of the activation of the limbic system completely overwhelms frontal lobe control. Disorders like episodic dyscontrol and frontal lobe damage are very rare, yet extreme fear and violence are not. The frontal lobes give consciousness a mighty instrument with which to integrate and regulate behavior. But that instrument can be misused or ignored by those with apparently normal brains. The criminal who coldly and senselessly kills an innocent bank clerk has catastrophically failed to absorb the most basic norms of social behavior and refused to exert even minimal frontal lobe control over his primitive limbic urges. Psychologists in the nineteenth century termed this kind of psychopathic behavior "moral insanity."

For more than fifty years, brain researchers have suspected that the prefrontal cortex of the frontal lobes is the center for self-control and inhibiting emotional outbursts. A. R. Luria, the Russian neuropsychologist, observed in the 1930s that patients with damage to the prefrontal cortex were often impulsive and subject to explosive anger and fear. Our massive, complex prefrontal area is so uniquely human that animal experiments have limited value in exploring its function. Researchers have had to content themselves with studies of the behavior of brain-damaged patients, who may have injuries that extend beyond the prefrontal region. With the advent of modern brain imaging techniques, however, neuroscientists can now explore the role of the prefrontal cortex in the living brain. One study using PET technology examined twenty-four men and women who had been convicted of heat-of-passion murders and found that they had lower than normal activity in key prefrontal areas.[14] Recent PET imaging studies of the effects of cocaine addiction on the brain indicate that the drug shuts off the inhibitory activity of the prefrontal cortex, which tends to eliminate moral restraints on behavior and increase impulsiveness and violence.

The modern era of brain imaging is part of the computer revolution. It began in 1972 with the introduction of computed axial tomography (variously called X-ray CT, CAT, or CAT scan). The technology—developed by British engineer Godfrey Hounsfield and South African physicist Allan M. Cormack, both of whom won the Nobel Prize for their achievement—allowed doctors for the first time to see the details of living tissue without having to cut through the skin. The CAT scan uses the fact that different tissues absorb differing amounts of X rays. A patient is placed inside a circular array of detectors and a beam of X rays is passed through the body at many different angles. Computers then use the X-ray data to reconstruct a three-dimensional image of the tissues. Although the CAT technology is used on all parts of the body, it represented a particular breakthrough for neuroscience. For the first time the structure of the living brain could be clearly seen and tumors and other types of brain abnormalities clearly identified.[15]

Prior to the CAT scan, researchers used four major techniques to study the living brain: conventional X rays, electroencephalogram (EEG), observations of brain-injured patients, and direct brain stimulation. Conventional X rays are only able to image the bone of the skull, fluid-filled spaces (ventricles), and large blood vessels in the brain. The EEG measures the overall electrical activity in the cortex as billions of cortical neurons fire their action potentials. But it is not precise enough to localize cerebral activity. Observing patients with brain injuries has provided many important insights, but prior to the CAT scan this discipline was severely limited by the fact that researchers usually did not know for certain the location and extent of a patient's injury until after the patient died and the brain could be autopsied. The CAT scan provided a three-dimensional image of the injury while the patient was being studied, a boon to both research and rehabilitation.

Studies using direct electrical stimulation of the brain were made famous by Wilder Penfield of the Montreal Neurological Institute, who with his colleagues published a series of groundbreaking papers in the 1950s. While Penfield was performing brain surgery on epileptic patients he would stimulate various portions of their cortex with a tiny electrical current. He uncovered a wealth of data on the functions of the cortex. (Only the outer covering of the brain has nerve endings sensitive to pain—this is where the pain of a headache originates. The brain itself has no such nerve endings. The pain caused by brain tumors comes from pressure the tumor exerts on the outer brain covering. Brain surgery is normally performed with a wide-awake patient under only a local anesthetic.) Penfield found that stimulating areas of the cortex that control movement would actually move the muscles. Stimulating other areas sometimes produced thoughts and feelings in the patient's mind. His technique is now a standard procedure in many types of brain surgery. Since no two brains are exactly alike, the neurosurgeon can use electrical stimulation to map out the function of different cortical areas in his patient before proceeding with the rest of the operation. This reduces the likelihood that anything of importance will be damaged during the surgery.

Penfield and other neurosurgeons found that stimulating the temporal lobes sometimes produces extraordinary sensory responses, particularly if the stimulation occurs at or around the amygdala. Patients report different kinds of vivid experiences including hallucinations, memories, emotions, déjà vu, sexual feelings, and physical sensations. The emotions are almost always fear, ranging from mild anxiety to intense terror. The hallucinations are unusual because the patients report that they seem spectacularly real, as if they are actually happening. The hallucinations normally involve the memory of a past experience. Many patients also report hearing a snatch of a melody when a particular part of the lobe is stimulated. One neurosurgeon reported that a patient heard Led Zeppelin music when he stimulated a specific site. When the site was stimulated repeatedly, the patient sometimes heard the same music but other times said he heard a different song from the same album. In patients who have multiple operations, however, stimulating the same site on different days sometimes produces different memories. This indicates that memory is dynamic and is constantly being reorganized.[16]

In extremely serious brain disorders, such as Julie's, electrodes may be inserted into brain structures to study behavior. However, this is a risky procedure sometimes used in laboratory animals but rarely in humans. The CAT scan allows us to study the structure of the amygdala. But it doesn't show us what is happening in the brain circuitry when the amygdala is activated. Nevertheless, the CAT scan held out hope that an imaging technique might be possible that could study the activity of a patient's amygdala without risking an operation. Its tremendous success led scientists and engineers all over the world to begin searching for such a technology.

Magnetic resonance imaging (MRI) was the next major breakthrough in our ability to image the internal organs. This technique uses computers to measure changes in the magnetic fields of subatomic particles that are contained in all living tissue. It employs powerful magnetic fields and radio wave pulses, which are much safer than X rays, to produce images of the brain far more detailed than CAT scans. MRI of the cerebral cortex shows every delicate fold of that convoluted structure. Although CAT and MRI reveal the detailed structure of the brain, they don't show the brain at work. Scientists searched for a new technology, and they found it: positron emission tomography or PET.

Of the many ways the activity of the brain can be monitored, blood flow has proven to be the most reliable. Whenever an area of the brain

becomes active, it uses more energy. This energy is provided by the glucose and oxygen carried by the blood. When activity increases, the flow of blood increases. The suggestion that blood flow should track brain activity was first made way back in 1890 by English physiologists Charles Sherrington and Charles Roy. It was Sherrington, one of the giants of neuroscience, who gave the name "synapse" to the critical point of connection between two neurons. It is the synapse that binds separate neurons into the circuits of thought and behavior. Not only was Sherrington an original thinker and a superb teacher—Wilder Penfield was his student—he was a great writer. His description of the billions of neurons at work in the brain has never been surpassed: "It is as if the Milky Way entered upon some cosmic dance. Swiftly the brain becomes an enchanted loom where millions of flashing shuttles weave a dissolving pattern, always a meaningful pattern though never an abiding one; a shifting harmony of subpatterns."[17] Sherrington would have been delighted that his ideas about the flow of blood in the brain would one day help make the flashing shuttles of the enchanted loom visible to the eye.

PET technology creates a series of colorful images of the brain in action. The patient receives an injection of glucose to which a tiny amount of radioactive material has been added. The glucose travels via the blood to the brain where it is taken up by busy neurons. The more active an area of the brain, the more radioactive isotopes are deposited there. (These decay into harmless byproducts in about ten minutes.) The isotopes emit elementary particles called positrons, whose patterns are electronically detected, and computers use those patterns to create images of brain activity. The images are color coded. Areas of the brain that are most active light up in red. Those that are least active are coded blue. For example, if you touch something with your index finger, the part of the sensory cortex associated with that finger lights up in red. More areas of the brain light up if the action requires additional analysis—say, a researcher has asked you to push a button if you see a particular pattern of symbols projected onto a screen in front of you. MRI and CAT show the detailed structure of the brain and its constituent parts. PET begins to tell us how these parts function together to produce the mind.

PET studies have shown that there is quite a bit of variation among individuals in their pattern of brain activity. To set up a baseline for each patient, scientists use a simple technique that is more than a century old. First they take a PET image of the patient's brain at rest. The activity

levels in that image are subtracted from future images so that the true variation in brain activity from the baseline can be calculated. Dutch physiologist Franciscus Donders introduced this technique in 1868. He used it to determine how long our visual system takes to process color. He told his subjects to press a key when they saw a flash of ordinary white light, then asked them to do the same thing when they saw a flash of colored light. By simple subtraction of the first reaction time from the second he determined that it takes about a twentieth of a second (fifty milliseconds) for the human brain to discriminate color. This illustrates an important principle of brain architecture: the more complex the information we perceive, the more processing areas in the brain it must be filtered through, and the longer it takes to process. Our brain processes a photograph in black-and-white faster than one in color.

Other technologies that also image the brain at work have been developed using the magnetic measurement approach. One is called magneto-encephalography (MEG). Its advantage is that it does not require an expensive radioactive tracer and it is faster than PET. MEG can record brain activity that occurs every few thousandths of a second, while PET can only record an image every quarter second or so. Over the last few years an exciting new version of MRI, functional magnetic resonance imaging (fMRI), has been developed that merges the strengths of the CAT and PET technologies. Not only can it make a three-dimensional picture of brain structure, it can also show the brain activity within that structure by measuring the faint magnetic differences between oxygenated and deoxygenated blood. Researchers are now exploring combinations of all the imaging techniques (MRI and EEG, for example), searching for even more windows on the living brain.

Neuroscientists have achieved many important insights into brain function with these technologies. They have noticed, for example, that the frontal lobes and prefrontal cortex don't turn on and off as dramatically as other parts of the brain. While we are awake they are constantly active, even when we are doing nothing in particular. It makes intuitive sense that their role in inhibiting the limbic system, monitoring our current experience, and planning for the future would require continuous activity.

In many ways, our brain is beginning to resemble a muscle. The more you use it—master new skills, acquire new knowledge, dynamically experience new people and environments—the stronger it gets. When we learn something, circuits light up all over the brain and there is a tremendous expenditure of energy as it tackles the new task. This is a bit like a couch potato who tries to run a mile. The sweat pours off him and his lungs burn as he expends a huge amount of energy attempting to go the distance. But if he starts training conscientiously, his body will begin to reshape and reorganize itself. His muscles will strengthen and the capacity of his heart and lungs will increase. Eventually, his running will show an economy of form and energy and he will be able to jog a mile almost effortlessly. Similarly, when you take the time to master a skill, the brain reorganizes its circuits to achieve maximum efficiency. We can watch this happen for simple tasks during fMRI or PET imaging. In addition, researchers are beginning to notice that different people have different styles of learning, some more efficient than others. Brain imaging might allow us to identify these individual styles and find ways to improve them. Not only could this spark a revolution in education, it could suggest important techniques for improving our conscious ability to unlearn phobias, prejudices, and other stubborn problems created by the primitive fear system.

Another extremely important finding of these imaging technologies is that the brain does not have one or two master control centers. Instead the brain recruits many specialized areas into networks to accomplish its task. Just focusing your attention on one finger increases activity in widely scattered parts of the brain. Take a moment and think about making a complex movement with your right hand—say, successively touching the tip of your right thumb with tips of the other fingers on your right hand. Think about it but don't move a muscle. Areas of your left frontal lobe are lighting up with activity, particularly in the supplementary motor cortex, a patch of the frontal lobe in front of the ear and toward the top of the left cerebral hemisphere. (Remember, the left side of the brain generally controls the right side of the body, and vice versa.) Go ahead and make the movement. The instructions flow to the left primary motor cortex, located just behind the supplementary cortex, as your fingers make the movement. We now know what areas of the brain are mobilized in certain intellectual activities. If you are undergoing PET imaging and a specific area lights up in your left supplementary motor cortex, the radiologist will know without your saying anything that you are thinking about moving your right hand. In a very general way the PET technology is able to read your mind.

There is, however, a more specific technique available: the polygraph or lie detector. Unlike the police, scientists use it to detect truths rather than falsehoods. In the form normally used by researchers, the polygraph detects subtle differences in the skin's ability to conduct weak electrical currents. Its accuracy depends on the preconscious emotional processing of the primitive fear system. Fear detector would be a better nickname for the polygraph. As we discussed in the last chapter, when you experience a threatening situation it is first processed—before you are even consciously aware of it—by the primitive fear system centered in your limbic system. Even with a mild threat the primitive system triggers a response in the autonomic nervous system. Increased heart rate is one reaction. But the most reliable response is sweating. The secretion of sweat may be so small as to be unnoticeable. But even a tiny amount of salty fluid is enough to reduce resistance to an electric current. In a polygraph examination, the subject is fitted with electrodes on the skin. A weak electrical current passes through the skin from one electrode to the other. The polygraph records the electrical current as a wave. In general, the greater the amplitude or height of the wave, the greater the change in skin conductance and the stronger the response. The wave can also measure the frequency with which responses occur to a particular stimulus. Theoretically if you lie to a polygraph operator you will generate a fear response.

But a criminal investigation adds many layers of complexity to the use of a polygraph. The polygraph operator might ask a question related to the crime: Have you ever owned a .22-caliber pistol? The primitive fear system processes and reacts to these words before you are even consciously aware of them. If someone is guilty, then his dread of being found out should trigger a significant fear response. He will be unable to suppress this response consciously because it has already happened before his conscious mind has come into play. In the same way, the preconscious processes that precede answering the question, particularly if his answer is a lie, should also generate a fear response. The polygraph operator does not necessarily look at the answer to any single question but instead seeks a pattern of lying. In a criminal case, however, the whole situation may be emotionally charged, even for someone who is perfectly innocent. This makes it more difficult to determine whether any fear responses are a reaction to the questions or simply a response to the general atmosphere of anxiety. Undergoing a polygraph examination is frequently stressful, whether someone is innocent or guilty. And innocent people may still wish to hide certain things from the police. The polygraph operator tries to compensate for these emotions by asking a series of preliminary questions to establish a baseline for this particular person. In later questions, the operator looks for departures from this baseline. Nevertheless, under these circumstances administering a polygraph is more of an art than a science, which is why it is not accepted as evidence in most courtrooms.

In contrast, scientists try to keep their experimental setting simple and straightforward. In one classic experiment, each adult participant was given a polygraph examination while sitting in front of a screen. Pictures of spiders and snakes were flashed on the screen, but too fast for conscious awareness. When asked, each adult said he had seen nothing. Yet an increase in skin conductance was recorded for each picture in the adults who admitted to an extreme fear of spiders or snakes. No such increases were recorded in the adults who said they had no fear of these creatures.[18] This is compelling evidence of the potency of preconscious processing by the primitive fear system. And it shows how a skilled investigator might read someone's mind without his knowledge.

Imagine that I have agreed to participate in some apparently innocuous research. I am led into a room and hooked to a polygraph machine. In front of me is a blank screen. The researcher asks me to stare at the screen. He says the examination will begin in five minutes. While I stare idly at the screen, he is secretly flashing pictures too fast for my consciousness to perceive and recording my subliminal responses. After five minutes he excuses me, saying my participation won't be necessary after all. I leave, puzzled. With the data he collected, he can tell whether I am afraid of spiders, snakes, blood, mutilation, or anything else he chose to flash on the screen. I, on the other hand, did not even know I had been questioned. If he had asked me, I might have refused to talk about these things.

Has neuroscience developed the technology necessary to read our minds and plumb our fears? Yes, at a rather primitive level. And as these techniques evolve, we can expect functional magnetic resonance imaging and other technologies to duplicate and probably exceed the ability of the simple polygraph to register the preconscious reactions of our primitive fear system. A clever investigator with such a souped-up lie detector might make us very uncomfortable with an artful set of true-false questions—that is, if we chose to cooperate. There is certainly a danger that this technology will be abused. Already use of polygraphs to screen and monitor employees is growing in government and the private sector. Just the threat of a polygraph examination can be intimidating. Yet our deepest fears and most complex thoughts remain safe for the foreseeable future. Our understanding of the brain and its infinite subtleties is still crude. Despite the risks, however, the revolution in imaging holds tremendous promise for treating brain diseases and providing insights into how we can better tap the limitless potential of this three-pound marvel.

{ Chapter 4 }

Why Are We Afraid?

Over millions of years, the human body has evolved elaborate systems to keep itself alive. Our skin is studded with millions of microscopic pain receptors, called nociceptors. By the time these receptors fire, however, the damage has already been done. The aching, burning, stinging, searing sensations frantically transmitted to the brain may signal a minor injury or a mangled limb. The real evolutionary trick is to find a system that anticipates pain-producing situations before they happen. This is where fear comes in.

Fear systems in the brain allow us to recognize in advance circumstances that may cause injury or death and take steps to avoid them. Fear is molded by our experience of pain, both as individuals and as a species. But what would happen if pain ceased to exist? What if you never experienced the pain of a cut finger, a twisted knee, a bruised arm, or even the fierce pain of childbirth? There is a rare condition called congenital absence of pain in which individuals from birth never know the sensation of pain. A malfunction in the development of their nervous systems keeps the brain from ever registering pain signals. What are these people like? Many of them are described as eternally cheerful, almost bubbly. Since they experience no pain, they feel no fear. This carefree attitude, however, is one of a number of behavioral anomalies in sharp contrast to their true situation. People with this condition frequently suffer from severe injuries. Bend your index finger back as far as it will go. What do you feel? Pain. People with congenital absence of pain don't feel that. They are constantly tearing their joints because they cannot tell when they have bent them too far. They burn themselves because they do not instantly pull away when they inadvertently touch a hot object, even a flame, unless they see or smell their skin burning. If they cut themselves they may not notice until they feel the blood. Pain and the fear that pain teaches create a wary respect for the environment that keeps us alive and well.[1]

Yet pain is a dangerous ally. It instructs us, but it can also destroy us. There are certain types of chronic pain so intense the sufferer's life is consumed by misery. Episodes of unbearable agony are followed by an overwhelming fear of the next attack. One of these conditions is trigeminal neuralgia, described by Antonio Damasio, a professor of neurology and leading neuroscientist, as affecting the face "generally on one side and in one sector, for instance the cheek. Suddenly an innocent act such as touching the skin or an even more innocent breeze caressing the same skin may trigger a sudden excruciating pain. People afflicted complain of the sensation of knives stabbing their flesh, or pins sticking in their skin and bone. Their whole lives may become focused on the pain; they can do or think of nothing else while the jabbing lasts, and the jabbing may come on frequently. Their bodies close in a tight, defensive coil."[2]

Somewhere between these opposite poles of torment and utter painlessness most of us live our lives, our minds filled with an ever-changing hierarchy of pain-inspired fears. Why are we afraid? From an evolutionary perspective the answer is straightforward: so we can survive, preferably injury free, for as long as possible, or at least long enough to reproduce and rear our children. Clearly most of our fears come from experience. But why is something like the fear of snakes so common, even among people who have never seen a live snake? Are we born with certain fears?

Fear in animals can be classified as innate or learned. Innate fears are wired into the brain and nervous system by the genes. They are common in animals. The chicks of many bird species will automatically freeze if they detect a pair of unfamiliar eyes looking at them. The chicks innately interpret this pattern as evidence of a predator. In the laboratory, two sticks with marbles glued to the ends are enough to elicit this behavior. Human infants do not show such a specific fear reaction. Nevertheless innate fears seem to play a part in their responses as well. An infant is born with a fear of falling and will automatically cling to whatever it is placed against. If an object looms in a baby's visual field—approaches the face rapidly—a baby as young as one week will widen its eyes, pull its head back, raise its hands in a defensive position, and utter a cry. All animals, including humans, will automatically flee, attack, freeze, or utter a cry of distress under certain circumstances. Sudden, loud noises provoke an automatic response in humans as they do in virtually every animal. A surprising intrusion into the space near your body also tends to produce a fear reaction. If you are reading this book quietly by yourself, and someone unexpectedly taps you on the shoulder, you may jump. These kinds of innate fear responses are triggered by the primitive fear system as it preconsciously scans the data streaming in from your senses.

Some animals are genetically programmed to respond to an extreme fear with dramatic deceptions. The hognose snake, for example, displays a truly unusual behavior. If threatened by a predator it will often feign death—going limp, its mouth open, tongue hanging lifeless. To complete the illusion, the snake has special glands near its mouth that secrete blood. Many predators will not eat a dead animal. Chicks of ground-nesting birds like the plover will also feign death if they detect a predator. Roughly every thirty seconds the chick will imperceptibly open its eyes to see whether the predator is still there. An adult plover that sees a fox or other predator approaching its nest will initiate a remarkable ploy called the broken-wing display. The plover holds one or both of its wings in a crooked position, making it seem disabled and easy prey. Over and over, the plover attempts to fly away, only to fall over flapping helplessly because of its "broken" wing. Actually it is leading the fox away from the nest. When the predator is lured away from the area the plover flies off. Studies have shown that this stratagem works almost 90 percent of the time. If the fox happens to surprise a plover and catch it, the bird will struggle briefly then go limp. Biologists call this behavior tonic immobility. If other birds are nearby, the fox will often drop the bird it thinks it has killed and chase the others. After a second or two, the "dead" plover scurries off.[3]

Broken-wing displays and tonic immobility may seem a long way from human behavior, but there is evidence that some vestiges of these primitive, innate responses are retained in our nervous systems. Consider, for example, the case of David Livingstone, the nineteenth-century African explorer and missionary. On February 16, 1844, he was working in some ditches near the village of Mabotsa in southern Africa when he heard shouts. A group of Africans ran up and asked him to help kill a lion that had just attacked some sheep. The thirty-year-old Livingstone was well aware of the dangers of lions. Two years earlier he had reported seeing a woman "actually devoured in her garden by a lion." Livingstone took his gun and went across the valley hoping to track down the beast. Instead, the lion came after him. As the lion charged, Livingstone fired both barrels of his gun but only managed to wound the animal. He was feverishly trying to reload when, as he recounted later, "I heard a shout. Starting, and looking half round, I saw the lion just in the act of springing upon me. I was upon a little height; he caught my shoulder as he sprang, and we both came to the ground below together. Growling horribly close to my ear, he shook me as a terrier does a rat. The shock produced a stupor similar to that which seems to be felt by a mouse after the first shake of the cat. It caused a sort of dreaminess in which there was no sense of pain nor feeling of terror, though quite conscious of all that was happening. It was like what patients partially under the influence of chloroform describe, who see all the operation, but feel not the knife. This singular condition was not the result of any mental process. The shake annihilated fear, and allowed no sense of horror in looking round at the beast."[4]

Livingstone's left shoulder was immediately splintered by the lion's powerful jaws. Just then, several Africans came running up, including an elderly man named Mebelwe, who had been working with Livingstone as a teacher. Realizing his friend would be dead within moments, Mebelwe grabbed a gun from another man, aimed, and pulled the trigger. The gun misfired. The lion, however, was distracted and, possibly seeing additional easy prey, dropped the limp body of Livingstone and attacked Mebelwe. In the struggle with the lion, Mebelwe was bitten on the thigh and another man who tried to help him was bitten on the shoulder. At that moment, when everything seemed hopeless, the lion dropped dead from the wounds inflicted by Livingstone. The men spent months recovering. Livingstone owed his life not only to the heroic Mebelwe, but also perhaps to the involuntary tonic immobility brought on by the shock of the attack, which may have fooled the lion into thinking he was dead.

Jumping when you hear a loud noise, flinching when an object flies at you, and similar reactions are automatic, subconscious fear responses. We don't learn to fear loud noises. We are born with it. There is, however, a second category of innate fears. We are not born with the fears themselves, but only with the tendency to develop them quickly under the right circumstances. These are the prepared fears. In every culture in the world, fears of spiders, snakes, heights, and closed-in spaces rank at the top of the list of the most common fears. Why is it so easy to develop a fear of snakes but so hard to acquire one of mushrooms? Yes, certain kinds of snakes are poisonous, but so are certain kinds of mushrooms. It's true that we don't run across poisonous mushrooms very often, at least not that we are aware of, but when was the last time you saw a poisonous snake? And snake phobia is common even in areas in which there are practically no snakes at all. Psychologist S. Rachman, who specializes in the study and treatment of fear, reports that many school-children "who have never left their virtually snake-free island of Hawaii express a fear of snakes, even of harmless snakes. Immediately, one thinks of the possibility that they might have acquired their fear of snakes by watching films or television, or read in books about frightening experiences with snakes, and it is probable that indirect experiences of this kind are largely responsible for their fears." But older residents informed Rachman that even when Hawaii was much more isolated, fear of snakes was not uncommon. That an intense and long-lasting fear of snakes can be developed indirectly is remarkable. Even more striking are studies showing fear of snakes to be twice as common as dental fears, even though dentists are both far more familiar to most people and far more associated with painful experiences.[5]

For much of this century, science under the influence of behaviorism believed that fear was completely determined by the environment. If you happened to have a consistently bad experience with flowers (you were allergic to them, for example), you could develop a significant fear of flowers, even a phobia. But years of research revealed that some objects and situations are much easier to become afraid of than others. A child can easily become afraid of snakes, but no matter how ingenious and persistent the researcher, it is almost impossible to make him afraid of a toy duck. Many scientists have been driven to the conclusion that certain fears have roots deep in our evolutionary heritage. Martin Seligman, the psychologist who formulated the modern theory of prepared fears, argues that these common phobias "are about objects of natural importance to the survival of the species."[6] Besides spiders, snakes, heights, and claustrophobia, common phobias involve fears of thunder, darkness, public or open spaces (agoraphobia), and deep water. There are also common social phobias like fear of public speaking and aversion to strangers. Few people have all these fears but almost everybody has at least one of them. These kinds of fears tend to be long lasting and easily acquired, especially in childhood. One negative experience as a child, even an indirect one (a scary story about snakes, for example), may be enough to activate a prepared fear for life, although we still don't know why one child (say, in a group of children who hear a scary snake story) will develop it while another won't. Prepared fears involve a form of rapid sensitization with a probable genetic component. These kinds of phobias are treated with various techniques that seek to habituate someone to the feared object or circumstance. Habituation in the case of severe phobias can be exceedingly difficult, but not impossible.

In my case, as I mentioned earlier, I have no particular fear of snakes. I admire them as beautiful, useful creatures. This may be because I had a series of excellent science teachers in grade school who would occasionally bring in snakes for us to touch and examine. I can't, however, say the same thing about spiders. As a child I spent seven happy years in Tucson, Arizona. My brother and I played and hiked in the vast Sonoran Desert surrounding Tucson. This is the living desert, with a hundred varieties of cactus, from giant saguaro to barrel, and an incredible variety of wildlife. We enjoyed it all—well, most of it, anyway. I remember one night when our family had gone out to dinner and a movie. It was dark when we got home and no one had remembered to leave the outside light on. In the darkness, we gathered around the front door as my father unlocked it and reached in to turn on the outside light. My brother abruptly yelled. I looked down and froze. Five large tarantulas were scuttling around our feet. It was a miracle we hadn't stepped on them. I was probably already afraid of spiders, but that experience reinforced the fear. Ever since, the thought of a spider, especially a big spider, makes me slightly squeamish even though I know that the vast majority of spiders—including the species of tarantula native to Arizona—are inoffensive, useful, and amazing creatures. "Even harmless snakes and spiders are extremely common objects of fear," says Rachman, "and many people who are frightened of them readily acknowledge that their fear is senseless. Often they experience additional embarrassment from the fact that their fears are so irrational."[7]

All the knowledge I have picked up about spiders over the years has substantially reduced my childhood fear. But it has never completely gone away. The persistence of prepared fears in the human psyche may be an important clue to the evolutionary nature of fear in human beings.

These deep-seated fears are our only direct link to the minds of our ancestors, the earliest *Homo sapiens*, who emerged around a hundred thousand years ago. The link may go back even further, a million years or more, to the minds of the apelike hominid peoples who were the direct forebears of our species. Our oldest written records are little more than five thousand years old. We have examples of cave painting and other artwork that date to about thirty-five thousand years ago. Beyond that we have only a scattering of fossilized bones, stone tools, and other artifacts. Prepared fears may be our most vibrant clue to the mystery of how early humans lived and, more importantly, how they thought.

The list of prepared fears contains one more significant clue to this mystery. It comes not from what's on the list, but what isn't. Animal fears vary by species. A grizzly bear, at the top of the food chain, has fewer fears than a mouse, on the bottom. Yet there is one instinctive fear shared by virtually every animal on earth: fire. Its omission from the list of human prepared fears is glaring. Not only do we normally have no innate fear of fire, children are usually fascinated by it. Very few children have to be taught not to play with spiders. Almost every parent worries about his child playing with matches. Some extraordinary event must have occurred in human evolution to allow us to shed this fear so completely.

One final aspect of the mystery of the early human mind needs explanation. When was it that humans became so anxious and fearful? Animal fears never extend much beyond their immediate environment. Why do we worry about everything from global warming to nuclear winter? I believe the answer is linked in an interesting way to the fear of fire. We lost our fear of fire for the same reason that we gained our fear of just about everything else. To see this link clearly and probe the origin of fear in the human mind will require us to go back millions of years to the beginning of the human family.

First, however, there is one alternative explanation of prepared fears to consider, an explanation that is completely independent of biological evolution. The source of this explanation is psychoanalysis, which views prepared fears as diverse manifestations of repressed sexuality. One psychoanalyst, reviewing the fear of spiders, concluded that the weight of opinion in psychoanalysis agrees "that the spider is a representative of the dangerous (orally devouring and anally castrating) mother, and that the main problem of these patients seems to center around their sexual identification and bisexuality."[8] As you can imagine, the psychoanalytic interpretation of the snake phobia overflows with genitalia metaphors, especially phallic symbols. The decisive trend in modern psychology, however, has been to treat the psychoanalytical view of prepared fears as speculative, unhelpful, and outdated. Rachman concludes that "after a century of study there is still no acceptable evidence that psychoanalysis is an effective treatment. . . . The psychoanalytic theory of fear is stagnant. There is no sign here of new discoveries, refinements of methodology, improved treatment, or growth. Instead of intellectual bustle there is lethargy, and the theory has been passed by."[9]

Human beings are the last of the walking apes, a family of upright-walking hominid species that began emerging around seven million years ago in Africa, evolving from an ancestral ape population. All the other species of walking hominids are extinct, including *Homo erectus*, *Homo habilus*, and the most recent hominid species besides ourselves, the Neanderthals, who died out only about thirty thousand years ago. No other apes or monkeys walk upright as we do. Our closest living relatives, chimpanzees and gorillas, are knuckle walkers. We are the last of a once-flourishing family of species, an unusual distinction we share with aardvarks. Usually when a group of related species has dwindled down to only one, it is heading for extinction. Perhaps we are. But in the meantime, we have become the most widespread and successful large animal in the history of life on earth. We live on all continents and breed in all climates and habitats. What happened?

Fifteen million years ago a colossal rain forest spread uninterrupted across Africa from west to east. Within it countless species of early apes and monkeys thrived. Over the next several million years, however, huge changes took place in the landscape because of the slow shifting of the gigantic tectonic plates on which the oceans and continents rest. Two great plates were pulling apart on a line that runs from Turkey through Israel and down into East Africa, through Ethiopia, Kenya, Tanzania, and Mozambique. Their movement forced pools of liquid rock up near the surface in Kenya and Ethiopia, creating huge blisters of land rising up to nine thousand feet in a series of impressive highlands. These highlands disrupted the rain flow from west to east, and areas to the east became drier. The uninterrupted rain forest became patchy, with areas of forest interspersed with large areas of shrub land. As the plates continued to pull apart, a long, steep valley was formed north to south: the Great Rift Valley, with forested plateaus and spectacular cliffs that plunge thousands of feet to arid lowlands. For a long time the prevailing view among anthropologists was that the first hominids emerged from the forest into the savanna, the broad African plain dotted with large migrating herds of animals. But recent work has shown that the savanna did not come into existence until about three million years ago, millions of years after the evolution of walking apes. Scientists now theorize that the Rift Valley became an immense engine of evolution because it separated once-unified ape populations. The populations to the east of valley had to adapt to a new way of life in a mosaic of forests, shrub lands, and widely differing climates. Within these populations, some apes began to walk.[10]

Great changes in the environment are the mighty millstones of evolutionary change. They grind existing species through a series of challenges that test their ability to survive. Many times they don't, and go extinct. Sometimes it is the less specialized species that have the flexibility to survive. Too much specialization may rob a species of its ability to adapt quickly. The giant panda, for example, lives exclusively in the bamboo forests of Asia. If those forests disappear, as they are today under the pressure of growing human populations, then the giant panda will disappear. Apes and monkeys, on the other hand, are usually not so specialized. They eat plant foods, including different kinds of fruit, and sometimes a little meat. Their brains are relatively large, giving them a degree of behavioral flexibility. Apes such as chimpanzees and gorillas can walk upright for short distances. Given the shape of their legs and pelvis this is awkward for them, and they quickly revert to knuckle walking. But around ten million years ago, somewhere in the shrinking forests of East Africa, a group of chimpanzeelike apes began to change.

Evolution is about genes and reproduction. Every living thing has a set of genetic instructions that dictate its form. In our case, these instructions consist of about one hundred thousand genes. Changes in a small number of genes can make a large difference in form and behavior. We share, for example, more than 98 percent of our genes with chimpanzees. Genes vary, however, not only between species but among members of the same species. Except for identical twins (produced by nature's version of cloning), no two human beings have exactly the same genes. Every baby contains a random mixture of genes contributed equally by its mother and father. In addition, genes occasionally mutate as mistakes in copying are made by the machinery of the cell. These small differences in genes make each of us genetically unique, and give each of us a slightly different mix of strengths and weaknesses. Today civilization largely insulates us from predators, climate changes, many diseases, and other direct selection pressures. But our hominid ancestors were under constant pressure from the environment. Even a slight genetic advantage—better eyesight, increased speed, greater cunning—might make it more likely that a particular hominid would survive the rigors of the environment long enough to produce offspring. These offspring, in turn, had a good chance of inheriting the genes that gave the parent a survival advantage. Over many generations, descendants with superior genetic traits would tend to produce more offspring than other hominids who lacked them. As different kinds of adaptive genetic changes accumulated over hundreds of thousands of years through natural selection, particularly in a population isolated from the mainstream of a species, the genetic differences between the isolated population and the rest of the species could become so great that the two groups could no longer interbreed successfully. This is called reproductive isolation and when it happens a new species has been born.

There are two surviving species of chimpanzees: the common chimpanzee and the bonobo, or pygmy chimp, of Zaire. They share 99.3 percent of their genes and only diverged from each other about 3 million years ago. Bonobos look so much like other chimpanzees that it took decades for zoologists to realize that they are a separate species. But separate they are. Bonobos tend to be smarter and less aggressive than the common chimpanzee. Most importantly, the two species cannot interbreed.

We don't know for sure why around ten million years ago one group of proto-hominids began undergoing the complex changes needed to walk upright. We probably never will. Evolution is a combination of chance and necessity and leaves only a smattering of evidence in the fossil record. But we can theorize that in the shrinking forests, with fruit trees and other food sources now more widely scattered, there was an advantage to moving on the ground from place to place more efficiently. And studies have shown that walking upright is about 50 percent more energy efficient than knuckle walking. This was the first step in the evolutionary process that led to modern humans. Its importance cannot be exaggerated. Walking upright freed the hands to specialize in exploring and shaping the world. Hands were our first and most important tools.

All primates originally evolved as tree dwellers. Monkeys still live in the canopy of forests, and chimpanzees and gorillas are excellent climbers. Their knuckle walking is an evolutionary compromise that allows them to move with moderate efficiency on the ground while preserving the long arms and other adaptations that give them their exceptional agility in the trees. By walking upright, however, early hominids made a decisive biological commitment to living on the forest floor. Hominids began to show signs of the anatomical changes that led to the fully human form. Modern humans have shorter arms and longer legs than apes. Our builds are slighter, probably to minimize the amount of weight that must be carried in the upright posture. Our chests are modified to allow the arms to swing freely as we walk and to enable the deep breathing necessary for running. There are a whole series of modifications to our pelvis, legs, and feet. The human hand has lost the curved shape of the ape hand, which is adapted to climbing, and now has an opposable thumb that gives it far more flexibility and precision. Though the brain of the first hominids was roughly ape sized—about a pound compared to the three-pound modern human brain—it showed a small but noticeable advance over the chimpanzee brain, both in relative size and architecture. These were walking apes with intriguing potential.[11]

No fossils have yet been found of any of these creatures older than about four million years. The estimate that the hominids branched off from the apes about seven million years ago comes from a new discipline called molecular anthropology. Molecular anthropologists study the genetic variations between species. They have discovered that genetic differences in the form of mutations seem to accumulate over millions of years at a relatively constant rate. This is a kind of genetic clock. The greater the genetic differences that are observed between two species, the longer ago they diverged from a common ancestral population. By studying the existing fossil record, this clock has been calibrated using species whose dates of divergence we know through carbon dating or other methods. The genetic clock can then be applied to pairs of species whose dates of divergence we don't know, like humans and chimpanzees or humans and gorillas. It shows that these pairs of species diverged about seven million and ten million years ago, respectively. Chimpanzees are our closest relatives among the apes.

Fossils of early hominid species that lived between three and four million years ago have been found. These apelike creatures are all classified as members of the genus *Australopithecus*, meaning "southern ape." They include the famous "Lucy" skeleton of an Ethiopian hominid barely three feet tall, belonging to the species *Australopithecus afarensis*, and an even older species, *Australopithecus anamensis*, found recently in Kenya. They show the characteristic pattern of upright posture and small brains. The evidence indicates that these hominids lived in heavily wooded areas. (Hominidae, or hominid, is the family name for all species in the human lineage including australopithecines.) In 1976 anthropologist Mary Leakey made an especially remarkable discovery: a trail of 4-million-year-old fossilized hominid footprints made through a layer of volcanic ash. The fossil record, however, is notoriously incomplete. It depends both on chance events preserving bones and other artifacts in exactly the right way to convert them into fossils and anthropologists being lucky enough to uncover these fossils. There may have been many different species of early hominids that radiated out from the original population into different environments, but we only have evidence for a handful.

It is easy to gloss over the brutal and terrifying environment in which these early hominids lived. Like their cousins the apes, the australopithecines were no match for any large predator. We assume that they searched for food in groups, constantly on the alert. A moment's inattention could be disastrous. The slightest illness or disability, even fleeting lameness, could prove fatal, and the old and the weak quickly perished. These creatures constantly faced the dangers of starvation, disease-carrying insects, and, quite possibly, attacks by other hominids. In the last few decades, biologists have discovered that killing within primate species is fairly common. Primatologist Jane Goodall carefully documented the calculated extermination over many months of one band of common chimpanzees by a neighboring band, which then usurped its territory. We tend to view chimpanzees and gorillas as gentle, funny creatures, and they often are. But in the wild, where the pressure to survive and reproduce is relentless, primate behavior can be cruel. "Recent discoveries about apes suggest," says physiologist Jared Diamond, "that a gorilla or common chimp stands at least as good a chance of being murdered as does the average human. Among gorillas, for instance, males fight each other for ownership of harems of females, and the victor may kill the loser's infants as well as the loser himself. Such fighting is a major cause of death for infant and adult male gorillas. The typical gorilla mother loses at least one infant to infanticidal males in the course of her life."[12]

For 4 million years the early hominid pattern of upright posture and small brains continued without much change. There is no evidence of toolmaking or any other sophisticated activity. Then about 3 million years ago, for reasons we don't yet understand, the earth's climate started to fluctuate. A long series of ice ages began (the last one ended only ten thousand years ago) and because of the periodic climate shifts, habitats were transformed. The broad African savanna emerged with its populations of big game. Hominid species were again ground through the millstones of evolutionary change. What emerged, possibly from one isolated population of australopithecines, was a new adaptation: the first species of our own genus *Homo*. Around 2.5 million years ago primitive stone tools began to appear: crude choppers, scrapers, and hammers. The first new species of which we have fossil evidence is *Homo habilus* (handy man), who lived about 2 million years ago. With this species we have a dramatic shift from the earlier hominid pattern of small brain, large teeth, and protruding jaws to the human pattern of large brain, small teeth, and flatter face. The structure of the new species' teeth indicates a dietary shift that added significant amounts of meat to the basically vegetarian hominid diet. The shift to meat may have been a crucial ingredient in the subsequent expansion of the brain. Although the human brain makes up only about 2 percent of total body weight, it consumes 20 percent of the body's total energy production. Meat is a high-energy food and an exceptionally concentrated source of protein and fat. Adding meat to the diet may have given early humans sufficient energy resources to evolve larger brains. It is not clear whether members of the early *Homo* species were hunters, scavengers, or a bit of both. The brain of *Homo habilus* weighed one and a half pounds, half again as large as the australopithecine brain. More significantly, there was a radical change in brain architecture. In the chimpanzee and gorilla, the occipital lobes in the back of the brain are relatively large compared to the modestly sized frontal lobes. This was the pattern in the australopithecines. But in *Homo habilus* the frontal lobes ballooned in comparison to the occipital ones, and the entire neocortex expanded. The occipital lobes, as you will remember, are primarily concerned with vision. With *Homo habilus* we see the unmistakable signs of a momentous shift from vision to imagination and planning. Australopithecines continued to exist side by side with early species of *Homo*, but by 1 million years ago they were extinct.[13]

Many animals have much keener senses than humans. We marvel, for example, at a dog's sense of smell. But with *Homo habilus* we see the beginnings of a peculiar sense that humans have in far greater measure than any other species: what I would call the sense of time, space, and possibility.

Because humans are so weak when compared to other large predators and have so few instincts, they are forced to deal with danger through elaborate anticipation. With the expansion of the frontal lobes we see the beginnings of a vastly extended and elaborated sense of time, whose components are a sense of the future that extends indefinitely forward, a sense of the past that extends indefinitely backward, and a spacious sense of the present. We are aware, for example, not only that we exist at this moment in a specific time and place, but that we live on a planet circling a star that is part of a galaxy and universe.

Other animals might be said to live much more in the past. Their genetic instincts that evolved in the past largely control their present and future behavior. If these instincts fail to keep up with changes in the environment—their niche disappears too quickly, as is the case with the giant panda's bamboo forests—they are unable to cope and go extinct unless their species can evolve fast enough to adjust to a new niche. They have little capacity to plan for change. But weak and fearful humans, with their sense of time, must plan. This planning capacity is the sense of possibility. Planning promotes the development of a sense of self, because we must visualize the same self in alternative possible future scenarios.

Consciousness—our perception of a unique self flowing through time, space, and possibility—may thus have evolved from this vastly expanded sense. Consciousness may be a byproduct of the fearful, planning brain. Our unique sense of time, space, and possibility helps explain both our fear of the unknown and our insatiable curiosity: we are helpless to plan effectively if we don't understand the world around us. This sense has led us to construct models of the entire universe all the way back to the beginning of time (the big bang), roughly 15 billion years ago, and visualize how the universe may evolve through the end of time. The obsession with time, particularly planning for the future, also helps explain the universal human fascination with life after death.

The fossil record that anthropologists rely on consists mostly of bits and pieces of skeletons. The bone of an arm might be recovered from one site, a skull from another. Often these fossilized bones are shattered into fragments that must be laboriously pieced together. But in 1984 something amazing happened. Richard Leakey—the son of the famous husband and wife anthropologists, Mary and Louis Leakey—was exploring the western shore of Kenya's Lake Turkana with his team. As they surveyed the area, his longtime friend Kamoya Kimeu noticed a small piece of fossilized skull mixed with the pebbles on a slope near a gully. Immediately Leakey and his team began a careful search for more of the skull. What they found astounded them. Leakey spent five seasons excavating the site, painstakingly sifting through fifteen hundred tons of sediment in a massive search for every last shard of the fossil. When he was finished, he had assembled the skeleton of a nine-year-old boy who had died of unknown causes 1.6 million years ago. Anthropologists were utterly flabbergasted when Leakey announced his discovery of a virtually complete skeleton, which he dubbed Turkana boy. Until then no complete human skeleton had ever been found that was more than one hundred thousand years old.[14] The only comparable find was the partially complete 3-million-year-old *Australopithecus* skeleton of the hominid Lucy discovered in 1974 by an American-French expedition. Turkana boy represents a new species of *Homo* with an anatomy that is almost completely modern. The brain has expanded to two pounds and the limbs are long and slender. It is estimated that if the boy had lived, he would have grown to be about six feet tall.

Turkana boy was originally assigned to the species *Homo erectus*, which was thought to be the ancestor of all subsequent species of *Homo*, including modern humans. But in recent years, with the discovery of more fossils, there has been a major rethinking of the fossil record. Many anthropologists now believe that the path that leads to *Homo sapiens* is much more complex than they once thought.[15] Turkana boy is now increasingly placed in his own species, *Homo ergaster*, which may be the actual ancestor of all subsequent human species. According to the latest theory—let's call it the multiple Out of Africa theory—less than a million years after early humans left the edges of the forest to wander the recently formed African plains they gained sufficient confidence to launch a series of monumental migrations out of Africa and into the rest of the Old World. The initial migration may have occurred between 1.5 and 2 million years ago. Groups of humans, possibly *Homo ergaster*, began migrating for the first time out of Africa. Over thousands of years they colonized the Middle East, parts of Europe, and Asia all the way to Beijing. Around 1.4 million years ago a new type of toolmaking technology, called Acheulean, evolved in Africa. These tools were larger and more carefully shaped than the older tools (called Oldowan), but they never showed up in eastern Asia. This suggests to some anthropologists that the early Asian population of humans had become isolated from its African roots. *Homo erectus* may have been a species of early humans that evolved from an isolated Asian population of *Homo ergaster*.

There is one important problem with the theory of an early migration of humans out of Africa and into Europe and Asia. How did these people survive the ice age climate? Turkana boy's tall, slender built is an adaptation to the warm African climate. Humans—and animals—that have lived in colder climates for thousands of years tend to have shorter, bulkier physiques, an adaptation that preserves body heat. We can see this today in the Inuit people (Eskimos). Clearly humans must have developed the ability to fashion warm clothing out of animal skins. But it is also tempting to think that their large brains had given them the ability to conquer their fear of fire. There are reports of East African sites several million years old containing fire-scorched stones that appear to be arranged as a hearth. But one cannot rule out that the stones could have been scorched in an accidental fire started by lightning or some other cause. If early humans had not yet harnessed fire, the colder climates of Europe and Asia would have been a powerful incentive to do so. Control of fire may have been discovered and rediscovered many times before it spread widely enough to become a permanent cultural fixture.

Thirty-five miles south of Beijing there is a place called Dragon Bone Hill (Chou-k'ou-tien, in Chinese) containing a limestone-filled cave. In 1926 scientists began carefully removing the limestone, looking for fossils. They were lavishly rewarded. By 1941 they had uncovered the remains of fifteen early humans, collectively called Peking Man, now classified as *Homo erectus*. Equally important, they had the first clear evidence that as of half a million years ago humans were using fire. Encased in the limestone were wood, wood ash, charcoal, charred animal bones, and seeds—compelling evidence that Peking Man used fire to survive the ice-age winters of north China.

According to the multiple Out of Africa theory, successive waves of migration followed the first great exodus of early humans to Eurasia. There were at least four more large migrations, occurring roughly every half a million years. This was a complicated process. In some places the new migrants competed with the older migrants, perhaps engaging in warfare, perhaps coexisting peacefully. In other places, colonies failed. Western Europe, for example, may have been recolonized repeatedly. The new waves of migrants may not even have reached the farthest corners of Asia, where *Homo erectus* had evolved.

Let me note here that among anthropologists the Out of Africa theory has one major competitor. It is called the multiregional theory and it posits that after a migration of archaic humans from Africa to Eurasia about 2 million years ago there were no further migrations of evolutionary importance. According to this theory, all the regional archaic human populations that were established by this initial migration eventually evolved modern human characteristics. Because of gene exchanges through interbreeding between the different regions, the human race remained a single species. But the theory is contradicted by several lines of evidence, especially genetic evidence, which strongly indicates that all modern humans descended from a single African population that evolved around one hundred thousand years ago. Today, the multiregional theory is a minority position among anthropologists, and its support has substantially eroded in recent years.[16]

While the multiple Out of Africa theory concedes that some regional populations of early humans in Eurasia evolved into new species, it argues that the most important site of human evolution was in Africa itself. One African population, probably of *Homo ergaster*, produced another new species, *Homo heidelbergensis*, with a two-and-a-half-pound brain, just short of modern human size. Members of this species may have made up the later waves of African migrants. One group of *Homo heidelbergensis* established itself in Europe and over hundreds of thousands of years seems to have given rise to another species, the Neanderthals, who appeared about one hundred and fifty thousand years ago, spreading through Europe and western Asia. Neanderthals have been caricatured as stooping, beetle-browed, hairy cavemen. Actually they are our closest cousins among the different kinds of early humans. Their brains, in fact, were on average about 10 percent larger than ours. The Neanderthals' powerful, bulky bodies adapted them to the ice-age climate of Eurasia. Neanderthal campsites consistently show evidence of the use of fire. And with these people, we have the first evidence of the ritual burying of the dead.

In the Zagros Mountains of northern Iraq lies a site that offers a window on the lives of Neanderthals: the Shanidar Cave. Excavated in the 1950s and 1960s, it contained the grave of an old Neanderthal man. Fossilized traces of pollen and other residue revealed that body had been laid on a bed of branches woven with flowers, some colorful and others with medicinal value. Several dozen Neanderthal burial sites have been discovered, none older than about one hundred thousand years. There is also evidence that Neanderthals cared for the injured and infirm. Some Neanderthal skeletons exhibit signs of degenerative diseases and long-term physical disabilities that would have required the individual to be helped by others. Despite this evidence of intelligence, Neanderthals lived in a relatively static society. For sixty thousand years, their tools showed no significant changes. And there are few signs of artistic expression or other forms of cultural evolution.

Many Neanderthal fossils have been found in caves, including the very first Neanderthal skeleton ever found, which was found in the Feldhofer Grotto above the Düssel River in Germany's Neander Valley. This led to the Neanderthals being nicknamed cavemen. Actually all early humans seemed to prefer caves when they could find them, even australopithecines. These not only provide shelter but are comparatively easy to defend against predators. Scientists have determined that certain caves were used repeatedly over thousands of years by humans. Large caves are particularly valuable in cold climates because their temperature tends to stay constant. The cave system in Dragon Bone Hill was used by Peking Man for a quarter of a million years. But caves are relatively rare and the probable social organization of most early humans—small bands of men, women, and children hunting, scavenging, and gathering plant food—may have led many to wander a fairly large territory. During winter or the rainy season some of these groups might have returned to a favorite cave.

Because they are protected by the elements, caves like Shanidar are an ideal environment for preserving fossils. Longuppo Cave in the Szechwan Province of China has recently yielded fossil fragments over 1.5 million years old that may belong to *Homo ergaster*, the predecessor of *Homo erectus*. The Gran Dolima cave site in northern Spain is yielding fossils of *Homo heidelbergensis*, possible ancestor of the later Neanderthals. Around one hundred and fifty thousand years ago, about the same time Neanderthals were appearing in Europe, a momentous evolutionary event was taking place in Africa. This event, too, is recorded in the recesses of caves.

Gouged out of a hill overlooking a vast expanse of southern ocean, the Klasies River Mouth Cave in the Cape Province of South Africa has been a favorite haunt of humans for tens of thousands of years. In 1968, pieces of two fossilized human jaws and other skeletal fragments found there showed an anatomy that is completely modern. Anthropologists were astonished when the fragments were dated to one hundred thousand years ago. Other findings in South Africa, East Africa, and the Middle East suggest that populations of modern humans, *Homo sapiens*, were well established between fifty thousand and one hundred thousand years ago.[17] Modern humans show the same general tall, long-limbed anatomy as Turkana boy, an adaptation to the hot African climate. But they are not as heavily muscled and have a brain that is one-third larger. Whereas stocky Neanderthals usually lived only into their thirties and almost never past forty-five, modern humans could live considerably longer, which meant they were able to accumulate much more survival-oriented lore in a lifetime. Over the long ages before the invention of writing, the older members of the group would pass along this lore to the younger generation by example and word of mouth. In most traditional societies, there continues to be a profound respect for the elders of the social group, who are the repositories of this wisdom.

Approximately fifty thousand years ago a remarkable and mysterious transformation began. At that moment in history, in the middle of the last ice age, at least three different types of humans were living throughout Africa and in large parts of Europe and Asia. Northern Europe, Siberia, the Americas, and Australia were empty of humans. Within forty thousand years—an incredibly short space of time by historical standards—all these areas would be occupied by humans, but only those of one species: ours. The change began in the Middle East where Neanderthals started disappearing, replaced by modern humans. Then the same process started in Eastern Europe and western Asia. In eastern Asia another population of humans, possibly late *Homo erectus*, began to vanish. Forty thousand years ago modern humans made their appearance in Western Europe. Anthropologists call these people Cro-Magnons, after the site in France where their remains were first identified. By thirty-eight thousand years ago, Neanderthals were gone from Eastern Europe. The process took longer in the western areas of the continent. In what is now southwestern France there is evidence that a population of Neanderthals tried to survive by adopting the new technology brought by the Cro-Magnons. They failed. By thirty-two thousand years ago they were gone, and by thirty thousand years ago not a single Neanderthal remained anywhere. They were extinct. In fact, all species of humans were extinct except *Homo sapiens*. This unprecedented surge of migration and replacement carried modern humans throughout the world. By fifty thousand years ago, they had voyaged from what is now Indonesia to Australia, rapidly colonizing the continent. With their fire-based technology, modern humans would go on to occupy the frigid territories of northern Russia and Siberia by no later than twenty thousand years ago. From there, they would move across the Bering Strait to Alaska. The Americas would be peopled by no later than eleven thousand years ago, just before the end of the last ice age.

With the rise of *Homo sapiens,* the key characteristic of the modern mind emerged: innovation. Cultural evolution rather than biological evolution became the dominant mode of change. Over the previous three million years new technologies had only materialized when a new, brainier species of *Homo* happened to evolve. Now modern humans began to build up layers of cultural change, in the form of new ideas and behaviors, that led to successive technological breakthroughs. The size of the human brain hasn't changed in at least a hundred thousand years, yet modern humans through their complex cultures have proceeded at an accelerating pace through the Stone Age into the age of agriculture and emerging civilizations, the Bronze Age, the Iron Age, and now the Industrial Age. All this change began with what is called the Upper Paleolithic revolution of forty thousand years ago, when modern humans swept away once and for all the older Oldowan, Acheulean, and other technologies. They replaced clumsy stone tools with an inventive, highly fluid technology featuring not only carefully crafted standardized stone implements of the highest quality but new materials such as bone, antler, and clay. There were compound tools, an unprecedented advance: ax heads set in wooden handles, spear points cunningly attached to shafts. Art emerged for the first time. There was sculpture and painting, such as the famous animal paintings in the caves of Lascaux in the Perigord region of France. A common feature of all prehistoric cave art was a poignant symbol of self-awareness, the handprint, produced by blowing paint around the hand as it was held against a rock surface. Tools became works of art, decorated with animal carvings. Beads, pendants, bracelets, and necklaces were crafted as part of the new art of body ornamentation. Instead of being static for hundreds of thousands of years, art and technology were dynamic, varying not only over time but from place to place, a sure sign of the activity of individual creative minds. Living sites increased in size as the social order became more complex and the population more numerous. Upper Paleolithic peoples began trading with each other over long distances, not just for necessities but for luxuries. The Neanderthal practice of burying the dead continued, but on a much more elaborate scale. The body was often decorated, and many different kinds of goods— some, perhaps, with religious significance—were included in the grave. All this is a clear indication that within the Cro-Magnon mind was a complex, self-conscious, and highly individualistic model of the world.

What was it that sparked the Upper Paleolithic revolution? Why did it take at least half a millennium after the first appearance of *Homo sapiens* for it to begin? The most popular hypothesis is that the revolution coincided with the full development of spoken complex language. But the question of when and how language developed not only in modern humans but in all species of early humans is tremendously controversial. The structure of the human neocortex leaves an impression on the inside of the skull. A number of researchers have concluded that even in the brain of *Homo habilus*, the first known species of human, the speech areas of the frontal and parietal lobes show the characteristic expansion necessary for speech.[18] Whether *Homo habilus* actually spoke, however, and what form that speech might have taken is purely speculative. Complex language might have existed all along in early *Homo sapiens*, but it could have taken thousands of years for them to learn how to tap the incredible power of their advanced brains and language for the purpose of innovation and sophisticated social organization. There is some evidence of experiments with new technology in northwest and southern Africa prior to the Upper Paleolithic revolution. Learning consciously how to counterbalance the urgent, simplistic demands of the primitive fear system with the sophisticated analytical, planning, and communication abilities of the rational fear system might have been a long, arduous process.

Once the revolution did start there remains the question of why the other types of human beings, particularly the Neanderthals, disappeared so quickly. Possibly new waves of modern humans expanding out of Africa killed them off, either violently or through the introduction of disease, just as European expansion introduced smallpox to vulnerable American Indians. Perhaps they simply lost out in a relatively peaceful competition for resources. Studies have shown that when just a small initial increase in mortality in a population is amplified over many generations it can lead to extinction in a millennium or two, which is about the time scale of Neanderthal disappearance after the Upper Paleolithic revolution began.

Out of the brutal environment of prehistory, our species miraculously emerged. Why had the human brain so dramatically expanded to more than three times the size of a chimp's? There are many theories, but I would argue that the short answer is fear. Compared to a lion, a tiger, a gazelle, our hominid ancestors were clumsy, unspecialized, and weak. No individual australopithecine or early human could take on a lion bare-handed. And modern humans are even weaker than many of our ancestral species. If Turkana boy had lived and grown to his full six feet or so, he would have been stronger than the strongest human alive today. His bones were twice as thick as a modern human's with attachments for huge muscles. Nevertheless he would still have stood little chance against a sixteen-hundred-pound bear. With modern humans, evolution moved away from strength and power as a survival strategy to one that relies almost completely on intelligence and cunning.[19]

Homo habilus did not have the teeth or claws to succeed as even a scavenger of dead carcasses so he invented primitive stone tools to slit through tough hides and carve the meat. Out of desperation, he probably threw some of these stones at attacking predators and learned a new survival technique. Throwing objects became a strategy not only for defense, but for hunting. Throwing stones led to throwing spears and allowed a slow, weak species to begin hunting larger animals. One theory behind human brain expansion is that larger brains are useful for the complex coordination of neurons and muscles required for accurate throwing. No gorilla or chimpanzee can throw like a human. Originally we hurled stones and spears, then moved on to bows and arrows. Now we throw ninety-mile-per-hour fastballs and intercontinental ballistic missiles.[20]

Even with a spear, however, no single human could withstand the attack of a pride of lions. This required a high degree of social cooperation to defend collectively against danger. Such cooperation was powerfully aided by the emergence of the most powerful tool of all for orchestrating social behavior: spoken language. Many theories seek to explain the expansion of the human brain in terms of language. A larger brain produced a richer language, which enabled the social structure to become more complex and efficient. Within a complex social structure, our weaknesses could become strengths. The human diet, for example, is not specialized. We can, and do, eat practically anything, even things that are less than minimally nutritious. We are not driven by instinct to seek out the proper foods. Instead, we must take the time to learn what is edible in our environment—whether a given mushroom, for example, is nutritious or poisonous. Elaborate social cooperation and a division of labor by sex enabled small groups of humans to make the maximum use of the food resources in a given area. Anthropologists carefully studied the hunter-gatherer peoples that survived into the nineteenth and twentieth centuries. They found that in most cases the women of these societies were primarily responsible for gathering plant foods and contributed at least 60 percent of the calories in the diet. Men hunted for animals, a less reliable source of food that nevertheless provided high quality protein. The hunter-gatherer diet included an enormous range of foods and required a large body of knowledge to identify each particular food, its location, and how best to prepare it. Generally the more diverse a diet an animal has, the larger its brain. Chimpanzees are the most omnivorous ape. Not only do they eat a wide variety of fruits and other plant foods, they will occasionally catch and eat small animals.

Our large brain is not only a speaking brain but a fearful one. Most of our fears are learned. But some seem to be genetically wired into our primitive fear system as special sensitivities. These are the prepared fears. How could a fear, or at least a fearful tendency, become a part of our genes? Presumably these fears had survival value for early humans, or their australopithecine ancestors. The actual course of evolution is complex, however. The genes for some traits are linked. When natural selection changes one of the traits, the others have to change, too. For example, genes controlling the shape of the skull might also affect the size of the teeth. When natural selection gave modern humans a flatter face and a larger braincase, the changes in these skull genes might have automatically provided us smaller teeth, not because smaller teeth have some sort of survival advantage. Similarly some of our prepared fears could have been the accidental result of other evolutionary changes in the brain. No one knows for sure. Yet it may well turn out that these fears do reflect adaptive tendencies that evolved in our early ancestors. Consider a few simplified examples.

We descended from ancient species of tree-dwelling primates and these acrobatic creatures have no fear of heights at all. The rare monkey who happened to be born with a fear of heights would not prosper in the tree-dwelling niche and would probably leave few offspring. When our hominid ancestors began walking on two legs, however, the situation changed dramatically. In the Great Rift Valley with its thousand-foot cliffs, a sensitivity to heights would be valuable. Those rare hominids that had a genetic predisposition to avoid heights would be less likely to die in falls and thus leave more offspring. This initially rare genetic tendency would become more common over hundreds of thousands of years as multiplying numbers of descendants continued to reap the benefits of shunning high places and left more offspring than their more fearless fellow hominids. The queasy sensation some people experience when they look over the edge of the Empire State Building's observation deck (assuming they will go up to the observation deck at all) is, in a sense, the same feeling that one of our ancient hominid ancestors experienced millions of years ago as it scurried away from some precipice in East Africa.

The prepared fears of snakes and deep water may be much older than that of heights and may also trace back to our tree-dwelling primate ancestors. Monkeys and other primates tend to be poor swimmers, so a genetic tendency to avoid deep water is highly adaptive. Snakes are a major predator of small primates, so this fear, too, would be adaptive. That monkeys have a prepared fear of snakes has been demonstrated in the laboratory. In one experiment, laboratory-raised monkeys who had never seen a snake were shown a videotape of other monkeys reacting fearfully to the presence of a snake. The primates quickly acquired the same fear. On the other hand, when a second group watched a doctored videotape showing other monkeys reacting fearfully in the presence of flowers, the laboratory monkeys did not acquire a fear of flowers.[21] The fear of thunder may be another ancient legacy from our forest-dwelling ancestors, reflecting a sensitivity to the dangers of lightning.

One night on a camping trip when I was twelve I was sleeping in my tent when I suddenly woke up feeling awful. My head was spinning and my arm was sore. I went out and sat for a while by the last glowing embers of the campfire. Then I tried to go back to sleep but could only toss and turn. The next morning I had a three-inch blister on my arm that took a couple of days to go away. The doctor said I had probably been bitten by a spider. The commitment by australopithecines and early humans to living and sleeping on the ground and in caves meant a greater exposure to insects, some of which can be dangerous. A greater wariness of insects would have been adaptive. This may be the reason many children show a fear of strange insects, just as they sometimes are afraid of large animals, which the primitive fear system may tend to equate with potential predators. Among the common insects, poisonous spiders represent the greatest threat, which may explain why spiders tend to provoke the greatest fear.

Early humans survived only through cooperation. A mountain lion is a solitary predator, more than capable of protecting itself. Humans, in contrast, are highly social, which compensates for their vulnerability as individuals. Several prepared fears seem to relate to the dangers of either wandering off alone or finding oneself alone in a threatening situation. The fear of darkness tends to manifest itself when we feel alone and vulnerable. This sense of isolation is an important element of agoraphobia.

In a typical case, a forty-five-year-old man "complained primarily of an inability to walk about in public and of a strong fear of being alone at any time. When he attempted to leave his home unaccompanied he experienced a severe fear reaction, which he described as a feeling that 'something dreadful was about to happen' to him."[22] The presence of a trusted companion substantially reduces agoraphobic fear, just as it reduces the fear of darkness. Agoraphobia is frequently related to panic disorder, a disease of fear that we will explore in Chapter 9. But agoraphobia also represents a more general fear of being out in the open alone and exposed to danger. This is a familiar fear during war. Even hardened combat veterans describe episodes of fear like the following, which took place during the Korean War: "So I took off afoot across the stretch with not another person in sight. Halfway, three mortar shells came in, exploding within fifty or so yards of me. The terror I knew was almost overwhelming. I ran until I was exhausted. It always happens that way. Be a man ever so accustomed to fire, experiencing it when he is alone and unobserved produces shock that is indescribable."[23]

This fear of being trapped alone in the open, which may be related to the primeval fear of lurking predators, is mirrored by claustrophobia, which is the fear of being trapped in an enclosed space. Claustrophobia is extremely common, affecting about one in ten people at least mildly. More women than men are claustrophobic and in a third of the cases the fear began in childhood. Severe claustrophobia affects about 2 percent of the population. One of its most common manifestations is a fear of elevators. It is not unusual for a severe claustrophobic to climb a dozen flights of stairs rather than take an elevator. A number of researchers have noted the similarities between claustrophobia and agoraphobia, and their probable origin in the distant past. "It is a curious fact," says Rachman, "that many people who are fearful of small, enclosed spaces are also frightened of being in large open spaces. This puzzle reflects neither confusion nor perversity, and probably can be understood as two manifestations of a fear of being trapped. There is no escape route available if a threat should arise. The persistence of these fears in modern man may be a vestige of the way in which primitive people reacted to the danger of being attacked while in a small enclosure or in a large unsheltered place—flight is impeded."[24]

The fear of being alone and threatened also plays a part in our relationships with other people. Although early humans evolved as social animals, their sociability was probably limited to their immediate tribal band or clan. "Like chimpanzees, gorillas, and social carnivores," writes Jared Diamond, "we lived in band territories." This characteristic can breed a potent fear of strangers, who may have hostile intentions and represent a real threat. The fear is intensified if one is alone and outnumbered by strangers. Diamond has spent years observing the aboriginal peoples of New Guinea, many of whom live in such isolation amid the rugged terrain that they knew nothing about the outside world until a Western expedition stumbled upon them in 1938. According to Diamond, "until recently, each tribe maintained a shifting pattern of warfare and alliance with each of its neighbors. A person might enter the next valley on a friendly visit (never quite without danger) or on a war raid, but the chances of being able to traverse a sequence of several valleys in friendship were negligible. The powerful rules about treatment of one's fellow 'us' did not apply to 'them,' those dimly understood, neighboring enemies. As I walked between New Guinea valleys, people who themselves practiced cannibalism and were only a decade out of the Stone Age routinely warned me about the unspeakably primitive, vile, and cannibalistic habits of the people I would encounter in the next valley."[25] This kind of apprehension about outsiders in early humans might have led to a genetically prepared tendency to fear strangers. This anxiety about strangers also seems to be an important element in the widespread fear of public speaking, since we tend not to be afraid to speak around our closest friends and family, even a large group of them. Our fear and embarrassment usually increase the more we perceive the members of our audience to be strangers, even if they are people we know casually. The primitive fear system may interpret speaking before a group as standing alone in the midst of a group of strangers. The fear of public speaking may also be related to a fear of losing status in the social group, a form of humiliation that would have had real consequences among early humans, jeopardizing access to food, shelter, and reproductive opportunities.

One striking aspect of claustrophobia does not seem to relate to the fear of being alone: the fear of suffocation. In one study, 80 percent of claustrophobic panics included the irrational fear of suffocation. One conceivable explanation is that people with claustrophobia misperceive the labored breathing that can accompany an intense fear response to an elevator or other enclosed space as a lack of oxygen. But this seems unlikely since people with other kinds of panic disorders do not often report that they have a fear of suffocation. The fear of suffocation in claustrophobia appears to be directly linked with the fear of enclosed spaces. Let's assume for a moment that the prepared fear of suffocation is adaptive. Why would our ancestors have had to be afraid of suffocating? Caves come immediately to mind. In the frigid ice age climate of Europe and Asia, certain populations of early humans might have lived in caves for most of the year. Was there a substantial risk of cave-in and suffocation, particularly in deeper caves, that gave a survival advantage to people with a genetic tendency to be wary of caves? The evidence is too skimpy to draw any definite conclusion. There is one other possibility, however, and it relates to the control of fire. Early humans living in colder climates were not only more likely to live in caves, but to build fires in them. Caves like the one at Dragon Bone Hill show scorch marks on the floor where these fires were made. But a fire in any enclosed area can be dangerous. It not only produces smoke, but a much more insidious by-product: carbon monoxide, a colorless, odorless gas generated by the incomplete oxidation of fuel. Carbon monoxide gradually binds with red blood cells, causing unconsciousness, suffocation, and death due to lack of oxygen. Every winter the newspapers carry tragic stories about people, sometimes whole families, who have suffocated in their sleep because they were using kerosene-burning space heaters in a closed room. A poorly ventilated cave could also have permitted a deadly buildup of carbon monoxide. Concentrations that exceed only about 1 percent are fatal. Claustrophobics are usually obsessed with having a constant supply of fresh air. This kind of concern in our early ancestors might have led them to choose the kinds of well-ventilated dwellings that are safest for building fires. Claustrophobics aren't the only ones with an irrational fear of suffocation, and it is often found independently in people with no claustrophobia. One survey reported that the suffocation phobia is twice as common as claustrophobia—another possible indication that this was a highly adaptive fear in our ancestors.[26] Although we no longer have an innate fear of fire, we apparently retain a related one of suffocation.

But how could we possibly lose such a powerful fear as that of fire? Other animals have been found to use primitive tools (chimpanzees use rocks to break nuts, or sticks to fish termites out of their nest), speak various languages (honeybees communicate the directions to a source of nectar using a kind of dance), even practice agriculture (some ants grow edible yeast and fungi in their nests and keep specialized species of aphids that excrete a sugary liquid), but no other social animal has been able to control fire. Humanity would be shocked indeed if some bearded researcher stumbled into a jungle clearing late one night and found a band of chimpanzees happily sitting around a campfire. Anthropologists are still debating when and how human beings first learned to control fire. But whether fear of fire was conquered a hundred thousand years ago, half a million years ago, or two million years ago, we can be reasonably certain that the breakthrough came as a by-product of the expansion and reorganization of the human brain.

With *Homo habilus*, the architecture of the brain shifted decisively away from the apelike architecture of relatively large occipital lobes and relatively small frontal ones, to the uniquely human architecture of large frontal lobes and relatively small occipital ones. Within these enormous frontal lobes was the rational fear system with its revolutionary capacity for sophisticated planning and analysis as well as its enhanced ability to inhibit the primitive fear system. Phobias like a terror of snakes are typical examples of the kind of reasoning carried out by the primitive fear system. Let's call this primitive limbic reasoning. Its hallmark is overgeneralization. It crudely joins cause (a general class of objects or situations) with effect (danger). The primitive fear system reasons, for example, that since some snakes, some heights, and some enclosed spaces are dangerous, they are all dangerous. Phobic individuals are thus afraid of all snakes, all heights, all enclosed spaces. Usually they know perfectly well that a garter snake is different from a rattlesnake, an elevator is different from the bottom of a cave, and the top of a sturdy skyscraper is different from the edge of a cliff. But they are afraid anyway. These distinctions mean nothing to the primitive fear system, and it is this that controls phobic behavior. The rational fear system easily makes these distinctions, however. Let's call its style of thought advanced cortical reasoning because it relies on the complex six-layer architecture of the neocortex. Cortical reasoning takes place throughout the neocortex as sensory data and other information are analyzed and interpreted. But advanced cortical reasoning takes place only in the frontal lobes, especially the prefrontal cortices just under the forehead, which contain the association areas that supply the highest level of abstraction and meaning to human thought. Not only does advanced cortical reasoning create more numerous, finely graded categories of thought than primitive limbic reasoning, it uses them to formulate strategies for the future. The rational fear system can make plans to avoid poisonous snakes, not simply all snakes, and only unstable caves, not all caves. The rational fear system can also inhibit the primitive fear system, though this can at times be extremely difficult. Nevertheless, even someone with a crippling phobia can often improve if they rationally, methodically work to desensitize themselves. The evolution of massive frontal lobes was perhaps the most important event in history of human evolution, and the unfolding of advanced cortical reasoning among early humans represents the beginnings of the modern mind.

The development of crude stone tools of the Oldowan type 2.5 million years ago was the first sign in the archeological record of this new kind of reasoning and planning. Instead of the random rocks that a chimpanzee might use to smash open a nut, early man began deliberately shaping rocks into different categories of tools for different uses. As the human brain enlarged over millions of years, so did the categories of tools and the quality of their manufacture, culminating in the rapidly evolving tool technology of the Cro-Magnon people, which led directly to the vast array of tools we have today and the profusion of machines that these tools are used to build.

As the categories of tools enlarged and with them the application of advanced cortical reasoning, there is evidence that the anxieties of early man were also growing. The burial rituals of first the Neanderthals and then the Cro-Magnons seem to reflect the frontal lobes' growing ability to generate anxiety-producing scenarios. Burial of the dead, particularly with elaborate ceremony, indicates not only sadness and respect, but anxiety about the fate of the dead person, about death itself, and perhaps about the community he or she has left behind. This division of the world into more and more categories has continued for the last hundred thousand years, endlessly multiplying our anxieties. Word of every new disease, every new risk from food, or water, or air is instantly flashed around the world, increasing our uneasiness. But the rational fear system does more than simply expand our fears—it gives us the means to control them and, at times, eliminate them altogether. This newly evolved system was undoubtedly the critical factor that allowed early humans to control their instinctive fear of fire.

Although no one knows for sure when and under what circumstances early humans first began to use fire, it cannot be an accident that this achievement, like the use of stone tools, coincided with the rapid expansion of the frontal lobes. To the primitive fear system, all fire is dangerous just as all snakes are dangerous, and this reasoning is inflexible. But the rational one provided another avenue of analysis, one that could conclude that not all fire is dangerous, and some kinds can even be useful. We can imagine many different scenarios in which humans were accidentally introduced to the benefits of fire. Perhaps they first tasted cooked meat when scavenging among the carcasses in the smoldering remains of a forest fire. Or they could have experienced the comfortable warmth generated by a small fire accidentally started from the sparks produced by pounding two rocks together to make a stone tool. The benefits of fire may well have been discovered and rediscovered many times under many different circumstances. Those early humans with rational fear systems strong enough to suppress selectively their terror of fire would have gradually discovered the tremendous value of controlled fire for providing warmth, cooking food, and scaring away predators. Such people would have tended to be more successful and leave more offspring than those whose unyielding instinctive fear forced them to shun fire altogether. Over thousands of generations, the genes of people who could control fire with relative ease would proliferate, ultimately eliminating the instinctive fear of fire altogether.

The importance of the conquest of fire to human culture and civilization cannot be overestimated. Our species has often been called the toolmaker. But it would be equally accurate to call us the fire maker, or even the fire master. Our mastery of fire has transformed every aspect of human life and changed the face of the earth. One of the early uses of fire was as a tool for hunting. Man-made fires drove game over cliffs or into box canyons where hunters were waiting. This is one behavior that humans shared with the only other animal known to exploit fire: the fire hawk (*Milvus migrans*), a bird of Africa, Asia, and southern Europe. This astonishing bird hunts along the edges of natural fires, preying on small animals fleeing from the flames. The fire hawk will even pick up a smoldering branch and fly some distance away before dropping it to start another blaze that it can use for hunting. The perfection of this hunting technique by modern humans may be one reason that so many large animals like mammoths became extinct all over the world by the end of the last ice age ten thousand years ago. Humans also used widespread fires, sometimes intentionally and sometimes accidentally, to change the ecology of large areas, thinning out dense forests and creating grasslands.[27]

Tools and fire are the technological foundation of human civilization. We sometimes forget what a breakthrough something as simple as cooking was for human evolution. Cooking allowed a huge expansion in the human diet. Many plant foods we take for granted are inedible or even toxic if they are not cooked. Kidney beans, soybeans, and lentils, for example, are some of the best sources of plant protein, yet they contain substances called lectins that damage red blood cells and can destroy the walls of the intestines. These toxins, like most plant toxins, are destroyed by cooking, which also eliminates the bacteria in raw meat. Manioc, a root plant that is a staple for South American Indians and in certain areas of sub-Saharan Africa, contains a significant amount of cyanide, which is eliminated by pounding and cooking.[28] One important difference between chimpanzees and early humans is that the food humans hunted and gathered was brought back to a base camp for preparation and sharing rather than being eaten on the spot. Cooking obviously reinforced this practice, which encouraged social cooperation and delayed gratification. It may have also promoted the development of complex spoken language as early humans communicated with each other during meals around the relative safety of the cooking fire.

Without cooking, agriculture as we know it would be impossible. And without agriculture's emergence about ten thousand years ago, the early civilizations that grew up in the heavily cultivated valleys of the Tigris, Euphrates, Nile, and other great rivers might never have arisen. Agriculture then and now is based on domesticated cereal grain like wheat, barley, rye, corn, and rice. Grain provides 70 percent of the world's calories. But the nutritious starches and proteins of these cereals are bound up in cells constructed out of cellulose, which is very difficult to digest. Cooking breaks down the cellulose and makes these grains highly digestible. Without cooking they are virtually inedible. Agriculture produces far more food per acre than hunting and gathering. It generated stable, permanent communities with increased population densities and surplus production: the common ingredients for the world's first civilizations that arose about six thousand years ago in Egypt, Mesopotamia, India, and China.

Without fire we would have no versatile source of heat, no cooked food, no civilization. We would be almost blind at night, relying completely on moonlight and starlight, and would lose our most effective protection from predators. We would have no fuel, no electricity, no chemical reactions (which require heat) that create steel, plastics, and a thousand other materials. In short, we would live in an extremely rudimentary hunter-gatherer culture with no metals, no baked pottery, uncooked food, and only crude tools. Every people on earth uses fire, so this would be a culture more primitive than any that has existed for at least half a million years. We have mastered fire for good or ill. Without it there would be no gunpowder, no explosives, no pollution. If we become extinct, it may happen in the cauldron of nuclear fire.

In the film *2001: A Space Odyssey*, director Stanley Kubrick and author Arthur C. Clarke wrote a scene in which an apelike ancestor of man uses the jawbone of a dead animal as both a tool and a weapon for killing. Overcome with excitement at his discovery, the hominid throws his newfound tool into the air. Kubrick cuts from the slow-motion ascent of the jawbone to the ascent of a space shuttle millions of years later. The primitive tool has evolved into the highest of technology. Imagine, for a moment, an alternative scene. A hominid cautiously approaches the smoldering edge of a recent forest fire. Among the ashes there is a small fire still burning among a pile of dead branches. The hominid hesitantly pulls one end of a thick branch out of the fire and curiously, fearfully examines his newfound torch. Suddenly there is a roar behind him. A charging panther is almost on top of him. Our hominid wildly waves his torch at the panther. The confused cat flinches, swerves, and runs away. In a fit of ecstasy at his survival, our hominid begins a frenzied dance and flings his torch into the air. As the torch spins upward, the director cuts to a shot of a gigantic Saturn rocket riding a plume of flame as it carries a group of Apollo astronauts to the moon, and we hear the opening chords of Richard Strauss's *Also Sprach Zarathustra*.

{ Part II }

Manifestations of Fear

All that each person is, and experiences, and shall ever experience, in body and mind, all these things are differing expressions of himself and of one root, and are identical: and not one of these things nor one of these persons is ever quite to be duplicated, nor replaced, nor has it ever quite had precedent: but each is a new and incommunicably tender life, wounded in every breath and almost as hardly killed as easily wounded: sustaining for a while, without defense, the enormous assaults of the universe.

—James Agee

{ Chapter 5 }

Children and Fear

Mom loved horror movies. When my brother and I were growing up, we would go see all the latest ones. She doesn't particularly like them anymore. She thinks they're too violent. I'm glad she didn't feel that way then, since my brother and I loved going. Some of my favorite memories are of standing in a long line of excited people on opening weekend at one of the big theaters in downtown Tucson, waiting to see such B-movie masterpieces as *House on Haunted Hill, The Tingler,* and *The Blob.* I would usually slump down in my seat, just peeking over the top of the chair in front of me, ready to duck when the monster jumped out.

Of course, all this fun had a few consequences. Sometimes I'd have nightmares about one of the movies I'd seen. I would wake up in a cold sweat, paralyzed with fear. For what seemed like an eternity, I would stay perfectly still, knowing that the slightest move would mean instant death from the monster under the bed or in the closet. Gradually I would work up my courage. In a flash, I would throw off the covers and flee down the hall into my parents' big bed. The feeling of relief was delicious. I would always spend a few minutes taunting the monster, daring it to come and get me now that I was safe with Mom and Dad.

My younger brother occasionally had the same kinds of dreams. His room was right across the hall from mine. One night he had an exception-ally vivid nightmare. He woke up in terror, frozen and sweating, too afraid even to open his eyes to see what awful fate awaited him. He finally poked his head out from under the covers and looked. To his utter horror he saw a ghostly skeleton floating out of the closet toward his bed. Summoning all his nerve, he jumped out of bed, ran into my room, and took a giant leap into my bed. He says he can still remember the blissful relief he felt in midair, knowing that he would be safe with me. Then he landed on my bed. To his complete shock, I wasn't there. As it turned out, I had a nightmare of my own a little while earlier and had run down to my parents' room. But as far as he knew, I was dead—a victim of the monster. My brother looked around and practically screamed when he saw the skeleton floating through my bedroom door. There was no escape. In what he still says is one of the most courageous moments of his life, he ran right through the spectral skeleton, down the hall, and into bed with the rest of us.

Children are much more vulnerable to fear than adults. The primitive fear system begins operating immediately after birth, whereas the frontal lobes—seat of the rational fear system—take years to mature. Without fully functioning frontal lobes, a child finds it difficult to suppress fears generated by the primitive fear system. This is why children are so often plagued by nightmares and fear of the dark. The most extreme form of nightmares is called night terrors *(pavor nocturnus)*. They occur within about half an hour of falling asleep. Covered with sweat and breathing profusely, the child will bolt upright in bed, eyes wide as if staring at something horrible, and scream. The attack usually lasts only a couple of minutes and the child often doesn't clearly remember the nightmare that caused the fright. Fortunately, this condition is unusual.[1] The night-mares my brother and I had were of the more ordinary variety.

Sleep is not a unitary process but consists of a number of stages. When you fall asleep, your brain—as measured by an EEG—generates a series of waves that become slower and slower as the sleep deepens. There are four stages of this initial slow-wave sleep. They last about forty-five minutes. Muscles are relaxed and heartbeat and blood pressure drop. Then for the next roughly forty-five minutes you move through the four stages of slow-wave sleep in reverse order, from deepest sleep to lightest sleep. At the end of ninety minutes, rapid eye movement (REM) sleep begins. The eyes dart behind the closed lids and the brain begins an intense pattern of activity, using more oxygen than it does during even intense mental activity while awake. Although some dreaming occurs during slow-wave sleep, the most vivid dreams and nightmares take place mainly during REM sleep. There are usually four to six periods of REM sleep during the night.

Since the frontal lobes continue developing all the way into the late teens, children who wake up from a nightmare find it more difficult than adults to comfort themselves with the knowledge that it was only a dream. It is not unusual for a terrified child to hallucinate, imagining that he sees monsters or hears strange noises. This represents especially strong activation of the amygdala. You will remember that electrical stimulation of the amygdala during brain surgery produces auditory and visual hallucinations, usually fearsome. Like all children, my brother and I found it difficult to control our fears, awake or asleep. If an imaginary fear occurred to us (a monster or murderer hiding in the basement), our primitive system would take over and generate a fear response. We used to marvel at my father's courage in taking out the garbage at night. The garbage cans were in the garage, which we thought of as an incredibly dark and scary place. We would ask him why he wasn't worried. He would just laugh and say there was nothing to be afraid of.

Mature frontal lobes endow adults with the capacity for advanced cortical reasoning, which gives them three huge advantages over a child. First, the frontal lobes analyze in a sophisticated way the world without and within. The mature mind is capable of dividing reality, both what we perceive and what we think, into an unlimited number of categories and using these categories to trace cause and effect. We can easily distinguish between the few dark places that are dangerous and the majority of dark places (like the garage) that aren't. Second, the frontal lobes plan. They generate complex scenarios about the future ("What will happen if I quit this job?"). They also generate scenarios about the present ("How do I get myself out of this mess?") and the past ("Why did bungee jumping ever become so popular?"). Scenario is just another word for story and we, as a species that not only walks upright but speaks, spend much of our lives fashioning stories and telling them to each other. One important aspect of consciousness is the narration of the story of our lives. As writer Kathryn Morton observed, the "first sign that a baby is going to be a human being and not a noisy pet comes when he begins naming the world and demanding the stories that connect its parts."[2] Finally, the frontal lobes inhibit the primitive fear system, sometimes more successfully than others.

The primitive fear system tends to dominate children's thinking. Thus in many ways children resemble phobic adults, with simplistic, generalized reasoning and an unsophisticated linking of cause and effect. Without frontal lobes mature enough to filter out naive inferences (all dark places are dangerous), children are particularly vulnerable to prepared fears. Fear of the dark is probably a prepared fear of predators that developed over the millions of years that the human family lived as hunter-gatherers. In a civilized setting, this fear is unnecessary. But most children must nevertheless suffer through it because their brains are not developed enough to suppress it. In part, this is an evolutionary accident. Species with big brains, like humans and primates, have a longer gestation period. If we use other primates as a yardstick, the human gestation period should be twenty-one months, not nine. But because the human pelvis is engineered for upright walking, the pelvic opening for the birth canal can only be so large. Thus the human infant is born a year early, basically a fetus, with twelve months' growth to go before reaching the stage a chimpanzee has already reached at birth. As it is, the size of the infant's head makes human birth uniquely dangerous among animals. The infant chimpanzee's brain is one-half adult size. The human infant's brain is one-third the size of an adult's. To reach that size it added 2.5 million neurons per minute during nine months of gestation. The full adult size of the brain is not reached by adding more neurons—actually, millions of neurons are pruned away as the brain sculpts the circuits for vision and the other senses—but by adding the trillions of synaptic connections necessary to wire the brain. By being born so early, the child and the brain mature that much later. But clearly much of the long period of dependency serves an adaptive purpose. When apes evolved from monkeys, the length of childhood doubled. When humans evolved from apes, it doubled again. Unspecialized humans require this unusually long childhood because we have so few instincts. We must learn an enormous amount to survive. Instead of claws and teeth we use tools to make our living, and these require both training and mature manual dexterity. There is one more oddity in the human development cycle. Once born, most animals grow steadily to adult size. But the growth of children is retarded until puberty, when they experience a growth spurt and catch up. Some biologists have theorized that children are smaller because it makes them easier to teach.[3]

One of the skills that takes years for children to master is advanced cortical reasoning, which involves both the detailed categorizing of reality and the successive filtering of those categories to determine cause and effect. The frontal lobes are so immature in infants that early fear experiences and other emotions are not subject to conscious processing and may leave subconscious imprints, perhaps in the form of phobias or other likes and dislikes, that were never subject to modification by the rational fear system at the time they were laid down.[4] Perhaps because advanced cortical reasoning is the most recent type of thought to evolve in the human brain, children find its abstractions far less intuitive than primitive limbic reasoning, which automatically teaches us not to touch a hot stove. Advanced cortical reasoning is no simple matter for adults either. Just ask anyone who has ever taken a course in organic chemistry or calculus. This is a bit like the difference between learning to speak, which we do intuitively, and learning to write, which must be taught and laboriously practiced. Writing is only a few thousand years old; speaking is far older.

Let's say a stream of sensory information just now registered by my skin is flowing into my thalamus. My brain might resolve that data into successively more specific categories in the following way. First the brain determines if the sensory information represents an object or simply a sensation, like heat or cold. Let's assume my foot pressed against something, so my brain concludes that it is dealing with an object. By then my eyes have turned to look at the object and another stream of information is being routed to the occipital lobes at the back of my head where features like shape, movement, and color are detected and the object as a whole takes shape. As this information moves forward in the neocortex toward the frontal lobes, the image of the object is refined and placed in a general category. In this case, assume the object is an animal. The next processing stage narrows that category to type of animal. At this point, my brain discovers that I've accidentally stepped on a snake. So far, about a tenth of a second has passed and the image has not yet flowed into my consciousness. Since the primitive fear system has been monitoring the neocortical processing of this image, any further cortical processing might be interrupted at this point by a fear response. Say our fear response is moderate, however, and we quickly control it. When the image of the snake flows into consciousness my neocortex may identify it as a garter snake if my knowledge base contains that information. Unlike primitive limbic reasoning, which is only concerned with preconsciously pigeonholing the object into a general category, advanced cortical processing continues into consciousness. The front-most portions of my frontal lobes, the prefrontal cortices, can loop the image back out into the neocortex for further refinement. Advanced cortical reasoning can refine the category of garter snake into successively more detailed categories—for example, the harmless behavior of this kind of snake, the area of the snake's brain (limbic system) that generates this behavior, the specific circuits in the snake's limbic system needed to produce the behavior, the functioning of the neurons of those brain circuits, the receptors of the neurons within the circuits, the molecules of the receptors, the atoms of the molecules, the elementary particles of the atoms, and the quantum fields that produce the elementary particles. This is about as far as science can go at the present time.[5]

Few children could carry through this kind of complex, nested analysis. Thoroughly understanding any one of the detailed categories that relate to the snake's brain or molecular structure requires mature frontal lobes and years of education. The implications of this ability to create an endless variety of nested analytical categories is profound, for it has allowed us to create all the complexities of the human mind, from art to science. I don't mean to suggest that this is exactly how the brain analyzes the image of a snake. The actual process is far more complex with many different things going on at the same time. At any point in the analysis the mind can branch off into another hierarchy of knowledge: what the snake eats, the environment in which it lives, and so on. But we can say with some assurance that sensory information in the brain flows from the back and sides to the front, and areas toward the back of the brain classify an object into the most general categories, while the areas further forward classify the object into successively more specific categories.

The husband and wife neuroscientists, Antonio and Hanna Damasio, have made an extensive study of brain-damaged patients to determine how this process works. They conclude that patients with damage to the front-most portions of the cortex, particularly the front of the temporal lobes, can continue to identify an object or event in general, but not specifically. One of their patients with temporal lobe damage, whom they call Boswell, is unable to recall any specific events from his past. He cannot recognize his family or friends. But his general knowledge has not been destroyed. He can classify something as belonging to a general category (tool) and sometimes further classify it into a middle-level category (wrench), but he cannot go beyond that to any specific instances in which he might have used a wrench. "In brief," write the Damasios, "when shown the faces of unique persons he was previously familiar with (e.g., Roosevelt or [Boswell's] wife) he was unable to recognize them, but he knows that their faces are human faces. He also knows the meaning of the basic facial expressions shown in those faces. . . . When asked to think about specific faces (or places), he cannot conjure up the face of any one particular person (e.g., he cannot conjure up his wife's face). Yet he can generate an internal representation of a 'generic' human face, or any part of a face (e.g., a nose), or of a geometric figure (a square), or of any color."[6]

This important finding, I believe, is the clue we need to unlock the secrets of the primitive fear system. Why are children so susceptible to phobias? Why are phobias so resistant to change? Why does someone who rationally knows that elevators are perfectly safe nevertheless freeze at the thought of getting on one? Let me suggest that it is because the primitive fear system, guardian of the primal fear response, cannot classify objects, events, or phenomena beyond middle-level categories. The primitive fear system is like Boswell, who can recognize that what he is seeing belongs to the general category of objects called pictures, and can further identify the picture as showing a human face, but can never take the next analytical step and identify the face as his wife's. No matter how many times he sees the picture, he only sees a generalized face, not his wife. Similarly, I would argue, whenever the primitive fear system sees a twisted moving form it first identifies the general category of the form (animal) and then the middle-level category (snake). But like Boswell it can never go beyond that middle-level category. It cannot distinguish between a garter snake and a rattlesnake. It only sees a snake, never a specific type of snake, just as Boswell only sees a face, never the unique face of his wife.

Of course, we can learn through experience to fear specific persons, places, or things. And the fear we feel can be horribly intense. But the primitive fear system is not able to identify these unique entities preconsciously. This does not mean that in the case of unique entities the primitive fear system is helpless in carrying out its alarm function. Say I am a free-thinking German liberal in the early 1930s who loathes Adolf Hitler. I might find myself instantly reacting with intense fear every time I notice someone of roughly Hitler's build with a small mustache. My primitive fear system has created a middle-level category that includes Hitler's general description. From then on I will have a preconscious fear reaction *to anyone who looks like Hitler.* Only when the image of the

Hitler-like person flows through the front-most portions of my temporal lobes and into my frontal lobes and consciousness will my neocortex be able to identify conclusively whether it actually is Hitler.

By neocortical standards, the primitive fear system is learning impaired. There are two reasons for this limitation. First, the limbic system is much older than the neocortex and its structure is not as complex. "The ancient two-layered limbic cortical tissue," says psychologist Rhawn Joseph, "has difficulty communicating with and comprehending data processed with the new brain [neocortex] as they speak different languages."[7] Second, and perhaps most important, the primitive fear system evolved as an alarm system that must act instantaneously to detect a threat. The primitive system is constrained by the few milliseconds—totaling perhaps a tenth of a second or so—it has prior to conscious awareness to identify danger. (The more complex a scene the more brain areas are required to process it and the longer preconscious processing takes. The brain processes a black-and-white cartoon sketch faster than a colorful scene that is full of motion.) As Joseph LeDoux pointed out, the primitive fear system is designed by evolution to store and detect primitive cues and ignore fine distinctions.[8] Its analysis must be quick and dirty, necessarily superficial. Human beings already have dangerously slow reflexes compared to other animals. Even a sixteen-hundred-pound grizzly bear can snatch a darting trout out of a mountain stream, something few humans could do. We make up for our slow reflexes with guile, but we still need a rapid alarm system to survive. Through trial and error over millions of years, evolution judged that only a system that stops its analysis at middle-level categories is fast enough. In preconscious processing, the brain essentially asks two questions about an incoming perception: "What is it?" and "How do I feel about it?" Sensory processing within the neocortex answers the first question and the limbic system answers the second. Preconscious neocortical analysis simply identifies the object, event, or phenomenon. Advanced cortical reasoning about the specific degree of danger does not appear to begin until the information flows into consciousness. The preconscious behavioral response (fight or flight) is wholly controlled by the primitive fear system. Primitive limbic reasoning completes its analysis on the threshold of consciousness, whereas neocortical reasoning directed by the frontal lobes continues into consciousness. From then on cortical reasoning is under no time constraints. We can consciously take as long as we want to consider a problem. Science, for example, required centuries of advanced cortical reasoning by tens of thousands of individual minds to develop its sophisticated categories and cause-and-effect relationships.

Children who develop intense phobias are sometimes labeled irrational, but this is both false and damaging to the child. The primitive fear system reasons in a much cruder way than the neocortex, but it reasons nonetheless. Phobias are perfectly consistent with the rudimentary associative logic of primitive limbic reasoning. If a young girl has a near escape from a rattlesnake, then it would be logical for her to conclude that rattlesnakes are dangerous. Yet though her neocortex sees a rattlesnake, her limbic system is only able to see a snake. Her limbic system concludes, therefore, not that rattlesnakes are dangerous but that snakes are dangerous, and may create a snake phobia in her mind. A claustrophobic's primitive fear system sees only an enclosed space, not an elevator. And since, to the claustrophobic, enclosed spaces are dangerous, the limbic system concludes that this one is, too. Incredibly, the primitive fear system is stuck in a world of midlevel categories that renders it incapable of distinguishing between an elevator and a deep cave whose ceiling is about to collapse. The primitive fear system is, I would argue, physiologically unable to make distinctions beyond midlevel categories, no matter how much rational knowledge about snakes or enclosed spaces is contained in someone's neocortex. Even the world's greatest biologist, if he had developed an intense snake phobia as a child, would still feel somewhat queasy around all snakes despite having an encyclopedic knowledge of every known snake species. "Phobics are capable of rationally judging the object of their fear as foolish," writes psychologist Andrew Mayes, "and yet obviously are terrified of that object. This suggests that a distinction can be drawn between a rational and a primitive type of appraisal, mediated by different parts of the brain, but still interacting. The former could weakly influence the latter . . . but it is the latter which has been evolved as a mode of perceptual appraisal closely tied to subsequent physiological responding, fearful expression and avoidance behaviour."[9] In treating the snake phobia of our young girl, it is pointless to try to teach her primitive fear system the difference between a rattlesnake and a garter snake. It will never learn. All she can do is consciously and methodically try to desensitize her primitive system to all snakes. With the help of a therapist, for example, she might gradually approach a harmless snake.

From a neocortical perspective, primitive limbic reasoning commits the twin logical fallacies of hasty generalization and misplaced causality.

Hasty generalization lumps all snakes—from garter snakes to anacondas—into one category of fear. Advanced cortical reasoning, through experience and study, can create many categories of snakes, based on a variety of criteria. I can divide them into nonpoisonous shy snakes, nonpoisonous aggressive snakes, poisonous shy snakes, poisonous aggressive snakes, and so forth. The number of neocortical categories is virtually unlimited. Science is a prime example of the neocortex at work, parsing reality into more and more sophisticated categories. The power that advanced cortical analysis gives us to shape our motivation and behaviors and control our environment is an important reason the neocortex has expanded so enormously over the last 3 million years. Misplaced causality erroneously links cause and effect. If I carry a rabbit's foot and something good happens to me, then primitive limbic reasoning—unless strongly contradicted by the rational fear system—may attribute the good luck to the rabbit's foot, making me positively fearful if I don't carry it with me all the time. Of course, the rabbit's foot didn't cause my good luck. That is misplaced causality. But the simplistic reasoning of the limbic system easily links things together if they happen to be present at the same time, even though they have nothing to do with each other.

Virtually all superstitions are created by primitive limbic reasoning. Most cultures—and individuals—are a mixture of primitive reasoning (superstitions, prejudices) and sophisticated reasoning. Cortical reasoning can sometimes reinforce prejudice and superstition. After carefully weighing the probabilities, for example, I might conclude that I should keep carrying around my rabbit's foot just in case it helps me in a way I don't completely understand. But in other cases, advanced cortical reasoning might be able to suppress the limbic system and short-circuit an incipient phobia by concluding, say, that there is no reason to be afraid of a garter snake. Primitive limbic reasoning and the alarm system it operates are an automatic part of every normal child's mind. How extensively children will be able to employ the sophisticated power of their neocortex, however, depends on their education, training, and experience. The application of advanced cortical reasoning acts as an important brake on primitive emotional responses. And the extent to which the neocortex is activated in advance can determine how strongly the primitive fear system reacts. In one experiment, a group of volunteer subjects were told they would receive vitamin injections. Actually, some members of the group were injected with a harmless placebo while others were injected with adrenaline, which tends to increase emotional responsiveness. Some of the subjects receiving adrenaline were told that a side effect of their "vitamin" injection might be a change in their emotional sensitivity. The rest of the adrenaline-injected subjects were told nothing about side effects. The researchers planted an actor in the group, posing as one of the volunteers. After the injections, the actor began to behave manically, pretending to be in an intensely euphoric mood. The subjects given an adrenaline injection and no explanation of side effects were quickly caught up in the mood, and began inventing manic antics of their own. The adrenaline-injected subjects who had been briefed on side effects along with those receiving the placebo tended simply to stare at the others in disbelief. With another group of subjects, the actor behaved in an angry and insulting way. Here the adrenaline subjects who were unaware of side effects became openly apprehensive, annoyed, or angry while the others tended to remain calm.[10]

The drama in the development of a child comes in the struggle of the frontal lobes and neocortex to break the chains of dread and uncertainty forged by the primitive fear system almost from the moment of birth. Researchers now know that an infant is not a blank slate, but possesses a wide variety of innate knowledge and tendencies that help it to survive and categorize the world. Infants react fearfully to the sense of falling and to objects that loom in their faces. They recognize adult facial expressions and can mimic smiles, frowns, and surprise. A dedicated set of neurons in the baby's temporal lobe next to the amygdala and hippocampus detects new stimuli. Since infants are easily bored and quickly pay attention to novel stimulation, researchers track infants' eye movements to determine what they notice and what they don't. If an infant is shown a violet light, at first it shows interest but then becomes bored. If the light is switched to blue-green, the baby remains bored and doesn't seem to notice the difference. But if the color is initially blue-green and then is changed to green-blue, the baby notices the switch. This kind of research has revealed that infants see the world in red, yellow, green, and blue.[11]

Every language in the world uses a subset of only about three dozen consonant sounds. Babies have been found to be able to distinguish between all thirty-six or so consonants though adults often lose some of this ability after they learn their native language. Most adult Japanese, for example, cannot distinguish between the consonant sounds of r and l. The acquisition of language seems clearly innate. No teaching is required, only exposure of the child to adult speech during the first years of life. The stages of language acquisition are basically the same in all cultures, although individual children will vary in how fast they go through them. On average, infants begin distinct babbling at six months. Around the first birthday, the child is using one-word utterances. At a year and a half, the child is using a vocabulary of thirty to fifty words. At two, the child uses two-word sentences and may have a vocabulary of several hundred words. At two and a half, the child speaks in combinations of three words or more. By three the child is speaking in full sentences. And by four most children can communicate easily and clearly.[12]

Children universally react to fear with three behaviors: crying, flight or avoidance, and freezing. But the display of these reactions changes as the child matures. Certain prepared fears, for example, don't seem to emerge until a certain age. Researchers have found that children under the age of two do not show signs of a fear of snakes. Between the ages of three and four, however, the fear definitely seems to emerge. The degree of general fearfulness shown by an individual child varies, depending on his or her temperament. Studies indicate that perhaps 10 to 15 percent of children tend to be more fearful than the average.[13]

Emotional cries are mediated by the limbic system and can be produced by electrical stimulation of the amygdala and other areas. Children are born with their larynx high in the throat, like all other mammals, so they can breathe and swallow at the same time. Only after the child is more than a year old does the larynx move lower so that the child can produce the entire set of human sounds. At about six months, a child's frontal lobes are starting to undergo the intricate and lengthy process of being wired to the limbic system. Connecting the frontal lobes to the rest of the brain is crucial for language, because the area for expressing language is located in most children just above the left ear and includes the lower rear portion of the left frontal lobe. Adults who have a stroke in this region—called Broca's area, after Pierre Paul Broca, the French neurologist who identified it in 1861—are sometimes left mute. As this area is fully wired to the rest of the brain by around one year, the child is able to make one-word utterances. About the same time there is another important change in the child's fear responses. In the first six months, most infants cry or fret because of discomfort, frustration, or boredom. They live basically in the present because their memories are poor. But as the frontal lobes and limbic system are wired, the child's memory rapidly improves. Around the first birthday, most children manifest two new fears: that of strangers and separation anxiety. They are familiar with their primary caregivers and may respond with distress if a stranger approaches. If they are left in an unfamiliar environment, they may also become upset.[14]

As children grow older, these fears tend to decline. The attachment to parents weakens and their relationships with other children become more important. The frontal lobes continue to mature and their imaginations blossom, but the rational fear system is not yet strong enough to suppress the terrors of the primitive fear system. From ages four to six, the fear of death and imaginary threats come to dominate the child's mind. These often include fear of the dark as well as fears of monsters, ghosts, murderers, tigers, lions, or other predatory animals, death by drowning, fire, traffic accident, or illness. A child often begins asking questions about death. Am I going to die? Why? Are you going to die? What will happen to me if you die? As children approach age twelve, fears of imaginary creatures decrease but realistic ones concerning death and personal safety often increase. With the rise in urban violence, the innate worry by children for their safety is strongly reinforced.

The fear of death and injury is virtually an obsession with many adolescents and teenagers. This helps explain the popularity of horror movies with this age group. Watching a horror movie allows an adolescent or teenager to face the fear of death in a controlled setting. Looking back, this was certainly part of the appeal of these movies for me. I was at an age in which I was having nightmares anyway. The movies allowed me, in a sense, to face my nightmares and enjoy them in a secure environment. "It is fear without isolation, with an instant escape, with familiar objects around us," writes critic Martin Tropp. "As a collective experience (made immediate in our century when film enabled us literally to be alone together in the darkness) the popularity of the horror story transformed private nightmares into communal events."[15]

For the same reason, we are fascinated by automobile accidents, and can't take our eyes off them when we pass. We constantly and instinctively monitor our surroundings for fearsome situations and orient ourselves in the world using fear, particularly anything that might trigger the fear of death. If we die, then nothing else we fear or desire matters anymore. We want vicariously to experience fear from a safe distance as a form of habituation. And it works. We tend to be less fearful of auto accidents after we have seen a number of them. Whether this is wise or not is another issue. Consciously and subconsciously, we are always trying to find ways to control our fears. There is a balance, however, that must be struck between adequate habituation so that a fear can be managed and overhabituating. If we overhabituate to brutality and death, we can become desensitized to violence and human suffering.

The hormones of puberty create a number of dynamic shifts in the adolescent's brain. The ability to learn a second language easily, accent free, is normally lost. The elaboration of the wiring between the frontal lobes and the limbic system gives adolescents more control over their primitive fear system. But this occurs at a time of emotional turmoil, during which fears concerning social approval become dominant and peer pressure is intense. Adolescents struggle to establish an independent identity, aided by the blossoming of advanced cortical reasoning, which often makes them worry about problems in the wider world.

When I was growing up, at the height of the Cold War, my friends and I worried a lot about the possibility of nuclear war. My imagination seethed with horror at the specter of hundreds of Soviet ICBMs heading over the pole to destroy the United States—and me. Since we might only have about fifteen minutes warning, I would generate scenarios in which the attack occurred when I was away from my family and there was no time to get back to them. Sometimes when the civil defense sirens were tested I would freeze. When we moved to Tucson, silos housing U.S. ICBMs—Titan missiles—were being built in the nearby desert. The father of one of my friends worked on the silos and he joked that if there were ever a war, Tucson would be ground zero. I didn't think it was funny.

Most of the children in my generation experienced similar fears. My wife clearly remembers a particular civil defense drill at her school when she was very young. Students were made to lie flat on the floor, face down with their hands covering their heads. Almost in tears, she asked her teacher if there was really going to be a war. She was terrified at the answer—"I hope not"—realizing instantly that if an adult wasn't willing to give her absolute reassurance then there really was something awful to worry about. In my wife's neighborhood, a center of attention for the kids was the underground bomb shelter that one family had built in its backyard. She and her friends were fascinated by it. They would sit for hours on the bunk beds that lined the metal walls of the underground room and talk about what a nuclear war would be like. Would the food in the bomb shelter last? What would happen if you had to go out when everything was still radioactive—would your flesh rot? The children of the family that built the bomb shelter said all their friends would be welcome in the shelter if there were a war. Every child in the neighborhood made a point of being nice to those kids.

The evolution of the human brain, with the frontal lobes and prefrontal cortex not only evolving last but maturing late in children, has created a neural architecture in which primitive limbic reasoning with its limited analytical categories precedes advanced cortical reasoning. Thus the primitive fear response with its fight-or-flight simplicity often overwhelms more sophisticated reactions. A quick-and-dirty emotional analysis by the limbic system precedes every conscious thought and generates an emotional reaction that can be highly resistant to change. It is much easier for the primitive fear system to influence the frontal lobes than for the frontal lobes to influence the primitive fear system. The nature of primitive limbic reasoning explains why our phobias involve general classes of things (snakes, spiders, heights, the dark) and our enemies ("the Communists") are often faceless abstractions. Undoubtedly there are important reasons for this architecture. Fear, particularly the fear of death, involves the survival of the organism and precedes all other motivations. The simplicity of the limbic system's preconscious organization allows it to react much more quickly and decisively than conscious cortical processes. But this evolutionary structure brings with it many problems, particularly in a modern setting. Not only does it lead to the phobias and anxiety disorders that torment millions of people, but it creates an alarming tendency for the mind to slip into primitive limbic reasoning and lump fellow human beings, each of whom is unique, into dangerously sweeping and ill-considered fear categories based on race, religion, ethnicity, class, gender, national origin, political doctrine or some other generalization. This fosters a climate of ignorance, bigotry, intolerance, and hatred, which when amplified by our technology can lead to the destruction of humanity and much of the earth's biosphere.

{ Chapter 6 }

Fear of the Unknown

The fear experience embodies a classic learning process. The brain, with its primitive and rational fear systems, tries to use past events to predict an inherently uncertain future. Since the future may bring disaster, it is always the object of at least a low level of fear. This is fundamentally a fear of the unknown and originates in the extraordinary ability our frontal lobes give us to analyze and plan for the future. The greatest unknown is death itself. For that reason, and the pain often inherent in the process, fear of death becomes in most people the primary fear.

Fear of the unknown profoundly affects our belief systems and perception of good and evil. In trying to explain a universe in which we ultimately suffer and die, we have developed an elaborate spiritual life that seeks to give us a greater sense of mastery over our own destiny. This type of understanding lessens our sense of anxiety and helplessness. Humans dread helpless terror more than any other kind of fear. We are the only species with a profound sense of the future and the only species that manifests religious beliefs. By providing insights into the purpose and meaning of life, religion gives us a sense of control over the fear of death and the unknown.

We are repelled and fascinated by death and the profound mystery that it represents. Reports of supernatural phenomena often gain widespread notoriety and spur furious debates. Near-death experiences are a recent example. Some people who have been close to death and then recovered describe strange, mystical sensations. These often include visions of light, feelings of joy and ecstasy, sensations of floating above one's own body, and encounters with the spirits of those who have already died. There is no evidence of the objective reality of these experiences. Scientists who have looked into the matter attribute them to the body's natural response to its extremely serious condition. When the body is near death it will sometimes release its store of natural opiates, known as endorphins, which can create intensely unreal feelings of the kind that David Livingstone reported. In addition, the limbic system may be receiving potent stimulation, which can produce exceptionally realistic hallucinations. There is no denying, however, the powerful subjective nature of these experiences. Many of those who have had a near-death experience report a sharply decreased anxiety over dying, or its disappearance altogether. They appear to have habituated to the fear of death.

For most people, however, the death experience is neither as dramatic nor pleasant. People who have experienced near-fatal heart attacks often describe experiencing a sort of slow-motion blackout as their oxygen-starved brain shuts down vision, hearing, and the other senses before consciousness fades away. Death is often accompanied by moderate to severe pain, though recently doctors have begun to use pain medications like morphine more aggressively. Nevertheless the terror of death for most people involves not just the pain but the helplessness and the dread of the unknown. This terror frequently expresses itself as a fear of disease, and no diseases are more feared than cancer and AIDS. As cancer cells lose their specialization and spread throughout the body, they can destroy the lungs and other organs. The tumors may cause cachexia, in which the multiplying cancer cells soak up almost all available nutrients while the body wastes away, absorbing its own muscles and organs in a vain effort to stay alive.[1] AIDS, of course, gradually destroys the immune system, leaving the body vulnerable not only to certain types of cancers but to a thousand other opportunistic infections. Great advances have been made in the understanding and treatment of cancer and AIDS. The most effective way to counter our primal fear of these diseases is by the application of advanced cortical reasoning in the form of medical science. Yet in the end we all die of some illness or accident. And no matter what the cause of death, the effect is always the same: the brain is killed. Legally and scientifically, when the brain dies, human existence ceases.

Who wants to live forever? The genes do. And because they have succeeded, perhaps we do too. The DNA pattern of every living thing stretches back in an unbroken line for 3.5 billion years to the beginning of life on earth. Every human being has a dimension of immortality. Each of us goes back, mother to daughter, father to son, parent to offspring, in an unbroken genetic chain through simpler and simpler organisms to the big bang of life nearly 4 billion years ago. Part of us has been alive for perhaps a quarter of the time that the universe has existed. That may be why the meaning of our lives is so deep and mysterious. If we could hold hands with our mother, and she could hold the hand of her mother, and so on all the way back through our hominid ancestors, we would eventually reach the common ancestor of humans and chimpanzees who lived around 7 million years ago. It would take about 280,000 generations. Our fear of death prods us to find ways to extend our lives. Science, among other strategies, is trying to understand the tricks that the genes have mastered. There search for greater longevity has had significant success. In 1900 the average life expectancy in the United States was fifty years. Today it is eighty-six for women and seventy-eight for men.

Fear motivates us to stay alive, but too much fear can kill us. Unending stress can wear our bodies down. It is even possible to be scared to death. The physical effect of fear is primarily mediated by the autonomic nervous system, which has the primary role in regulating the internal state of the body. The largest organ in our body is the skin. It encloses a liquid environment in which the tissues and organs, including the brain, float. As the great French physiologist Claude Bernard wrote: "The living organism does not really exist in the *milieu exterieur*—the atmosphere it breathes, salt or fresh water if that is its element—but in the liquid *milieu interieur* formed by the circulatory organic liquid which surrounds and bathes all the tissue elements. . . . The *milieu interieur* surrounding the organs, the tissue and their element never varies. . . . Here we have an organism which has enclosed itself in a kind of hothouse. The peripheral changes of external conditions cannot reach it; it is not subject to them, but is free and independent. . . . All the vital mechanisms, however varied they may be, have only one object, that of preserving constant the conditions of the internal environment."[2] Fear, mediated by the autonomic nervous system, is one of the primary mechanisms designed to protect us from threats to this liquid environment.

The autonomic nervous system has three principal divisions: the sympathetic nervous system, which activates the fight-or-flight response on command from the hypothalamus, the parasympathetic system, responsible for keeping the body calm and the digestive system working properly, and the enteric system, which also affects elements of the digestive system as well as the pancreas and the gall bladder. Noradrenaline secreted by the sympathetic nervous system increases heart action, promoting the fear response, while acetylcholine secreted by the parasympathetic nervous system decreases it. The interaction of these two neurochemicals determines heart rate. The control is so fine that adjustments can be made within a single beat.

Fear is designed to be self-correcting, to turn itself off by motivating us to take the appropriate action to eliminate the source of the stress. In that manner, it is like hunger. We turn off hunger by eating. We turn off fear by fighting or fleeing. Although we also have the option of engaging the neocortex and generating a much wider range of options than fight or flight, even advanced cortical reasoning ultimately must decide whether and under what circumstances we should approach a potential threat, and if we should not approach it, how we should withdraw. The constantly shifting dynamic balance between noradrenaline and acetylcholine, as well as the concentrations of hormones and other chemicals, determines the relative state of fear or relaxation that the body experiences from moment to moment. These chemical interactions are complex. For example, adrenaline circulating in the bloodstream powerfully reinforces the effect of noradrenaline on heart rate. The sympathetic nervous system originates in the gray matter of the spinal cord, while the parasympathetic nervous system is supervised by several nuclei in the brain stem. The vagus nerve, which runs from the brain stem to the heart, regulates the heart rate. Positive emotions like love and happiness activate the parasympathetic nervous system and put us in a relaxed state. Think of the interaction between the sympathetic and parasympathetic nervous systems as a tug of war between two formidable teams. Whenever the sympathetic one has the advantage, the body goes into a fear response. But the parasympathetic system then redoubles its efforts to bring the body back into equilibrium. The primitive fear system and the rational fear system compete to influence the hypothalamus, which oversees the autonomic nervous system and the fear response.

An unexpected shock or fright, including a loud noise, can cause a sudden decrease in heart rate. "My heart stopped," someone might say, describing their reaction. A strong fear can also cause the heart to race. Both a sudden increase or decrease in heart rate are capable of causing abnormal heart rhythms that can lead to sudden death. Thus someone may be scared to death. This phenomenon helps explain the mysterious deaths that are sometimes reported in folk religions like voodoo. The person who dies has often experienced a sudden fright. Shocking the system by jumping into very cold water can also cause an abnormal heart rhythm and sudden death. Long-term stress is also dangerous. The sustained increase in stress hormones can result in irreversible organ damage, wasting, and death.[3]

Certain psychedelic drugs that cause bizarre distortions of perception, particularly LSD (lysergic acid diethylamide), have also been associated with horrific fears and sudden death. The Swiss chemist Albert Hofmann, who first synthesized the chemical, experienced these kinds of stressful symptoms. LSD is the synthetic derivative of a plant fungus that is the psychoactive ingredient of certain mushrooms used in religious ceremonies by Central American Indians. Hofmann was investigating the medicinal uses of synthetic derivatives of this fungus. After working on purifying a batch of LSD, he noticed some strange sensations. He decided to test the drug on himself and on April 19, 1943, took a seemingly tiny dose of the drug. What happened next completely overwhelmed him. "Everything in my field of vision wavered and was distorted as if seen in a curved mirror," he said. "Pieces of furniture assumed grotesque, threatening forms. . . . Even worse than the demonic transformations of the outer world were the alterations that I perceived in myself, in my inner being. Every exertion of my will, every attempt to put an end to the disintegration of the outer world and the dissolution of my ego, seemed to be wasted effort. A demon had invaded me, had taken possession of my body, mind, and soul. I jumped up and screamed, trying to free myself from him, but then sank down again and lay helpless on the sofa. . . . I was seized by the dreadful fear of going insane. I was taken to another world, another place, another time. My body seemed to be without sensation, lifeless, strange. Was I dying? Was this the transition? At times I believed my self to be outside my body, and then perceived clearly, as an outside observer, the complete tragedy of my situation."[4] It took Hofmann about fourteen hours to recover. After LSD became popular with the counterculture in the 1960s, it was associated with suicides, psychotic reactions, and permanent changes in the thinking processes of chronic users. Yet researchers continue to study psychedelic drugs because of what they might tell us about the nature of human consciousness. The mechanism by which psychedelic drugs act is still not well understood, but seems to be related to rapid changes in neurotransmitter systems involving serotonin, noradrenaline, and dopamine. There is a large increase in the production of noradrenaline in the brain, which may explain the peculiar alertness and vivid memories stimulated by these drugs. The flow of serotonin to the cerebral hemispheres seems to be disrupted, possibly reducing the ability of the neocortex to inhibit the limbic system. This could explain the fearful reactions.

By taking LSD, Hofmann unexpectedly confronted the unknown. Sometimes the events of history conspire to do the same thing, stressing the mind and sympathetic nervous system to their limit as individuals are forced to confront uncertainty and death. Around the same time Hofmann tested his drug, Abraham Pais, a theoretical physicist and friend and biographer of Albert Einstein, was in the middle of a terrible ordeal of his own, hiding from the Nazis in occupied Amsterdam. His experiences embody in a striking way many of the themes we have been exploring in our analysis of fear and illustrate the vibrant and complex responses of the brain's interlocking fear systems during times of crisis.[5]

Pais comes from an old, well-established Jewish family in Amsterdam. He was almost twenty-two when the Germans invaded the Netherlands as part of the blitzkrieg (lightning war) that conquered Europe. He vividly remembers his father rushing into his bedroom in the early hours of May 10, 1940, to tell him of the invasion: "Bram, get up. There is war." Five days later the Dutch government capitulated. For five years he struggled to survive the Nazis.

Pais was well aware of the implications of the recent breakthroughs in nuclear physics. Once when his teacher George Uhlenbeck was visiting Enrico Fermi at Columbia University in New York, Fermi walked over to the window of his office and said: "Do you realize, George, that fission may make possible the construction of bombs so powerful that just a few of them can destroy this whole big city?" But Pais was trapped in Holland with no job because the Nazis had banned Jews from all academic posts.

The Nazis relentlessly and shamelessly appealed to primitive limbic reasoning in their grotesque race war against the Jewish people and other ethnic and religious groups. They tried to play on people's sensitivities to prepared fears by explicitly portraying their enemies as roaches and rats. Research has shown that it is much easier to condition the sympathetic nervous system to react fearfully to biologically prepared fears.[6] Prior to shipping them to concentration camps, the Nazis methodically stigmatized and dehumanized Jews. Pais had to wear a large Star of David on his outer clothes whenever he went out. Four members of Pais's family survived the occupation. Seventeen died in the Holocaust. Pais had his first taste of the German occupation one night in his room at his parents' home. "[S]uddenly I heard yelling and shrieking in the room next to mine, in the house next door. It was the bedroom of an old man in his eighties, a Jew. I knew at once what was happening. . . . The next morning I learned that my old neighbor, in his nightclothes, had been clinging to his bed, refusing to move and yelling for mercy. He was gone."

Not long afterward, he went into hiding. Many Dutch families courageously took in Jewish families and concealed them from the Gestapo. Pais lived with the family of a tailor on one of Amsterdam's old canals, not far from the hiding place of Anne Frank and her family. He had a room on the top floor and a tiny hiding place in the attic that he could slip into if the house was searched. One night he was having dinner with the family and Hans Kramers, a professor of physics and friend, who had joined them. One of the children went to answer the door and pressed a secret alarm bell indicating something was wrong. Pais rushed to his tiny hiding place. "Then, dammit, I was so nervous that I could not work the inside lock," Pais said. "I therefore held the panel in position by hand. That way it did not fit perfectly; a narrow open crack remained. The Gestapo people came upstairs and went into the attic. One man carried a strong torchlight which he at one point shone straight at my panel. I could see the light through the crack—I can still see that light even as I write these lines. He played the light around for a while. Then they left." A few minutes later someone entered Pais's room and sat next to the wall in which Pais was hiding. The person began reading from a volume of lectures on Shakespeare. "It was Kramers," Pais said. "What this good man was doing now was reading to me from that book, in order to calm my nerves."

Pais found that despite the terrible stress, his powers of concentration had improved tremendously. Prior to going into hiding he had worked hard at his physics but found himself easily distracted. "Now, in hiding, it all worked differently," Pais said. "I would get up, exercise, have breakfast, then sit down at my little worktable and, presto, thoughts emerged totally unforced, by themselves, you might say." Pais began switching his hiding place, trying to stay ahead of the Gestapo. By early 1945 he had moved in with an old friend, Lion Nordheim, and Nordheim's wife and sister. The women were Jewish but had blond hair and blue eyes and could pass for gentiles. By then Pais and Lion were working with the Dutch resistance. After lunch one day the bell rang. Friends had been in and out so Pais didn't pay any attention. "Moments later the door to my room opened," Pais said. "There stood a tall man in SS uniform, the skull and bones symbol on his cap, a drawn revolver in his hand. My first reaction was a quick look at the window. Could I jump out? Impossible?" The young people in the apartment were herded together. "My strongest recollection of the next moments is the total collapse of Lion," Pais said. "He was visibly in total panic, had lost all semblance of composure, and moved erratically, causing one of the Germans to hit him in the face, sending his glasses flying. . . . As we drove off, I experienced fears more intense than I have ever felt in my life. It was a degree of fear that caused physical pain. My body ached all over."

In conditions of extreme terror, not only can the overexcited sympathetic nervous system cause the body to collapse, but the mind can disintegrate as well. A noradrenaline surge ordinarily pumps up alertness and lays down vivid memories. But when noradrenaline overwhelms the brain, the result is often panic and confusion. Excessive noradrenaline and other neurochemicals rivet the attention on the object of fear, disrupt working memory, and reduce one's focus, like a contracting tunnel, until the person can concentrate on only the narrowest fear goal (escape, for example) or the fear itself ("I'm going to die"). This narrowing of focus makes it difficult for the fearful person to shift his attention to anything else. He is unable to process other stimuli and everything around him becomes a blur.[7]

The men were taken to Gestapo headquarters and placed in separate rooms. Pais was extremely apprehensive but tried to keep his mind clear. "I remembered some advice given to me by resistance members on how to behave in such situations," he said. "First, and most important, try not to show any fear. Behave politely. Ask for an interpreter who could translate spoken German into Dutch to gain time for replies." During his interrogation he was manhandled and threatened, but he steadfastly denied being in the resistance. Pais and Lion were imprisoned together. As the days went on they were periodically interrogated separately. They fell into a routine. "Days in prison were mostly quiet," said Pais, "but nights were bad. We would hear heavy metal doors clanging, shouts, shrieks. We know that some poor bastard was being taken away, but had only grim forebodings as to where." One day Lion stumbled back from an interrogation, pale and shaken. "What happened?" asked Pais. "I've been condemned to death," Lion said. "My immediate very brief reaction was and still is astounding to me. It was as if, inside my head, a blinding light shone and a voice spoke: *I shall live.* I had not been condemned. Lion had fallen on his cot. I picked him up and cradled him in my arms, as one does a young child. I spoke calming words to him; I do not recall what I said. He quieted down somewhat but remained deeply withdrawn and hard to reach these next few days, staring out of our little window, unseeing." When Pais left the prison he spoke to another prisoner who was working as a clerk. "Where is Lion?" Pais asked him. "He was shot several days ago," the man said.

Calm words and gentle physical contact are two of the surest methods of calming someone. They tend to decrease the activity of the sympathetic nervous system's fight-or-flight response and increase the parasympathetic nervous system's rest-and-digest pattern. The limbic system reacts powerfully to the sound of the human voice and personal human presence. In brain-imaging studies, the amygdala responds most strongly to words and faces. If infants are not held and stroked, their limbic systems actually begin to wither. If this isolation continues long enough, the infants will lose the ability to express and experience emotions and will ultimately withdraw, displaying no interest in their environment, behaving peculiarly, even dying. Tragically, in the late 1930s the Nazis began a pilot program to try to breed the master race. Couples were selected according to strict standards. The children were immediately removed from their parents and sent to a special home where they could be raised in a superior environment. But the children received virtually no mothering because the Nazi designers of the experiment believed it would make them soft. Nineteen out of the twenty children that were raised in this environment showed severe abnormalities in their social and emotional development.[8]

Pais's ordeal exemplifies the many dimensions of fear. His memories remain phenomenally vivid after half a century. His ability to concentrate was dramatically enhanced and he was amazed to find that when he would sit down to do physics his mind worked effortlessly a peak levels. This is a state some psychologists term flow.[9] Pais constantly struggled to manage his fear by maintaining as much control as possible. His first step was to go into hiding to avoid arrest. But even after his arrest he tried to follow the advice of the resistance and show no fear to his interrogators. After two years in hiding, Pais showed signs of habituating to the dangers—probably overhabituating. When the doorbell rang on the day of his arrest, he ignored it. This kind of habituation to potentially threatening signals is common even in everyday life. How many people pay any attention to car alarms anymore? At the moment of his arrest he instinctively searched for a way to escape. Helplessness caused Pais the greatest terror: the helplessness of the old man clinging to his bed as the Gestapo arrested him, the terrible apprehension he felt as he watched the flashlight shining through the crack in his hiding place, the physical pain he felt after his arrest, the screams in the night in prison. Helpless terror is compounded by being alone. Companionship, which is so important in easing the fears of phobics, helped sustain Pais. He was fortunate to have friends like Kramers and Lion. Although his close friendship with Lion was the cause of "the most tragic moments of my life," Pais was painfully honest about his instinctive and overwhelming relief when he realized he wasn't going to die. The fear of death has a power that is primitive and tenacious.

Pais's story is remarkable, but not unusual for those days. He endured dreadful mental suffering as he faced an unknown future in the heart of a Nazi killing machine that cost him most of his family and many of his friends. His is also a story of incredible resilience in the face of this agonizing uncertainty. He used the full resources of his mind to continue working until the terrible cold and famine of the winter of 1944–45 when thousands died of hunger and there was practically no heat. He was able to trade his tuxedo for a bag of potatoes and felt very lucky. He and his friends managed to keep up their spirits: "I have memories of those evenings spent together, cheery in spite of everything, during which I, like nearly all the Dutch, could think of only one thing: food."

Pais was extremely fortunate to escape serious physical injury. Even after he was captured, he was not tortured, only punched and slapped at times. The worst stress was mental, as his interrogators constantly threatened to shoot him. Throughout his years of hiding and period of imprisonment, he went through mental torture agonizing over all the hideous things that could happen to him, and probably were happening to his friends and family.

This kind of pain comes straight from the frontal lobes, which contain our awareness of the future and allow us to contemplate all the multiple possible directions that our life might take. This is the mechanism of anxiety. Even when things seem to be going well we all know that we are at risk from disease, accident, the suffering or loss of friends and family, or other reversals. Anxiety is the fear of the future. The word derives from a Greek root meaning "to strangle." Anxiety is part of the human condition because the set of things we love is small compared to the list of things we fear. We love only certain people, certain foods, certain places but we fear many things. Oddly, loving or desiring something increases our fear. At the very least we fear losing what we love, or failing to get what we desire. Usually there is much more to it than that. We love our children, but think how many fears we have about their future. There is a deep asymmetry as we look out on the world. Every love or desire creates at least one fear, but every fear does not create love.

The rational fear system through the prefrontal cortex spins out a stream of plans and possibilities. These are produced from the constantly updated synaptic model of the world created by our frontal lobes. This system also generates scenarios that attempt to explain our past actions and seek to understand how we came to be where we are. The big bang is the favorite scenario of modern cosmologists who study how the universe came to be where it is today. Generating scenarios about the future can be a source of immediate anxiety (what if my plane crashes?). And generating scenarios about the past is an important element of regret. We can endlessly replay in our minds scenarios of things we could have done differently that might have led to a different present and a future with less fear and pain. (If I had only worn my seat belt I wouldn't be sitting in this wheelchair. If I had only stopped smoking, I wouldn't be facing a lung cancer operation.) This is an essential part of anguish, sorrow, humiliation, shame, and despair. Emotions like grief and sorrow also stem from our strong emotional attachments to others. When someone close to us leaves or dies, the sorrow we feel may be mixed with elements of regret. (If I had only insisted that he go to the doctor, he might not have had the heart attack.) Fear not only involves avoiding physical or mental injury for ourselves, but worrying about others we care for as well—and not only the people we love but the things we love. Fear of mental pain expands our range of fears beyond ourselves. It is a fundamental source of sympathy and empathy because our minds can create a scenario in which we experience the mental and physical pain of others. Yet generating scenarios is also a source of happiness and pleasure, as when we contemplate how fortunate we are that things worked out as well as they did.

Although scenarios are generated by the frontal lobes, particularly the prefrontal cortices, this mechanism can be controlled by primitive limbic reasoning. The baseball player who refuses to wash his jersey because he is on a winning streak exemplifies this kind of control. We are dealing again with misplaced causality. Just because the player won several games while wearing that jersey, doesn't mean the jersey was responsible for the wins. Yet because human consciousness is highly suggestible and fear-ridden, superstitions like this are common among athletes. They can become self-fulfilling prophecies. The baseball player generates scenarios foreseeing that he will play poorly if he doesn't wear the dirty jersey. The player will then only feel comfortable and confident with the dirty jersey. Yet if we could secretly replace the jersey with an identical one that was just as dirty, his frame of mind and the outcome of the game would be identical. Superstitions like breaking a mirror or having a black cat cross your path can generate similar bad-luck scenarios among people who believe in this kind of thing. These types of superstition—for example, avoiding the number thirteen (Friday the thirteenth, the thirteenth floor of a building)—are a form of cultural phobia. Primitive reasoning driven by an intense fear of the unknown is alive and well in the form of psychics, astrologers, ouija boards, and even fortune cookies.

Because of our sense of the future, we wonder about the purpose and meaning of life. One expression of this kind of thinking is religion, which is a feature of every human culture and goes back at least as far as the Cro-Magnons. Fear of unknown and the unknowable, fear of death—all these uncertainties cause mental pain. Religion seeks to address that pain. It is a fundamental expression of human culture because it provides a sense of understanding and comfort, helping to stave off despair. It was the priests of the earliest civilizations who systematically studied the earth and the stars and began accumulating a written body of knowledge. Though they sometimes seem in conflict today, philosophy and science evolved from religion and its preoccupation with the nature of the universe and our place in it.

Religion not only assuages fear, it can create it. The fear of eternal damnation or other spiritual consequences is sometimes used to seek conformity. Fear always motivates us to avoid certain things, and with religion it is no different. Religion can create a new hierarchy of fears that shifts our emotional perceptions. If a close friend dies, this may occasion intense sorrow in one individual. But another highly religious person, who believes the friend has entered an eternal paradise, may treat the death as an occasion for joy and celebration. The fear of death has been, if not eliminated, then significantly curtailed.

Every religion or other moral system is built on judgments of good and evil. The initial source of these judgments is the preconscious processing of the primitive fear system. Researchers have found that people of different languages and cultures always divide objects, individuals, and events into good or bad as the first step of any further evaluation. This initial determination of goodness or badness colors their subsequent judgments.[10] If someone believes that showing fear is bad because it is a sign of weakness, for example, he may be less able to evaluate his own fears objectively. The primitive fear system judges everything we see as good or bad and all thoughts and sensations enter our consciousness with a preconscious emotional coloration. But advanced cortical reasoning can recognize these prejudices and find ways to compensate for them.

Religious cults like those led by Jim Jones and Marshall Applewhite build on the simplistic preconscious judgment of good and evil by the primitive fear system. Within the cult, and particularly within the leader, resides all goodness. The rest of the world is wicked. Cult leaders, through various combinations of charisma, indoctrination, and intimidation, provide a false sense of security to vulnerable people. These leaders try to create a euphoric belief among their followers that they are a messiah or prophet and have new energy and power to suppress all the uncertainty of life and the fear of the unknown, including the fear of death. In extreme cases the cult will try to convince its followers that through suicide they will become immortal. The results, of course, can be tragic: seven hundred and eighty dead at Jonestown and thirty-nine dead at the Heaven's Gate compound at Rancho Santa Fe near San Diego.

We can read about the past and learn from the mistakes of others. But writing gives us only a glimpse of what went before us. Human memory is fragile and the scenarios writers produce always contain errors at some level. Every moment of reality possesses an infinite amount of information. As we move further and further back, history dissolves into stories and myths. Yet the ancient wisdom often contains important truths. What was the first human emotion? In the Book of Genesis, after Adam and Eve disobeyed the Lord and ate of the fruit of the Tree of Knowledge, their eyes were opened to good and evil. They made clothes for themselves and hid when the Lord came walking in the Garden. Adam said, "I was afraid." The eyes of Adam and Eve were opened not only to good and evil, but to the future and the past. Human beings have used this knowledge to create a world civilization and scientific theories that encompass the entire universe from its very beginnings. But the price is fear.

{ Chapter 7 }

From Anxiety to Terror

hy does fear, ranging from mild anxiety to outright terror, play such a dominant role in our emotional lives? The answer reflects the immediacy of pain and fear in our survival. Something we fear can lead almost instantly to our injury or death, whereas most pleasurable activities do not have such instant life-or-death consequences.

We live in an ocean of fear fed daily by torrents of alarming news pouring out of the mass media. We are overwhelmed by reports about crime, disease, terrorism, and a million other dangers. We pay attention because our primitive fear system is innately tuned to fixate on alarm calls. A huge percentage of the stories selected by the media for reporting deal explicitly or implicitly with fear. It is a fascinating exercise to take any newspaper or newscast at random and mentally note how many different kinds of fear are woven through the stories.

To illustrate my point, I randomly picked an evening newscast by a Los Angeles television station in the spring of 1997. Here is a list of what was reported. First came the story of a brushfire near Los Angeles that destroyed one house and threatened several others on a day of high winds. There was footage of a woman rushing back to her burning house to rescue her cats. The second story involved a just-released videotape made by the dashboard camera of a New Mexico state trooper who had pulled over a car on a routine traffic stop. The tape, which also recorded the conversations outside the police cruiser, showed a twenty-year-old driver getting out of his car with a handgun and threatening the officer, who tried to calm him down. After a few moments, the officer grabbed the man and there was a struggle off camera. Next we saw the man holding his gun to the officer's temple. The officer repeatedly pleaded with the man to take his finger off the trigger so the gun wouldn't go off accidentally. The man forced the officer into his car and they drove off. The newscaster reported that the car was stopped at a roadblock a few miles away and the officer, who was praised for his presence of mind, persuaded the man to surrender peacefully. Los Angeles is famous for its news helicopters, and has more of them than any other city. The next story featured the station's chopper flying over the scene of an accident that happened a few minutes earlier in which a car jumped a curb and hit two people who were sitting on a bus bench. Fortunately the injuries weren't life-threatening. Then there was a follow-up on a terrible traffic accident the night before involving ten teenagers from a wealthy suburb who were coming home from a party. The teenagers were packed into a small truck, which went out of control and crashed. One of the teenagers was killed and five others were severely injured. Only one of the ten was wearing a seat belt. Next came videotaped footage of an accident earlier in the day in which a passenger train struck a car towing a trailer. The driver was killed. Then there was a report about an expensive car that slammed into a gas main, starting a spectacular blaze. The driver got out of the car and fled the scene. Police said the car was registered to a municipal court judge, but they didn't yet know whether he was driving.

The next story showed taped footage of a wild police pursuit of a car at speeds reaching a hundred miles per hour. It ended when the car flipped over and the driver disappeared into a nearby neighborhood. The police were still looking for him. Next came a story about a baseball coach who made a racially insulting remark to an African-American teenager. The coach apologized but many people were upset. The newscaster then reported that there had been a moderate earthquake in a sparsely populated area of central California. This was followed by an unusual human-interest story about a high school teacher and baseball fan who has moonlighted as a popular and colorful peanut vendor at Dodger Stadium for the last thirty-eight years—since the day the ballpark opened. A few days earlier he had bought a couple of extra packages of peanuts from another vendor. These were promotional packages that were not supposed to be sold. He sold them anyway for a profit of two dollars. When he admitted to his employer what he had done, he was promptly fired. In an interview with a reporter, the ex-peanut vendor expressed deep remorse, quoted John Steinbeck, and voiced the hope that he might get another chance. Fans at the stadium were outraged at the harshness of his punishment. So far, however, the Dodger Stadium concessionaire had refused to rehire him. Next came a report about plans for a new sports arena near downtown Los Angeles. The city council approved the plans but worried that the city would have to pay too much of the arena's annual operating expenses, which could put pressure on taxes. Then there was the story of a lottery player who claimed he was swindled by the man who sold him a lottery ticket. He said he took the ticket back to the man—the operator of a small deli—to see if he had won anything. The deli operator told him he won a free game and the man turned over the ticket. Later he saw the winning lottery number and realized it was the one he always plays. The prize was almost $7 million. Meantime the deli operator had claimed the prize, saying that he had found the ticket. He was charged with grand larceny. Next came a story about a home burglary in San Diego a few nights earlier. As the burglar approached the bedroom, he was jumped by the pet cat, who clawed him on the shoulders and back. The burglar fled but was later arrested. The cat was being treated as a hero. Then there was a story about a Marine Corps helicopter crashing near Dallas. The two men in the helicopter were killed. One witness said the pilot acted heroically because he steered the crippled helicopter away from a school. Finally there was the story of a San Francisco–area computer hacker arrested by the FBI after stealing information about thousands of credit cards through the Internet and trying to sell the information on the World Wide Web.

Fear of being shot to death, fear of random violence, fear of crime, fear of losing your house, fear of being hit by a car, fear of your children being injured or killed in an accident, fear of being persecuted because of your race, fear of earthquakes, fear of losing your job, fear of government taxes, fear of being cheated, fear of dying in a helicopter crash—this was an eventful news night in Los Angeles. Yet these stories are fairly typical of the kinds that are seen everywhere. Some of them were carried throughout the country. There are, however, some regional differences in emphasis. Different parts of the country tend to habituate to certain unique local problems that jar outsiders. In Kansas City, Missouri, for example, the malls have tornado shelters and warning sirens that locals take for granted but outsiders often find distressing. In Los Angeles, the locals tend to ignore or laugh off the hundreds of small earthquakes that occur every year, earthquakes that tourists find unnerving. A large earthquake like the Northridge quake of January 1994, however, puts everyone's nerves on edge. Every little aftershock makes people jump, particularly those near the epicenter of the original quake. It takes a year or so for people to rehabituate. On the other hand, different areas of the country are permanently sensitized to certain local dangers. In the upper South, where winter snowfall is usually fairly light, the worry is ice. Freezing rain can glaze a road—or even more dangerous, only a patch of road—and turn a morning commute into a treacherous nightmare. I've had several experiences in Kentucky and Virginia in which I've been driving on an interstate highway in weather that just turned cold enough to freeze the roads and watched as car after car coming in the other direction spun out of control on the ice. Fortunately the accidents were never serious. In the Los Angeles area, people are sensitized to the danger of wildfire. Television stations will break into their newscasts for live reports about efforts to contain the latest ten-acre brushfire. But there is good reason for concern. The long dry season and occasional high winds in southern California's monsoon climate quickly fan a fire out of control. Everyone is vulnerable. A few years ago my wife and I were driving in the hills above Laguna Beach and saw the blackened ruins of spectacular homes overlooking the Pacific Ocean.

Los Angeles is notorious for its high-speed police pursuits on the freeways, many of which are reported live by the fleet of news helicopters. But there has been a concern by police in recent years about a phenomenon that has been dubbed post-high-speed-chase syndrome. Police officials now acknowledge that pursuing a suspect who is often driving recklessly at extremely high speeds creates a powerful fear response in police officers. There is a massive surge of adrenaline and noradrenaline. In some officers there is a propensity for this response to take the fear-fight-anger pattern. The primitive system takes over and rational judgment is impaired. Once the suspect is apprehended this can lead to an excessive use of force by the officer. The most famous case, of course, involved Rodney King, who on March 3, 1991, led police on a dangerous high-speed chase before being apprehended and beaten—on videotape—by pursuing Los Angeles police officers. Just over a year later, the acquittal of those officers on most of the charges connected with the beating began the Los Angeles riots, which killed fifty-five people in one of the largest civil disturbances in the history of the country. Police now receive training on how to suppress their fear response in this kind of pursuit.

The beating of Rodney King and the subsequent riots severely damaged the reputation of the Los Angeles Police Department with many segments of the community. The sympathy of most of those who saw the beating on videotape was with the prostrate King. People identified with him, not the police. They felt afraid for him. The LAPD regained a great deal of credibility in many people's eyes during another highly publicized confrontation: the astonishing shootout in February 1997 between police and two bank robbers in North Hollywood. The two armed robbers clad in body armor sprayed automatic weapons fire at everything in sight, including news helicopters, as the clearly outgunned police courageously fought back. This was all carried on live television. I happened to turn it on myself in the middle, and like everyone else I felt terribly afraid for the police and bystanders until the gunmen were finally shot and killed. This strong identification with the police led many people to have a better sense of the dangers they face.

Our interest in fearsome stories goes beyond their role as alarms. We are fascinated by them in multiple ways. We want to experience fear in a safe setting to learn what to be afraid of and how to behave in fearful situations. Watching these stories is a form of habituation, and there is also an element of relief in seeing someone else undergo a terrible experience. This is a bit like the feeling Abraham Pais experienced when his inner voice said, *I shall live.* Yet we can also be sensitized by news about crime and violence if we believe the threat to our own safety has increased. That's why the pervasive coverage of appalling crimes makes people fear crime more strongly than is statistically called for. Paradoxically the sensational coverage of violent crime makes us less fearful but more anxious. By being confronted with this vicarious violence almost daily, our primitive fear system tends to become habituated. We can watch a violent news story or violent movie and take it in stride, whereas someone who had never been exposed to such images of violence would be deeply shocked. But at the same time our primitive fear system is habituating, our rational fear system is being sensitized. Our frontal lobes have absorbed the message of the omnipresence of violence (which is actually exaggerated in most communities) and generate constant anxiety-producing scenarios. What if we had a flat tire late one night like Bill

Cosby's son Ennis? What if we are targeted by some maniac on the highway? Our anxiety about crime has dramatically increased in recent years, even though the crime rate has generally remained steady or fallen.

The alarm call method of communication seems to be more and more pervasive. Much of the media lurches from one sensational story to another, emphasizing the primal emotions, especially fear, and making little sustained effort to report overall trends or underlying causes. It is a triumph of primitive limbic hysteria over advanced cortical reasoning.

Just as fear dominates the flow of information in our society, it permeates the structure of society itself. In his classic work, *The Prince*, Renaissance political philosopher Niccolò Machiavelli advised rulers that given the choice between being loved or feared they should choose to be feared, since fear is the more impressive, powerful, and stable emotion.[1] More than four centuries later, an American president echoed those words. "People react to fear, not love," said Richard M. Nixon. "They don't teach that in Sunday school, but it's true." States have consistently used fear to enforce the social order. Even in the freest societies, laws are not obeyed solely on a voluntary basis. There is always an underlying fear of the government's power to fine and imprison. Governments often use propaganda to stir up fear and hatred of their enemies and rivals, especially in times of war. Candidates for public office frequently use similar propaganda techniques in the form of attack ads and negative campaigns to stir up fear and doubt about their political rivals. Propaganda, like sensational news reporting, seeks to appeal directly to the primitive fear system, bypassing the rational fear system and advanced cortical reasoning.

Individuals can be fearful or fearless, and so can societies. A society's attitude toward fear profoundly shapes its response to issues of individual liberty, change, and personal security. Crime has become such a pervasive fear in our society that many law-abiding people now carry guns for their own protection. The results are sometimes tragic, sometimes ridiculous. A Texas newspaper reported on the case of a woman shopper, loaded down with bags, who returned to her car in a shopping mall late one night. She was shocked to find four teenagers sitting in the car. She screamed at them to get out, but they ignored her. She dropped her bags, reached into her purse, and pulled out a small pistol. As soon as the teenagers saw the gun, they jumped out of the car and fled into the night. Only after the woman got into the car did she realize it wasn't hers. Her car— the identical make and model—was parked several rows away.

Relatively fearful societies are more likely to have coercive governments, limited civil rights, resistance to change, and hostility toward outsiders. A fearless society, in contrast, is more likely to have the maximum latitude toward individual liberties, outside influences, and social change that is consistent with public order. Fearful societies run the risk of stagnation and decay. Fearless societies are vulnerable to rampant individualism and fragmentation. But in any society under severe stress, fear can spread wildly. The irrational reactions of the primitive fear system overwhelm rational thought and mass hysteria follows. This happens in times of war and during major epidemics. The *War of the Worlds* scare revealed incipient hysteria prior to World War II. We saw it in the early years of the AIDS epidemic. Terrorists know that a few selective acts of violence can set off a mass panic. Yet even from a strictly rational point of view, societies have reason to be concerned for their survival in the face of global environmental damage, the proliferation of nuclear, biological, and chemical weapons, and other possible catastrophes.

When humans use their conscious abilities to cooperate in a modern social setting, the advanced societies we create expend the majority of their resources allaying our most basic fears—our fear of death through starvation, exposure, disease, accident, attack by others. For example, we support a military to protect us from outsiders, a police force to protect us from each other, a transportation system to make our travel safer, a health system, and vast water and sewer systems to protect us from disease. We create a complex network of public and private institutions and mechanisms to provide us with a huge array of goods and services to meet our needs for shelter, nutrition, and comfort. We take for granted that our civilization has practically eliminated the danger from predators. To combat micropredators like bacteria and viruses as well as genetic malfunctions like cancer and other forms of illness and injury, we have set up a huge medical research establishment. If all this enormous infrastructure collapsed in a destructive war or massive natural disaster, and no help was forthcoming, a large proportion of the population would rapidly die of exposure, starvation, and disease. In many ways civilization is a vast elaboration of the role of the individual neuron within the brain, which the great Spanish neuroanatomist Santiago Ramón y Cajal described as "the aristocrat among the structures of the body, with its giant arms stretched out like the tentacles of an octopus to the provinces on the frontier of the outside world, to watch for the constant ambushes of physical and chemical forces."[2]

Our innate fear systems work in concert with our social nature to create civilizations that protect us as much as possible from the fear of death and other threats to our physical well-being. Civilization is a kind of fortress against our most primal fears. Within it, we can pursue our desires and curiosity, not constantly expend most of our energy on avoiding starvation, injury, and death as we did for the first 95 percent of our species' existence. Clearly fear is not banished by civilization. Everything we do in a civilized setting is motivated by a balance of fears and desires. But the fear of death is usually less imminent than it would be if we were still struggling for our living with stone tools.

Fear is a powerful organizing principle for both the individual and society. Neither individuals nor societies can ever be truly understood unless we understand their fears. The American Revolution was motivated by a fear of oppression. Because of this fear, the U.S. Constitution created a federal government constrained by checks and balances. Like the history of every society, American history has always been molded by fear. In the nineteenth century, the period leading up to the Civil War was dominated by the fear of slavery and the fear of the dissolution of the Union. In the twentieth century, the modern Democratic party was created by Franklin Roosevelt in response to the rampant fear of economic insecurity spawned by the Great Depression. The modern Republican party emerged from the fear of Roosevelt's New Deal with its commitment to an activist role for government. The fear of economic insecurity and the fear of big government continue to shape American politics almost seventy years later along with many other fears, including the fear of environmental degradation, the fear of permissiveness, the fear of crime—the list is endless.

When fears compete, as they do in every mind, the one that produces the strongest activation of the brain's fear systems is that which normally controls behavior. But this can be a complex process. It begins with an assessment by the primitive fear system of any primal fears involved. The rational fear system and consciousness weigh distant fears against immediate fears and desires—a teenager might weigh whether the supposed pleasures of smoking now are worth the risk years from now of developing lung cancer or heart disease. The context and neurochemical state of the person at the time plays an important role. If someone is hungry, that will influence how he weighs fears with regard to eating. A hungry Cro-Magnon might have taken risks in hunting large animals that his well-fed peer would have shunned. Hormonal changes in teenagers make them more sensitive to peer pressure. A teenager might override an otherwise strong fear (the risk of lung cancer) if the reward of a specific behavior (smoking) is immediate acceptance by peers. Everyone has to weigh a huge number of fears, and this process can be confusing and frustrating. Take, for example, the sometimes conflicting information about what foods are healthy and how much we should eat. As we go about our daily lives, we are motivated by a hierarchy of fears that can shift from moment to moment. If we knew that tomorrow we would be diagnosed with a fatal illness, the competition from the fear of death would eliminate whole arrays of other fears.

Much of the progress toward world peace in the last half of the twentieth century resulted from the emergence of a new and specific fear that personally affects every human being on earth: the prospect of dying in a nuclear war. This dread very likely deterred the outbreak of a third world war, though it did not stop smaller wars that could be fought without nuclear weapons and with little risk of nuclear escalation. Machiavelli would have been the first to point out that human beings often must be motivated by fear, not love, to seek peace. "For love is sustained by a bond of gratitude which, because men are excessively self-interested, is broken whenever they see a chance to benefit themselves," he wrote almost five centuries ago. "But fear is sustained by a dread of punishment that is always effective."[3] Nuclear weapons were never used so long as there was a fear of mutual destruction. Only at the end of World War II, when the United States had a monopoly on nuclear weapons and there was no such fear, were atomic bombs dropped on Hiroshima and Nagasaki. There is no doubt that if, instead of the United States, Japan or Germany or the Soviet Union had had a monopoly on these weapons they would have been used as well. The summit meetings between the Soviet Union and the United States were pervaded by an air of fear. There was a powerful incentive for these negotiations to succeed in improving relations or the superpowers might find themselves, even against their will, in a war that would destroy humanity. For half a century, nuclear weapons kept a shaky international peace—until the Soviet Union collapsed. Even today their existence remains a potent inducement for the major powers to engage in responsible statesmanship.

Nuclear weapons represent one of the ironies of the modern world. Humans create civilization to protect themselves from the ravages of nature and of each other, yet the by-products of civilization—weapons of mass destruction and global environmental damage—create even more formidable threats to the human race. Civilization can sometimes make a mess of things. Evolution, however, gives us a tool to dig our way out: advanced cortical reasoning. But since it is easily swamped by the preconscious alarms of the primitive fear system, we need to have the clearest possible understanding of how best to make advanced cortical reasoning work. That will require a further exploration of the mysteries of the primitive fear system and the complexities of the frontal lobes.

As we discussed in Chapter 3, the primitive fight-or-flight response plays out in two basic ways from the initial fear. One response is fear-flight-panic, the other is fear-fight-anger. Alarm calls quickly activate the primitive fear systems of individuals and deactivate the frontal lobes because the brain interprets alarm calls as signaling a threat to survival, which takes precedence over all other thoughts and behavior. Among a group of people, the fear-flight-panic response to an alarm call can lead to mass panic of the kind that occurred in the Beverly Hills Supper Club fire or the *War of the Worlds* scare. The fear-fight-anger response within a group can lead to mass anger and the formation of a mob. I can clearly remember the mob atmosphere at the meeting at Harvard's Memorial Church in the spring of 1969 after the crackdown on the demonstrators who had taken over University Hall. The mood became increasingly volatile and electric as one speaker after another poured out his rage. Rational thinking was almost impossible. Just as we have inherited the tendency for mass panic from our animal ancestors, we seem to have inherited and embellished the mobbing response as well. This can be seen most clearly in birds and is quite amazing. I once saw a group of blue jays launch a mass attack that drove away a cat. "Nesting birds routinely mob predators such as owls, crows, and cats," write biologists James L. Gould and Carol Grant Gould. "Mobbing behavior includes a series of short scolding 'chats' (with easily localized wide-band frequencies) combined with physical group attacks on the trespassing predator. The sight of a myriad small birds in spring attacking a flying crow several times their size is familiar to many of us."[4]

Whether a group of human beings responds to fear with mass panic or mass anger depends on the circumstances, including the degree of the threat and the comparative likelihood of the success of fighting versus fleeing. One of the most important variables for human beings is the attitude of the leaders of the group. Adolf Hitler perfected the mob event at his gigantic Nuremberg rallies, complete with walls of light, banners, uniforms, singing, and martial displays. He used his venomous rhetoric not only to reinforce racial hatred and stimulate a fighting spirit among his followers, but to terrify and panic his enemies. Winston Churchill is justly admired for taking the tremendous fear of Hitler felt by the British people and, with stunning oratory, turning it from panicky capitulation to gallant resistance. Martin Luther King, Jr., is revered for using his exceptional eloquence both to reduce fear among the races and channel a sense of fearful helplessness by many African-Americans into a fighting response that involved civil disobedience and nonviolent resistance. King was influenced by the example set by Mohandas Gandhi, the great spiritual leader of India and an apostle of nonviolence. King, in turn, influenced another healer of racial hatred, South African President Nelson Mandela. King not only appealed directly to the emotions, he appealed to reason by arguing that it was only simple justice that the rights enumerated in the Declaration of Independence and the Constitution be guaranteed to African-Americans. The civil rights movement matched King's eloquence with a sophisticated campaign in the courts that required a brilliant application of advanced cortical reasoning.

Leaders can not only channel fear from flight into fight, they can seek to increase the fear of something the group has overlooked. In the years leading up to World War II, Churchill tirelessly warned of the rising danger of the Nazi party. He was appalled that many Western leaders made the mistake of underestimating Hitler. In the 1960s a consumerist and environmental movement sprang up, warning of the dangers of unsafe automobiles and polluted air and water. People were sensitized to risks they had generally ignored, and a series of important reforms and social changes followed.

What exactly does it mean to be sensitized? We have discussed at length how the primitive fear system generates a fear response prior to conscious awareness and can trigger a behavior—jumping or freezing—before we are even aware of it. Nevertheless, we feel fear and other emotions consciously, not just subconsciously. How do these emotions that we are sensitized to enter our consciousness? A growing body of research indicates that just as language functions are specialized in the different hemispheres of the human brain, with 95 percent of people having their dominant speech centers in the left cerebral hemisphere, each cerebral hemisphere has different emotional specializations. The degree of specialization is striking. For most people negative emotions like fear, hatred, and anger enter consciousness and are expressed through the right frontal lobe, whereas positive emotions like love, happiness, and euphoria enter consciousness through the left. The implications are striking for measuring people's personalities. A recent study by two Harvard researchers found that by taking a mere one-minute EEG measurement of the frontal lobes of a group of men, they could tell which of the men were optimists and which were pessimists. Optimistic men, who also tend to have fewer fears, activate their left frontal lobes more strongly than the right. Men who are more likely to resemble the kinds of characters that Woody Allen plays in the movies—anxious, pessimistic, fearful— activate their right frontal lobes more strongly than their left.[5]

This differential activation is most prominent at the very front of the lobe: the prefrontal cortex under the forehead, which is the center of the rational fear system and advanced cortical reasoning. Neuroscientists are not yet sure why this differential emotional specialization occurs. There is some evidence that the right prefrontal cortex is more sensitive to fear than the left because it contains an extra amount of the sensitizing neurochemical noradrenaline. The final explanation will undoubtedly be quite complex. Whatever the reason, the fear systems in the two cerebral hemispheres behave very differently. The circuit in the right frontal lobe that connects the right prefrontal cortex, the right amygdala, and the other limbic structures on the right side of the brain specializes in making us feel fearful. It is this circuit that seems to go awry in illnesses like episodic dyscontrol. The violent patient, Julie, in Chapter 3 had a malfunction in her right amygdala that stopped when that amygdala was destroyed. This pattern of a malfunctioning right primitive fear system is common in this disorder. Neurologist Richard Restak describes another such case involving a twenty-one-year-old man who began having suicidal impulses and violent episodes that included attacking his spouse. "When I hit my wife," he said, "it would be just like something I couldn't control. Like getting into a car accident on an icy road and the car loses control and there is nothing you can do to stop it. And then afterwards I would feel a lot of remorse, and I would find myself crying and begging her forgiveness."[6] A CAT scan showed that the man had a tumor at the tip of his right temporal lobe, just where the right amygdala is located. After the tumor was removed, the episodes of violence stopped completely.

If a monkey loses both its right and left amygdala, it also loses its fear. A bad-tempered monkey will become completely tame, its primitive fear system seemingly completely destroyed. This is not true for humans, however. If both amygdalae in the human brain are destroyed, emotional reactions diminish but don't disappear. This is clear evidence that human beings have evolved a more complex primitive fear system than monkeys. Destroying the human primitive fear system involves a much more widespread destruction of brain tissue, that includes not only damaging both amygdalae but the hippocampus, uncus, cingulate gyrus, insular cortex, temporal cortex, and orbitofrontal cortex. Of these structures, the orbitofrontal cortex seems to play an especially important role in human fear. The orbitofrontal cortex is actually the underside of the prefrontal cortex. It rests on top of the eye sockets and extends upward into the fissure that divides the two cerebral hemispheres. The right and left orbitofrontal cortices are so intimately wired to the right and left amygdala and other limbic structures that they are generally classified as part of the limbic system. It is best to think of the orbitofrontal cortex as the transitional area between the primitive and the rational fear systems.

Studies of patients with injuries to the orbitofrontal cortex have found distinctive patterns of behavior, depending on whether the right orbitofrontal cortex or the left is damaged. If the injury is to the left orbitofrontal cortex, then the patient tends to become extremely profane and impulsive, freely expressing the negative emotions flowing out of his intact right prefrontal cortex. If the injury is to the opposite orbitofrontal cortex, then the patient is often polite, cheerful, and intelligent, but unconcerned about his damaged brain. He exhibits the positive emotions of his intact left prefrontal cortex. He still reacts instinctively to sudden shocks or fears, but he does not seem to be able to feel fear consciously. Skin conductance tests show that such patients have lost the ability to empathize with the fear of others. Patients with damage to either right or left orbitofrontal cortex are similar in that they have great difficulty making decisions. It appears that for the rational fear system to work properly, and interface with the decision-making capacity of consciousness, both positive and negative emotions must be integrated into the fully functioning frontal lobes.[7]

The two hemispheres of the brain give us a form of depth perception or three-dimensional view of the world. This is provided by the different types of simultaneous and parallel processing by the hemispheres. There are two parallel tracks for preconscious processing of sensory data. Among the most important differences in hemispheric processing is the fact that the left hemisphere processes information rationally and sequentially while the right hemisphere processes the same information more holistically. This simultaneous processing is particularly important in decoding the information contained in language. Proper hemispheric processing of language gives us both the intentions of the speaker (rational content) and his motivations (emotional content). If the right hemisphere processing is damaged, a person might know what a speaker is saying in a rational sense but have no idea about his motivation—whether he is sad, angry, or joking. If the left hemisphere processing is damaged, a person may be able to judge accurately the emotional state of the speaker but not be able to decode the rational content of what is being said.

This simultaneous rational-emotional processing developed in a specific evolutionary context: as a crucial tool for human beings as highly social animals to interpret the motivations and inventions of other human beings. The problem with this form of processing is that it leads to distortions when we apply it to contexts outside of human social interactions. These distortions consist primarily of imputing human emotions or motivations to contexts in which such emotions or motivations are completely absent, or in which they are very different from human emotions and motivations. Among the errors that this leads to is anthropomorphism: that is, imputing human motivations and intentions to nonhuman phenomena. What might be called the Walt Disney view of nature—in which animals have human emotions and intentions—is an example of this. Animals, particularly complex animals, may have intentions and emotions, but they are very different from human ones.

Severe damage to the human orbitofrontal cortex impairs both the primitive and the rational fear system and tends to destroy a person's ability to function in the social domain in four important ways. First, it prevents people from empathizing and thus accurately judging the emotional state of others. Second, it prevents them from rapidly learning from their own emotional experience to change their behaviors in ways that are socially appropriate. The amygdala's emotional reactions tend to be rigid and difficult to change. It is the orbitofrontal cortex that gives consciousness and the rational fear system their emotional flexibility.[8] The third reason is a bit more subtle. Since people with orbitofrontal damage have impaired rational fear systems, this tends to push them into the primitive limbic reasoning mode. They get stuck in the present, unable to use future scenarios or past experiences to make decisions. Thus, if there is a decision to be made that involves no strong emotion in the present, they have difficulty making it, because they have no strong sense of the future emotional consequences (generalized from past experience) and can only loop endlessly through a futile rational analysis, listing all the pros and cons but unable to give them their appropriate emotional weight. This is why patients with orbitofrontal damage are consistently unable to take care of themselves in the social domain. Finally, research indicates that the more active the left orbitofrontal cortex, the more quickly one can unlearn fears established by the primitive fear system.

An important finding by researchers is that a certain type of serotonin receptor—the serotonin-2 receptor—is concentrated in the orbitofrontal cortex and the amygdala. In primates (but not necessarily in other species) serotonin inhibits aggressive behavior. If serotonin is blocked in primates, they behave impulsively and aggressively. Monkeys that have a high concentration of serotonin-2 receptors in the orbitofrontal cortices, amygdala, and parts of the temporal cortices, but not elsewhere in the brain, show well-tuned, cooperative social behavior, while those with low concentrations of these serotonin-2 receptors show noncooperative and antagonistic behavior.[9] In humans the strongest neuronal connections are between the prefrontal cortex and limbic system in the left cerebral hemisphere. This may help explain why activating the left orbitofrontal cortex is associated with inhibiting the primitive fear responses of the limbic system.

In *The Prince*, Machiavelli took a cold and cynical view of human nature. Basically he argued that since human beings cannot control their primitive and selfish instincts, a ruler owes them nothing and is justified in doing whatever is needed to remain in power. "This advice would not be sound if all men were upright," said Machiavelli, "but because they are treacherous and would not keep their promises to you, you should not consider yourself bound to keep your promises to them."[10] The founders of the American republic took a more optimistic view. Although they were not naive about human nature—James Madison stressed that if men were angels there would be no need for government—they believed that through the exercise of reason, people could control and transcend their primitive urges. They were products of the Enlightenment, an age of reason. Later, America became the first country to offer free public education and this innovation has spread around the world.

Modern neuroscience has located within the brain the source of the best and the worst of our nature. From the primitive fear system can emerge a mass of panicked people trampling over each other as they flee from danger, or an angry mob capable of committing violent acts. From the rational fear system and advanced cortical reasoning can emerge art, science, and civilization. The struggle between these two, one old and entrenched, the other young and potentially powerful, will determine how much we rationally control our lives, both as individuals and a society.

{ Chapter 8 }

The Pleasure of Fear

Fear is inextricably bound to pain, but it is also linked with pleasure. Successfully overcoming a fear or emerging from a fearful situation unscathed can be a highly pleasurable experience, for surviving a scare often triggers the release of a flood of opiatelike neurochemicals.

The fearful experience itself vividly focuses our attention and memory, making us feel more alive. The fact that we often find surmounting a fear to be exhilarating and pleasurable explains many things about human behavior, including the appeal of amusement park thrill rides, horror films, and daredevil activities such as skydiving, hang gliding, and race car driving.

This is part of our human nature and makes us, as a species, dynamic risk takers for good or ill. We climb Mount Everest and go to the moon not solely for the sake of our curiosity but because the pleasure of surmounting the danger is its own reward. One problem with this aspect of human nature is that frequently experiencing fearful situations leads to habituation, even boredom. To reproduce the same intensity of feeling, the level of risk taking must increase. That is one reason films tend to grow more violent and daredevil activities tend to become more extreme.

I was nine when I rode my first roller coaster. We had driven from

Tucson to Los Angeles for a vacation and were visiting a large amusement park near the ocean. At the center of the park was a giant wooden roller coaster. My brother and I had never seen anything so big and we were fascinated. We were too small to go on it by ourselves, so we begged Dad to take us. He wasn't especially enthusiastic about the idea, but eventually relented. I clearly remember getting into the car, Dad in the middle and my brother and I on either side of him. The safety bar didn't even go back far enough to hold me in. Dad put his arms around my brother and me and held us tightly. As the chain lift pulled us to the top of the first hill, I was excited and apprehensive. We must have been almost a hundred feet in the air. We went over the top of the hill and dropped what seemed like straight down. I remember the sense of complete weight-lessness as we fell and had this overwhelming feeling that I would have gone flying out of the car if Dad hadn't been holding on to me. The sense of speed and danger was overpowering as we rattled through drop after drop and around hairpin curves. Any second, it seemed, we would go hurtling off the tracks into oblivion. When the ride ended, my brother and I were breathless with excitement. We begged Dad to take us again, but he said that was enough for one day.

Roller coasters are the classic thrill ride. They combine terror and exhilaration into a seductive experience that attracts millions of people every year, including me. I've enjoyed riding big roller coasters ever since. Roller coasters have had a passionate following throughout this century. They are an offshoot of the age of railroads. The precursors of the roller coaster were railroad cars that rolled at high speed along tracks that went straight down the sides of mountains. By the 1920s there were twenty thousand wooden roller coasters operating throughout the United States, including the Cyclone at Coney Island, one of the most famous of them all. Charles Lindbergh reportedly said that riding the Cyclone beat the thrill of flying. The Cyclone is still operating and still attracting large crowds. But most of the rest of the big roller coasters of that era went out of business and were torn down during the Depression.

Yet ever since the opening of Disneyland in 1956 transformed the concept of an amusement park, which had slightly seedy connotations, into the clean, family-friendly theme park, roller coasters have enjoyed a revival. There are now around five hundred large ones in America and more are being built all the time. The biggest theme parks compete to have the wildest, tallest, fastest roller coasters. I've ridden on one of the longest roller coasters in the world: the Beast at King's Island outside

Cincinnati. It is around seven thousand feet long, twice the length of most others. The power for most roller coasters is strictly the force of gravity. Once they are pulled to the top of the first big hill, the acceleration they achieve provides more than enough momentum for the entire ride. But The Beast is so long that it requires two big drops—one at the beginning of the ride and another chain lift to the top of a huge hill in the middle—to get you through the entire ride. The longest roller coaster in the world is The Ultimate in the north of England, which stretches about nine thousand feet. The Beast is a wooden roller coaster, but steel roller coasters have been the technological breakthrough that has led this era of roller coaster popularity. The steel technology allows roller coasters to do things that no wooden roller coaster can: loop-the-loops, corkscrews, and other mad gyrations as you are twisted and turned upside down and in all possible directions. In some steel roller coasters, you sit in ski-lift-type chairs and your legs dangle freely as you fly along the rails above you. The current tallest and fastest roller coaster is Superman: The Escape—a steel coaster at Magic Mountain, a theme park north of Los Angeles. It's not unusual for the first big drop of a wooden roller coaster to be around two hundred feet with top speeds of seventy-five miles per hour. Superman: The Escape is 411 feet high and accelerates from zero to one hundred miles per hour in seven seconds. It is not configured in the usual manner. Two parallel steel tracks take two sets of cars up to the top of the hill. Then the cars slow, stop, and reverse direction so you ride down the tracks in reverse. It's like falling backward out of a forty-story building. As you decelerate at the top of the hill, you experience several seconds of weightlessness. The ride uses mechanical means, not gravity, to accelerate you to the top of the hill—a high-tech version of the wooden roller coaster's chain lift. The acceleration is so rapid that you experience more than four Gs of force. The Air Force and NASA have extensively studied the effects of G forces on the human body because pilots of supersonic aircraft, as well as astronauts, routinely experience high levels of gravitational force. The studies have shown that about seven to ten seconds of a sustained G force of 4.5 is enough to cause most people to black out—flow of blood is hampered by the high gravity and the brain shuts down because of lack of oxygen.

Many people passionately hate and fear all roller coasters. A few years ago I was in Harrisburg for a series of meetings with the governor of Pennsylvania and his staff. A group of us decided to go one evening to Hershey Park, a nearby amusement park. Of course the first thing I wanted to do was try its big roller coaster. I was surprised how the group divided up into those eager to go on the ride and those who were horrified at the idea. Even a friend of mine who had been a Green Beret in Vietnam said he couldn't stomach the idea of going on it. Why are roller coasters so appealing to some people and so unpleasant to others? The answer highlights not only the nature of fear but the nature of pleasure.

Why do we experience some things as painful and others as pleasurable? What is it that is going on in our bodies and brains? Surprisingly science understands fear and pain far better than it does desire and pleasure. Although opium and its active ingredient, morphine, have been used to control pain and stimulate euphoria for thousands of years, the receptors in the brain on which morphine acts were only discovered in 1972. Morphine imitates the natural opiates that the body produces.[1] These were isolated in 1975 and are called endorphins. Scientists call this class of neurochemicals, opioids. Opium is derived from the opium poppy, *Papaver somniferum*. Somnus was the Roman god of sleep. Opium, morphine, and the modern synthetic version of morphine—heroin—are highly addictive. The mysteries of addiction are still being explored. One theory of the addiction process is that when an addictive drug, like heroin or alcohol, is taken frequently, the body automatically compensates for this unnatural opiate increase by cutting back on the number of receptors for the substance. As the number of receptors is reduced the same amount of heroin or other addictive substance causes a smaller and smaller response. This is the phenomenon of tolerance. To receive the same amount of pleasure, the person must take more and more of the drug. If the drug usage stops, the person experiences withdrawal, which usually involves symptoms that are the opposite of those produced by the drug. For example, morphine produces a sleepy, contented sense of well-being. But in morphine withdrawal the addict experiences an unpleasant hyperarousal as the body chemistry begins fluctuating as part of the process of restoring itself to the preaddiction state. Since the addiction has cut the number of opiate receptors, there are now too few receptors for the natural opiates to bind to and do their job of calming the body and brain. Eventually the number of opiate receptors increases to normal and the withdrawal symptoms stop. But the addict may continue to yearn for the drug-induced euphoria and slip back onto the path of dependence, tolerance, and withdrawal. There are large individual variations in addictive behavior. Just as many people drink socially and never become alcoholics, some people are less susceptible to becoming severely addicted to narcotics than others. During the Vietnam War there was a widespread heroin abuse problem among American soldiers. But after returning to the United States, most of these men stopped taking heroin and showed no sign of any long-lasting craving. A minority, however, continued their drug abuse. Scientists believe that the qualities that separate the addict from the nonaddict involve some combination of biology, genetics, personality, and experience. But one fact is undisputed. Whether a person becomes an addict or not, these drugs have a tremendously powerful effect on the brain.[2]

In studying opiate receptors and opiate drugs, rats are the experimental animals of choice. Like humans, rats react to opiates with intense pleasure. Solomon Snyder, a codiscoverer of the opiate receptor, described an experiment using laboratory rats that helped identify one of the brain's own morphinelike endorphins. The rats were initially given regular morphine. "Each rat had a small tube implanted in his skull so that a drug or other substance could be injected directly into the periaqueductal gray of the rat's brain," Snyder said. "First, the rats would leap as much as five feet in the air, squeal, and rotate in a peculiar way. This intensely hyperactive period was followed by a prolonged period of sedation during which the rats were clearly unresponsive to painful stimuli." Then they were given tiny quantities of a brain extract containing what was believed to be a natural endorphin. "We witnessed the same leaping and squealing, followed by the sedation and lack of response to painful stimuli," Snyder said.[3] Snyder and the other researchers were delighted. Clearly a natural opiate had been found.

Similar behavior is found in rats whose brains are electrically stimulated. Certain areas in and around the limbic system produce intensely pleasurable sensations. If, for example, an electrode is implanted in a rat's hypothalamus and the rat by pushing a lever can deliver a short pulse of electricity to the brain, the rat will quickly develop a pattern of pressing the lever as often as possible, to the point of exhaustion. Some rats have been observed to stimulate themselves as much as seven thousand times an hour, ignoring hunger and thirst. And unlike hunger and thirst, there is no point of satiation when the desire for stimulation ceases. It continues as long as the rat is able to push the lever. Why is there no tolerance? It turns out that natural opiates are immediately inactivated by peptides in the brain. Receptors are only exposed to natural opiates for about a thousandth of a second, long enough to generate a pulse of fear-reducing pleasure but far too short a time for tolerance to develop.[4]

Heroin and other drugs are not inactivated by natural enzymes so the receptors are exposed to them for prolonged periods and the tolerance response unfolds.

Rats become passionately addicted to this kind of self-stimulation. According to one University of Michigan researcher, "Animals that had not received any brain stimulation for several days have been known to jump from the experimenter's hands into the test chamber, where they would immediately make the responses that had been previously rewarded by brain stimulation."[5] Experiments were also done with human subjects. These volunteers described marvelous feelings of elation and profound well-being when certain areas of the limbic system were stimulated. But the stimulation of nearby areas produced feelings of fear, dread, and isolation. It is thought that the stimulation of the brain's pleasure centers promotes the release of the opiatelike endorphins. There also appear to be nonopiate pleasure systems in the brain that involve neurotransmitters like serotonin, dopamine, and acetylcholine. The effect that a neurotransmitter produces depends on the type of receptor that it stimulates. There are at least fourteen different kinds of receptors for serotonin alone. Some of these may be pleasure receptors.

What does drug addiction have to do with roller coaster rides? The heaviest concentrations of opiate receptors are in areas of the brain associated with fear. In fact, the heaviest concentration of opiate receptors in the entire brain is in the amygdala. This implies a radical revision of our notion of pleasure. Certain kinds of pleasure—perhaps most kinds— are not independent sensations. They are what we perceive when our subjective level of pain and fear decreases. The fundamental reality is fear and pain. Pleasure is our perception of the reduction of fear and pain. Sometimes a surge of natural opiates can reduce our fear and give us a paradoxical sense of well-being under the worst of circumstances. This was what appeared to happen to David Livingstone. Remember that when he was attacked by the lion his overwhelming fear was suddenly replaced "with a sort of dreaminess in which there was no sense of pain nor feeling of terror. . . ."[6] When we feel fear the sympathetic nervous system is aroused. A whole series of neurochemical and hormonal changes takes place to enable us to meet the threat. But this is an unnatural state for the body to be in for long periods of time. The body attempts to restore the former equilibrium, reducing the activation of the sympathetic nervous system and increasing the activation of the parasympathetic nervous system, which promotes relaxation. One way this equilibrium is restored is through the secretion of natural opiates. These endorphins decrease sympathetic activity and increase parasympathetic activity.

If pleasure involves a reduction in fear, then there are two basic ways that we can manipulate fear to produce pleasure. The first is to increase our fear artificially and then enjoy the sensation of our body pushing the fear back down to normal levels through the secretion of natural opiates and other fear-suppressing chemicals. This is what the roller coaster is all about. The second is to reduce our current level of fear directly. This is what drugs do. A drug need not be a powerful narcotic like morphine. The caffeine in coffee is a relatively harmless drug that produces a mild sense of euphoria and well-being as well as stimulating alertness. Similarly, small amounts of alcohol tend to increase our sense of well-being by reducing our fear. Alcohol is a depressant that reduces the function of the frontal lobes, including the right orbitofrontal cortex through which most people consciously experience fear. It is popular at social occasions, in part because it reduces our anxiety about mingling and talking with other people.

Humans are unique in both the intensity of our thrill seeking and the single-mindedness with which we use substances, addictive and nonaddictive, to reduce our fear. We are the most fearful of species and our lives, in a real sense, are an endless quest for ways of coping with this situation. Even our desires are bound up with fear and pain. If you haven't eaten for a long time, you feel the unpleasant sensation of intense hunger. If you were lost in the woods, this would also be accompanied by a fear of starvation. When you eat, the level of pain and fear declines and you experience an unmistakable sense of pleasure. This increased sense of well-being is a common feature of many different kinds of positive experiences, including being in love. As the Roman poet Lucretius wrote: "Nature cries aloud for nothing else but that pain may be kept far sundered from the body, and that, withdrawn from care and fear, he may enjoy in mind the sense of pleasure."[7] Humans are remarkably inventive when it comes to ways of lowering levels of pain and fear. You may seek to become financially successful, produce a great work of art, or win the Nobel Prize. But all these goals have a tendency to increase your sense of well-being.

Roller coasters and other thrill rides are one way we can increase our fear in a controlled setting. During the roller coaster ride your primitive fear system is going full tilt but your rational system knows that you are safe and keeps the primitive under control. The human brain consists of a complex set of interacting systems: the instinctive urges of the brain stem (hunger, thirst, sex), the fear and other preconscious emotions of the limbic system, and the more complex emotions and thoughts of the right cerebral hemisphere, left cerebral hemisphere, and consciousness. Each one of these systems may be doing different things simultaneously, which is why we often feel conflicting urges. On a roller coaster, we scream and laugh at the same time. Our primitive fear system is screaming while our rational fear system is laughing. The rational system is able to keep the primitive reaction under control. Each burst of primal fear is followed by a quick reduction of fear to normal levels, a process we experience as pleasurable. People who for some reason don't feel they can keep their primitive fear system under control avoid roller coasters. They may have a fear of heights. Or they may have a more sensitive limbic system that makes it difficult for them to suppress a fear response once it has started. This is what we might expect of people who have a greater activation of the right frontal lobe. And, in fact, these people do tend to be more fearful of situations in which they are not in complete control of their fear responses.[8]

Even when experiencing an uncontrolled fear event, the relief of coming out unscathed can be highly pleasurable. This was the case for me as a child when I ran into my parents' room, terrified of a nightmare. A delicious sense of pleasure and triumph accompanied my relief at escaping from the fear into the complete safety of my parents' protection. Unfortunately this is also true in more sinister situations, as when a gang member survives a shootout with another gang. The fear during the shootout is intense and the pleasure and exhilaration at having survived can be equally intense.

The fact that a reduction of pain and fear is perceived as pleasurable provides a framework for explaining many puzzling aspects of human behavior. For example, why do we laugh? I believe laughter may, in large part, be related to a sudden release of tension that triggers a relaxation response in the body. This relaxation response is, in turn, related to the dissipation of an implicit fear. The dissipation of one common implicit fear takes the form of a sense of relief: "I'm glad it wasn't me." If someone's feet fly out from under him as he slips on a patch of ice, we sometimes have to catch ourselves to keep from laughing. Our preconscious processing and the sudden relaxation response we experience ("I'm glad that didn't happen to me") generate an instant desire to laugh, particularly if the person doesn't seem to be hurt. When a fear suddenly dissipates, the parasympathetic nervous system (the rest-and-digest system) increases its activity with respect to the sympathetic nervous system (the fight-or-flight system), producing positive emotions like happiness and contentment. Humor and laughter seem to be part of this relaxation response. Humor often has the element of surprise (the punch line) which ensures the suddenness of our relaxation response. Perhaps we laugh so often because we fear so much.

As a highly social species attuned to the emotions of others, we can generate an undertone of sympathetic tension simply by watching a person walk out on stage (we implicitly fear that they will embarrass themselves), or even having someone telling us a joke (we implicitly fear that the joke won't be funny, they will stumble in telling it, or they will be offended if we don't laugh). When the person on stage doesn't make a fool of himself and the joke is moderately funny, we relax and laugh. Laughter can also be triggered by the dissipation of the fear that we will not like other people or they will not like us—normal fears in a social animal. When a stranger suddenly does or says something that we can identify with (tells a story about his child, for example), we experience the relaxation response and smile or laugh. The more unexpected the action or words (and thus the more rapid and intense the relaxation response), the harder we laugh. Doctors have known for many years that smiling and laughter are good medicine because they relax the body. Comedians have an intuitive sense of this as well, which is why they joke so often about our fears and frustrations. The pleasure generated by the dissipation of an implicit fear ("I'm glad it wasn't me") is also partly responsible for our morbid curiosity about terrible crimes and disasters and the almost irrepressible desire we have to rubberneck when we pass an accident on the highway.

Clever Hans was the nickname of a beloved horse belonging to a retired German mathematics professor. The horse became world famous in the early nineteenth century. The professor had some unconventional ideas about animal intelligence and began teaching the horse to count, spell, and even do simple mathematics. He was amazed at the horse's intellect. Hans always gave answers by tapping his hooves. If the professor asked Hans to add two plus two, Hans would tap his hoof four times. If the professor wanted Hans to identify the color of an apple, he would tell Hans to tap once if it was green, twice if it was red, or three times if it was blue. Hans would tap his hoof twice. The professor was not a publicity seeker and only invited small groups to witness Hans's ability. He included in these groups highly skeptical students of animal behavior. He encouraged them to make up their own questions and would sometimes leave the room while they questioned Hans. No matter what questions the skeptics devised, Hans always answered correctly. Even the doubters would laugh in amazement at Hans's uncanny accuracy. Many academics were convinced and proclaimed Hans to be one of the wonders of the world.

The secret of Hans's ability was finally uncovered after an intensive study by developmental psychologist Oskar Pfungst. Pfungst noticed that Hans was able to answer any question at all—whether it concerned higher mathematics or even if it was asked in a foreign language—as long as the questioner knew the answer. But if the questioner didn't know, then neither did Hans. Pfungst also discovered that Hans was completely unable to answer questions if the questioner stood behind an opaque screen and no one else was present. "The horse, it turned out, was taking his cues from unconscious, almost imperceptible shifts of head and body posture in the members of the audience—movements created by the involuntary relaxation of the tension among the observers when the number of hoof taps reached the correct value," write biologists James and Carol Grant Gould. "Pfungst himself, even after he understood the process, found it almost impossible not to cue the horse."[9] Clever Hans could detect the involuntary tension that pervades human life but that we often fail to notice.

We are such a fearful species that we go to extraordinary lengths to seek relief from fear and pain. Take our odd food choices, for example. "Almost uniquely among animal species," writes Paul Rozin, a professor of psychology at the University of Pennsylvania, "humans regularly come to like substances that are innately aversive. Tobacco, coffee, the irritant spices, and the various forms of alcohol are among the more popular foods of humans around the world. . . ." It is not unusual for a young person trying his first cigarette to become nauseous. Yet some people persist in smoking because the nicotine in tobacco crosses the blood-brain barrier and activates a type of acetylcholine receptor in the limbic system that has been linked to the reduction of fear and the stimulation of the parasympathetic nervous system. This is why many smokers say that smoking relaxes them. Recent research also indicates that nicotine may enhance memory.[10] Rozin considers another innately aversive substance, the chili pepper, which stings the mouth and produces defensive reactions including increased salivation, watery eyes, and a runny nose.

"Two possible explanations of the acquired liking for chili (and perhaps other innately unpalatable substances) depend on its initial unpalatability," writes Rozin. "The mouth pain of chili may become pleasant as people realize that it is not really harmful. This puts the pleasure of eating chili pepper in the category of thrill seeking, in the same sense that the initial terror of a roller coaster ride or parachute jumping is replaced by pleasure. People may come to enjoy the fact that their bodies are signaling danger while their minds know that there really is no danger. . . . Alternatively, the many painful mouth experiences produced by chili may cause the brain to attempt to modulate the pain by secreting endogenous opiates, morphinelike substances produced in the brain. . . . At high levels, they might produce pleasure."[11]

The pleasure of fear also involves the heightened sense of awareness provided by a novel fear experience—the acute feeling that we are really living life, not just drifting along. This is particularly true of people who are risk takers and have little trouble suppressing their primitive fear responses under normal circumstances. The neural machinery of the brain is tuned to detect novelty because anything new may pose a threat. We quickly become habituated to everyday life. The rush of adrenaline, noradrenaline, and other stress hormones generated by fear snap us out of this habituation. Our senses become more alert, our perceptions sharper, and our memories more vivid and long lasting. Noradrenaline, in particular, sensitizes the frontal lobes and the limbic system and turns on the sympathetic nervous system. This is why wartime memories are usually so clear, even the memories of civilians who were nowhere near a battlefront. War is a time of uncertainty, when the mind is more on edge because of the potential danger. My father loves to reminisce about his years in England during World War II, of watching the spectacular nighttime air attacks on London and of listening to the drone of German V-1 rockets overhead—when the droning stopped everyone ducked, because the rocket was diving to the ground with its payload of high explosives. Abraham Pais can still remember his reaction when he first heard the news that war had broken out: "It was one of thrill, intense excitement, rather than fear or gloom."[12]

The craving for novelty and excitement is an integral part of our culture. Hollywood, for example, has turned the action film into the artistic equivalent of a roller coaster ride. These movies play on our primal fear of death in the most direct possible ways. Steven Spielberg has had a spectacular string of hit movies—*Jaws, Jurassic Park, Lost*

World—centered around the fear of being eaten by a terrifying predator, from great white shark to Tyrannosaurus rex.

In nearly every action movie the hero or heroine, like Sigourney Weaver's character in the *Alien* series, lives in constant fear of death, often an especially hideous form of death. The signature of these films is that most chilling of human sounds: the scream of terror. Screams are the primal cry of the limbic system—virtually all larger animals scream in fear. The scream serves three purposes. First, like hair standing on end, it makes us seem more menacing to a possible attacker. Its startling effect may make the attacker, if not retreat, at least hesitate so we have more time to flee or prepare to fight. Second, the scream alerts those nearby who may come to our aid. Finally, the scream serves a social function by warning others of the danger so that even if they cannot help us they may at least avoid it themselves.

The extraordinary film *Titanic* memorably brings to life the terrible tragedy of the sinking in April 1912 of that fabulous ocean liner and the horror endured by those who went through it. The 1997 film lays out an immense tapestry of fear and creates a microcosm of the human condition. The Titanic's passengers and crew blithely ignored the danger surrounding them until it was too late. This reflects a characteristic human tendency to deny and defy our transient existence by living life as if there is no end—at least no end in sight. We laugh, we fall in love, we plan, we create and procreate, we strive for our future as if we can count on it. Sadly, we cannot.

Not long after the film opened I talked to its multitalented writer, director, and coproducer James Cameron.[13] "I've spent my whole career making films about helpless terror," he told me on a stormy day in Malibu. "The Titanic was a perfect subject." Cameron, who was born in Canada in 1954, fuses the passion of an artist with a consuming interest in science and technology. A physics major in college, he was drawn to Hollywood, where he became known for suspenseful, high-energy films like *The Abyss*, *The Terminator*, *Aliens*, and *True Lies*.

"In *Titanic* I wanted to show a realistic human response to a horrifying event by people of many different backgrounds," Cameron said. "Other movies about the Titanic have shown the passengers standing on the deck singing *Nearer My God to Thee* as the ship went down. I wanted to show the panic and the terror. I was fascinated by the story of the disaster because it's a tremendous example of a wide range of personalities facing their own mortality. There were some amazing responses, ranging from a desperate fight for survival to fatalistic acceptance. Some people have tried to characterize this film as a kind of metaphor of disaster as civilization goes sailing into the new millennium. The reality is much simpler. *Titanic*, in my mind, is just a metaphor of the individual dealing with imminent death. As I told the actors, the Titanic's passengers were like all of us. We think: 'It can't happen to me. I've never died before.' "

Cameron described the acting techniques used by Leonardo DiCaprio and Kate Winslett, the film's stars. "Actors are fascinating people," Cameron said. "Most of us try to hide our emotions. Actors are trained to express theirs. The methods individual actors use to express fear vary wildly. Leo is more the technician. He creates an emotion, and when the scene is over the emotion is instantly gone. But when Kate acts fearful, she truly feels afraid. She would often become very emotional while shooting. During one of the scenes in the flooded corridor, Kate was convinced she was dying. Actually, I was two feet from her, but she said she felt as if she'd had a near-death experience. After shooting the scene of Leo's death, Kate went off by herself and cried for an hour. Kate and Leo use completely different techniques to create the appearance of fear, but on the screen the results are exactly the same. It's a surprising, mysterious process."

When we intentionally frighten ourselves by seeing movies like *Jurassic Park* and *Titanic*, what we seek in part is a measure of habituation to the greatest mystery of them all. "For the ultimate horror of all horror stories, the corpse that will not stay buried, is our own dead future, the body we bury and disinter with every retelling of the tale of terror," writes Martin Tropp. "A century of horror stories, in versions from the ridiculous to the realistic, all have one underlying secret—they draw their power from our fascination with repeatedly confronting our fear of our own mortality."[14]

Movies are only one method that we have contrived to heighten our fear in a controlled setting. Auto racing, air shows, and daredevil stunts are all enhanced by the element of danger. Circuses feature death-defying acts on the high wire and animal trainers braving cages full of snarling lions and tigers. This ingredient of danger also exists in sports like boxing, football, and hockey. There is a growing interest in extreme sports that often generate intense fear—skydiving, bungee jumping, mountain climbing, hang gliding, whitewater rafting, and skiing on treacherous slopes. In some cases there is more than a hypothetical risk of injury or death. A chorus of critics have pointed out that several of the recent expeditions to the summit of Mount Everest have included too many thrill seekers with minimal mountain climbing ability. The result has been a spate of deaths.[15]

This illustrates an important danger inherent in any reckless quest for thrills and excitement. The pleasure of fear can become an addiction. To our primitive fear system, there is no difference between real and contrived fear. It reacts the same to each. If no real danger is forthcoming, it habituates so as to be ready for the dangers yet to come. But that habituation creates a tolerance for fear that resembles the tolerance that an addict develops for his drug, though fear tolerance is more subtle. The craving for excitement does not bring with it the physical dependence of the drug addict, but it can lead to a strong psychological dependence. And this psychological dependence is built out of changes in the wiring of the brain that can lead, if the excitement is not forthcoming, to dark moods and even depression. We step onto a treadmill, always looking for that elusive ultimate thrill. The hard-core roller coaster enthusiast searches for a bigger, faster ride. He has habituated to existing rides and needs a more sensational thrill to reawaken his jaded senses. In a way, our entire culture is going through this process of addiction, tolerance, and craving for more. As the media and entertainment industries compete for our attention, the violence and sensationalism in movies, books, and on television becomes more graphic, the scandals and revelations that are shrieked by the media more shocking. Violence and scandal that would have horrified us a generation ago we now dismiss with a shrug. The way to stop this escalation of tolerance and craving is through rationality and moderation. If we ride roller coasters every day, we will quickly become bored. But if we ride them once or twice a year, the excitement will not diminish. The degree of habituation depends on the frequency of exposure. It is the steady drumbeat of scandal and violence that is numbing our senses and degrading our civility. If we can muster the will to exercise self-restraint and limit our exposure to this material, then our normal sense of sympathy and outrage will have some hope of returning.

Our thrill-seeking nature makes us dynamic. We are always exploring new frontiers and challenging ourselves. This can be done rationally or foolishly. Think of the space program. For all its faults, it has been a systematic effort to accomplish a series of extremely difficult and dangerous missions by controlling as much of the risk as possible to ensure a maximum chance of success. A measure of the space program's achievement is our complete shock when something like the *Challenger* disaster occurs. Overcoming fear is an important part of maturing; it is part of developing the confidence and ability to surmount the many obstacles in life, both as individuals and as a species. Yet there is a balance that each individual and each society must strike between facing fear and tempting fate.

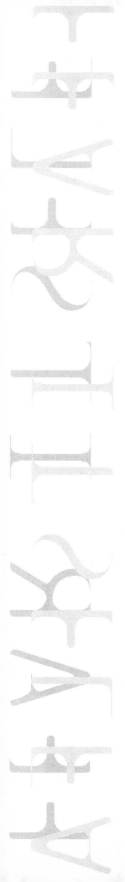

{ Part III }

Transcending Fear

*So first of all, let me assert my firm belief that
the only thing we have to fear is fear itself—
nameless, unreasoning, unjustified terror which
paralyzes needed efforts to convert retreat into
advance.*

—Franklin Delano Roosevelt

{ Chapter 9 }

Diseases of Fear

Too much fear can cripple the mind, but so can too little. The diseases of fear split along these lines. Phobias, anxieties, obsessive-compulsive disorder, panic attacks, anorexia, bulimia, post-traumatic stress disorder are conditions in which the amount of fear in people's lives overwhelms and crushes them. But psychopaths have too little fear. Their actions are unconstrained by anxiety, guilt, or shame. They do what they want and take what they want unless society stops them.

There is a common thread between these two extremes. In each, the rational fear system has been disabled in some way. The primitive fear system, with its primal instincts of fear and aggression, has been released from the control of the neocortex. In the anxiety disorders it is primitive fear that is out of control. In the psychopathic disorders, it is primitive aggression. Anxiety disorders are the number-one mental health problem in the United States, affecting about 25 million people. They can be treated with antidepressant drugs that act to restore the balance between the rational and primitive fear systems. Nondrug therapies that teach new behaviors and normal thought patterns have been shown to be just as successful as antidepressants, if not more so. Antidepressants can also help control some types of psychopathic behavior. But there has been less success in treating psychopaths with behavior therapy.

The diseases of fear are the extremes of two common types of human personality: the fearful and the fearless. Every species of mammal includes individuals that exhibit high and low fear, and there appears to be a genetic component to this behavior. Fearful and fearless populations of rats can be selectively bred. Studies of infants and children indicate that some are born with limbic systems and sympathetic nervous systems that are unusually sensitive to stress. Others have fear systems that are unusually insensitive. Are there evolutionary advantages to unusual fearfulness and fearlessness? Is that why these genetic tendencies have not been weeded out by natural selection over millions of years? It does appear that both groups have certain adaptive advantages. Studies of monkeys show that more fearful animals are less likely to harm themselves by acting impulsively. Fearless animals are sometimes killed when they attack a more powerful monkey or stray too far from the group and are caught by a predator. But fearless monkeys also can be more aggressive and successful in gathering food and competing for mates. In the case of human beings, there is evidence that natural selection has preferred fearlessness to fearfulness. Roughly 15 percent of people are classified as more fearful than normal. About twice that percentage are classified as relatively fearless.[1]

Human behavior is extraordinarily complex and psychology and neuroscience have only begun to give us hints of the underlying mechanisms. Children born with more sensitive fear systems do not necessarily develop into inhibited adults; neither do children born with less sensitive fear systems necessarily become uninhibited. Upbringing, environment, and conscious choices also mold the temperament. Nevertheless, psychologists have noted certain tendencies. Some fearful individuals are introverts, who are often quiet, introspective, somewhat distant with people, except for close friends, and sensitive to negative experiences and the opinions of others. The introvert tries to keep emotional outbursts to a minimum and tends to be serious and orderly. Some fearless individuals are extroverts, who are often sociable risk takers enjoying excitement and not particularly concerned about what others think. Extroverts tend to be less introspective, and prefer to stay active to keep from becoming bored. They are often emotional, impulsive, and sometimes aggressive. Introverts seek to control their fears. If this control is lost, they can be consumed by fear and develop anxiety disorders. Extroverts often have little desire or need to control their fears. But if they lose touch with them completely, they can become psychopaths, capable of lying, stealing, cheating, and bullying others without any sense of remorse or shame. The psychopath tends to have a very low heart rate and a sluggish sympathetic nervous system. In one study of boys who become psychopaths, the investigator concluded: "From age eleven onward there is significant evidence to suggest a relation between low heart rate and aspects of antisocial behavior. . . . Psychopaths are less capable of experiencing fear."[2] Although the extrovert tends to be self-centered, the psychopath is concerned only with himself. The psychopath may appear sociable on the surface, but there is no genuine concern for other people. They are only instruments for getting what he wants.

The violent psychopath can become the most dangerous of criminals: the serial killer. This is Ted Bundy, the murderer of college women, and John Wayne Gacy, who killed thirty-three boys and young men. "They are not insane, and delusions or other signs of irrational thinking are usually absent," says psychiatrist Frank Elliot. "They are egocentric and lack the capacity to feel empathy and love. They have little or no conscience or sense of guilt, tend to project blame when they get into trouble. They are unreliable, untruthful, and insincere, but they are often convincing because they believe their own lies. There is a vast gulf between what they say and what they do. They are impulsive, the whim of the moment being paramount. They are given to periodic and often senseless antisocial behavior which may be either aggressive, passive, or parasitic."[3]

The psychopath haunts the modern world not only as the serial killer but as the type of terrorist who would callously kill innocent men, women, and children along the boulevards of London and Tel Aviv or in the buildings of Oklahoma City. The mass media amplifies the power of the terrorist and the serial killer by trumpeting their actions, methods, and demands, spreading fear to millions. We think of the terrorist and serial killer as recent phenomena. But their modern incarnations have been with us for more than a century. World War I was started by a terrorist's bomb thrown into the carriage of the Archduke Ferdinand, heir to the throne of the Austro-Hungarian Empire. And the most infamous serial killer of them all was Jack the Ripper, who terrorized London in 1888.

Jack the Ripper was one of the most vicious and mysterious psychopaths in the history of crime. His victims were impoverished women, mainly prostitutes, who lived in the Whitechapel district of London's poor but bustling East End. He always killed at night, often committing his crimes with people—and police—nearby. After one murder the acting police commissioner of London arrived at the scene in time to see the last trickle of bloody water flow out of an outdoor basin where the Ripper had washed his hands. Another murder occurred in a square constantly patrolled by the police. At one-thirty on the morning of September 30, 1888, the police saw nothing unusual. Fifteen minutes later they stumbled upon the slashed and mutilated body of Catherine Eddowes. Once the Ripper killed two women in one night. "The criminal withdraws himself from all eyes as securely as though he possesses the charm which could make him invisible at will," wrote one reporter. The Ripper's methods were atrociously brutal. His victims were butchered and disemboweled. Usually some of their internal organs were removed. After the killing of another victim, Anne Chapman, *The Times* commented that the Ripper "must have left the yard in Hanbury Street reeking with blood and yet . . . he must have walked in almost broad daylight among streets comparatively well frequented, even at that early hour, without his startling appearance attracting the slightest attention."[4]

The public outcry was unprecedented. The newspapers were full of Ripper stories, and the latest murder was often covered in special editions. The police swarmed through the district, some dressed as prostitutes. Because of the way the victims were dissected, the police suspected a doctor might be the killer and many doctors were questioned along with hundreds of other suspects. The Ripper taunted the authorities through a series of letters and poems that he mailed to various officials. Some of the letters included evidence of the crimes, predicted future killings, and purported to give clues to his identity. Often they were signed, "Jack the Ripper." "What fools the police are," wrote the Ripper in one. "I even give them the name of the street where I am living." People were afraid to leave their homes at night. In a sense, Jack the Ripper was more than a serial killer—he was one of the first and most fiendish urban terrorists. George Lusk, chairman of the Whitechapel Vigilance Committee, was sent a piece of Catherine Eddowes's kidney with a note: "From hell, Mr. Lusk, sir, I send you half the kidne [sic] I took from one woman, prasarved it for you, tother piece I fried and ate it; was very nice."[5] Scotland Yard believed the poor grammar and misspellings were intentional. Clearly Jack the Ripper was a model for one of the most vivid modern fictional incarnations of the psychopath: Hannibal the Cannibal, the psychiatrist turned ghoulish serial killer played by Anthony Hopkins in the film

Silence of the Lambs. The primal fear generated by the serial killer is a favorite Hollywood plot device.

The Ripper case attracted a bizarre assortment of characters that sounds familiar: psychics, conspiracy theorists, amateur detectives, purveyors of false confessions, phony witnesses, and other publicity seekers. According to one popular theory the murders were part of a plot by the royal family to get rid of any witnesses to the secret marriage of a royal prince. Thousands of letters and tips poured in to police, none of which proved reliable. Many suspected a foreigner. Queen Victoria herself suggested that police check the crews of foreign ships docked on the Thames. The hysteria became so great that mobs formed and attacked foreigners and others they suspected might be the Ripper, including an American actor who was starring in a theatrical production of Robert Louis Stevenson's *The Strange Case of Dr. Jekyll and Mr. Hyde.* The climate of terror highlighted larger issues of social reformers, including the squalid condition of the East End and the treatment of women. On October 2, 1888, journalist Florence Fenwick Miller published an article pointing out the irony of the enormous public outrage at the Ripper, when it was commonplace for women to be "kicked, beaten, jumped on, chopped, stabbed, seamed with vitriol, bitten, and deliberately set on fire—and this sort of outrage, if a woman dies is called 'manslaughter,' if she lives, a 'common assault.' Common indeed. . . ! Now that men's consciences and imaginations are aroused by the Whitechapel murders, I ask them *what* are they going to do to check the ever-rising flood of brutality to women, of which these murders are only the latest wave."[6]

On November 9, 1888, the Ripper killed Mary Kelly. This time, the killing took place indoors in her shabby lodgings. When her dismembered body was discovered, the police were jeered in the streets. Yet this was the last of the killings. Jack the Ripper was never heard from again. Who was this merciless psychopath? Over the last century, there have been many suspects and many theories, but no one has ever been conclusively identified as the Ripper.

The criminal brain is a heavily studied but still highly controversial area of neuroscience. Serial killers like Jack the Ripper appear to have different patterns of impairment from impulsive mass murderers like Charles Whitman, the sniper who destroyed so many lives from the top of the University of Texas tower. Whitman had the classic brain anomaly associated with episodic dyscontrol: a tumor pressing against his amygdala. This kind of tumor seems to cause extreme stimulation of the limbic system that can overwhelm frontal lobe controls and lead to overpowering fears and violent episodes that are totally out of character for the victim. Although no two serial killers are exactly alike, these psychopaths—who are almost always men—tend to be more methodical than impulsive killers. Victims of episodic dyscontrol are often remorseful after their violent episodes, but serial killers usually show no sign of remorse. Some studies of violent psychopaths indicate that these men's frontal lobes and neocortex often display lower than normal activation. Other studies indicate that many psychopaths may not have the typical left-hemisphere dominance for language, but instead have processing centers in both hemispheres. There are also signs of lower levels of serotonin in the violent psychopath's brain. Higher levels of serotonin and certain kinds of serotonin receptors have been linked to a greater level of socially acceptable behavior.

None of these factors by themselves necessarily leads to violence, but they seem to indicate problems with the frontal lobes, which are primarily responsible for reining in our primitive impulses. There may be particular problems with orbitofrontal areas of the prefrontal cortices. These are the structures that allow us to put ourselves in other people's places imaginatively and empathize with them. Antonio Damasio has studied patients with damage to their orbitofrontal cortices. In one test, two groups of volunteers, one normal and the other with orbitofrontal damage, were shown a series of slides. Some of the slides contained very disturbing images—of murder victims and other gory scenes. Each volunteer was hooked to a polygraph machine so that changes in skin conductance measuring subliminal emotional response could be recorded. "The results were unequivocal," said Damasio. "The subjects without frontal damage—both the normal individuals and those with brain damage which did not affect the frontal lobes—generated abundant skin conductance responses to the disturbing pictures but not to the bland ones. On the contrary, the patients with frontal lobe damage failed to generate any skin conductance responses whatsoever. Their recordings were flat. . . . During one of the very first debriefing interviews, one particular patient, spontaneously and with perfect insight, confirmed to us that more was missing than just the skin conductance response. He noted that after viewing all the pictures, in spite of realizing their content ought to be disturbing, he himself was not disturbed."[7]

Although head injuries and frontal lobe damage are sometimes associated with increases in violence, Damasio's patients were not violent or aggressive. Many patients with damage to their frontal lobes, particularly the right frontal lobe, retain a sense of humor and optimism. This is understandable since, in most people, the right frontal lobe is associated with the conscious perception of negative emotions like fear, while the left is linked to positive emotions like cheerfulness and optimism. As a matter of fact, people with right frontal damage are often cheerfully unconcerned about the terrible brain injury they have suffered. Damage to the right orbitofrontal area not only eliminates an important source of anxiety but also the source of empathy. These patients experience no preconscious emotional reaction to disturbing slides of other people being injured or killed. But other tests by Damasio confirmed they still react to immediate threats to themselves—they jump at a loud noise for example.[8] Their primitive fear system remains intact, but they have lost the ability to empathize with others because their damaged orbitofrontal cortex is no longer able to generate scenarios that put themselves in other people's places ("That could happen to me"). Similarly they don't worry about their own future because they can no longer generate the negative emotional scenarios that would normally cause them concern.

Studies of violent psychopaths have found that they, too, do not react to stimuli that elicit sympathetic responses from most people. The serial killer also seems to have lost the ability to feel the suffering of others. When combined with the low level of activity in the neocortex and frontal lobes, we may have an individual who not only has a reduced ability to inhibit the violent impulses of the primitive fear system, but has no desire to inhibit them. Why should the serial killer spare the life of someone for whom he has absolutely no sympathy? Serial killers usually retain the superficially sociable nature of the extrovert, and use this charm to lure their unsuspecting victims to their deaths. But there are also cases of introverts who lose their empathy for others and become serial killers. One of the best known is the Unabomber, an antitechnology zealot who over a period of almost two decades, from the mid-1970s on, mailed a series of often lethal mail bombs to people of whose political views and occupations he disapproved. Whereas most serial killers dispatch their victims in face-to-face confrontations, the Unabomber never confronted anyone. This implies a much more introverted individual. Theodore Kaczynski, who pleaded guilty to committing these bombings, lived for many years as a virtual hermit.

Serial killers show strong evidence of primitive limbic reasoning at work. The serial killer does not normally kill at random. He selects a specific category of victims. Often this involves a sexual obsession. For Jack the Ripper and many serial killers since, it was prostitutes. For Ted Bundy, it was young, college-educated women. For John Gacy, it was boys and young men. With the Unabomber, however, the category of victims involved a political obsession. This appeared to be the case as well in the bombing of the federal building in Oklahoma City. In the case of another notorious serial killer, Donald Harvey, it seemed to involve a demented moral obsession. Harvey, known as the angel of death, was a nurse's aide at a Cincinnati hospital. He pleaded guilty in 1987 to killing twenty-four patients under his care. He told his lawyer that he had killed twenty-eight other people but couldn't remember their names. Harvey usually injected poison into his victims, then carefully disguised the deaths so that they appeared to result from natural causes. The people at Harvey's hospital considered him a charming man who seemed to care for his patients. Harvey said that he killed his patients "out of mercy."[9] Apparently in Harvey's mind, since some patients in extremely hopeless situations might welcome death, everyone under his care should die. Other serial killers may have a grievance against one member of a class of people, but their primitive fear system reasons that every member of that class deserves to be killed. This pattern of thinking is something like the person who has a frightening experience with a rattlesnake, develops a phobia, and now tries to kill every snake he sees. The horror of the serial killer is that his phobia involves a group of human beings.

Serial killers are rarely found to be legally insane. The calculated nature of their crimes and their attempt to avoid detection is strong evidence that these psychopaths know what they are doing is wrong—in the eyes of society, if not their own eyes—and can choose not to carry out their loathsome acts. If a potential serial killer seeks medical help there are treatments that may be effective in stopping this behavior. Antidepressant drugs can sometimes reduce aggression, in part, researchers believe, by increasing the amount of serotonin in the frontal lobes, allowing the patient to inhibit the limbic system more effectively. Lithium, which is used to treat severe depression, is also sometimes effective. Behavior therapy, which seeks to develop healthier thought patterns, may also be helpful, particularly if started at an early age. Yet drugs have side effects and behavior therapy may not work. Science has much more to learn about the serial killer, and psychopathic behavior in general remains a severe social problem.

The general picture for anxiety disorders is more optimistic. There has been rapid and accelerating progress in the last two decades in both the understanding and treatment of these hideously painful disorders. The disorder of the psychopath is linked to the freeing of the fear-fight-anger response pattern from the controls of the rational fear system centered in the frontal lobes. The anxiety disorders flow from the freeing of the fear-flight-panic response pattern of the primitive fear system from the restraints of the rational fear system. Let me sketch in a simplified way some of the key circuits through which these disorders take place. Remember that fear is expressed both preconsciously and consciously. The preconscious fear response is produced by the primitive fear system as it constantly scans our environment for threats. The conscious perception of fear appears to flow into the frontal lobes from the primitive fear system through, in most people, the right orbitofrontal cortex and the right prefrontal cortex of the right frontal lobe. This increase in fear in the right frontal lobe registers in our consciousness as a series of negative emotions: dread, pessimism, unhappiness, anxiety. People who routinely activate their right frontal lobe more strongly than their left tend to be pessimistic, inhibited introverts. These negative emotions are shared with the left hemisphere and the left frontal lobe through the corpus callosum, a thick band of fibers connecting the two hemispheres. There are other less prominent connection points between the two hemispheres as well. The left frontal lobe in most people has the strongest connections with the limbic system. The left frontal lobe—through the left orbitofrontal cortex—can more easily suppress the negative emotions of the primitive fear system, using natural opiates and other nonopiate systems. When the left orbitofrontal and prefrontal cortex are strongly activated, not only are preconscious limbic system fears controlled and even extinguished at times, but the negative conscious emotions flowing from the right frontal lobe are also muted or suppressed through a mechanism that we don't yet clearly understand. This reduction of fear through left prefrontal and orbitofrontal suppression we consciously perceive as positive emotions, in the form of happiness, optimism, and well-being. That is why people who routinely activate their left frontal lobe more strongly than the right tend to be optimistic, uninhibited extroverts.

The psychopath's underactive neocortex and frontal lobes seem to have lost touch with the primitive fear system in both the left and right hemispheres. Since primitive fears do not flow into the psychopath's consciousness (through the right orbitofrontal cortex, let's assume), he is unable to generate the scenarios that would allow him to empathize with the pain and fear of others. At the same time, with little or no conscious perception of fear he is unable to perceive the emotional consequences of his actions to himself or others. When a normal individual considers doing something wrong, the right orbitofrontal cortex generates a scenario of what would happen if the individual went through with this possible behavior. The guilt, shame, regret, and other negative feelings that fill the right frontal lobe at the prospect of doing something wrong act as a strong disincentive to take the action. The psychopath does not feel these emotions. He realizes intellectually that his actions could have negative consequences for him if he is caught, and he plans accordingly, but he does not feel those consequences as potential emotional pain. This is generally a problem with the right orbitofrontal cortex. But at the same time, the psychopath's left orbitofrontal cortex is not functioning normally and thus is not suppressing the primal impulses of anger, aggression, and desire generated by the primitive fear system. In short, the psychopath can neither use the conscious perception of fear to orient his behavior through the rational fear system, nor suppress the preconscious, impulsive fear, anger, aggression, and desires of the primitive fear system.

People suffering from anxiety disorders normally have an intense conscious perception of fear. Their right orbitofrontal cortex works well, often too well, in that they may be highly sensitive and emotional. The major problem is with the suppression of the fear-flight-panic response that is (normally) conveyed into consciousness through the right orbitofrontal cortex. In this case either the limbic activation is too strong to be controlled by the left frontal lobe—something like what happens with episodic dyscontrol, except that this involves fear and anxiety only, not violent behavior—or there is some problem in activating the left orbitofrontal cortex to suppress these fears. Anxiety disorders seem to occur more frequently in people who are classified as inhibited or introverted and whose primary mode of frontal activation is through the right frontal lobe, specifically the right prefrontal cortex. Since the right frontal lobe is the seat of negative emotions and a pessimistic outlook, the comparatively low activation of the left frontal lobe makes it more difficult to activate strongly the left orbitofrontal cortex, which appears to be the primary center responsible for suppressing these anxieties. The left frontal lobe may also be weakened with respect to the primitive fear system by problems with neurotransmitter activation. A shortage of serotonin, for example, may diminish the orbitofrontal cortex's suppression capability. One way antidepressants may improve anxiety disorders is to increase the availability of serotonin in the frontal lobes. But recent studies indicate that multiple neurotransmitters, not just serotonin, are affected by drugs that treat diseases of fear like obsessive-compulsive disorder.[10] Each different anxiety disorder may have different patterns of malfunctions of brain circuits, neurotransmitters, natural opiates, and hormones.

The frontal lobes are responsible for shifting conscious attention from one thing to another, as the context warrants from moment to moment. This gives consciousness its emotional and intellectual flexibility. The primitive fear system, on the other hand, tends to fixate on the object of fear. In anxiety disorders the frontal lobes' flexibility to shift conscious attention at will is severely diminished. Instead, consciousness is forced by the primitive fear system to focus on the object of fear. In the case of phobias, it is the object of the phobia. If someone with the snake phobia sees a garter snake, his attention fixates on that snake to the exclusion of everything else. If someone is a constant worrier, then he spends most of his time fixated on an unending stream of worries, unable to shift to more positive modes of thought. A student who is consumed with worry about his grades wastes valuable time in which he could actually be studying. If someone with hypochondria hears about a new type of infection that is resistant to antibiotics, he will immediately fixate on his fear of coming down with the disease, unable to shift his attention away from this unlikely possibility. In the eating disorders anorexia and bulimia, the anorexic fixates on the fear of being fat, while the bulimic fixates on the related fear of overeating. In obsessive-compulsive disorder, the victim has both unwanted and intrusive thoughts and fears (the obsession) and ritualized acts (compulsions) that are usually undertaken to try to diminish the obsession.[11] The victim may have an obsession with germs that causes him or her to fixate on anything in the environment that may be a source of germs. This leads to frequent, compulsive hand washing. Someone with post-traumatic stress disorder remains sensitized to fear and fixated on a past trauma, just as Paul Reed remained locked into his traumatic Vietnam experiences.

The orbitofrontal cortex plays a critical role in providing consciousness with the ability to flexibly shift its attention. The amygdala seems to focus on analyzing and making connections between events and emotions involving immediate likes and dislikes. Working with the hippocampus, it codes emotional responses to immediate experience emphasizing the specific internal and external context.[12] If I unexpectedly come upon a snake, for example, my amygdala working with my hippocampus will record exactly where I am, what I am doing, what the snake is doing, and how I am reacting. If I have a snake phobia, these memories will be burned into my brain as the amygdala orders the brain stem to release the sensitizing neurotransmitter noradrenaline throughout my limbic system and neocortex. The orbitofrontal cortex, on the other hand, takes the database built up by the amygdala as well as knowledge absorbed by the neocortex and constructs cognitive maps that create general knowledge about what to expect in the future. This involves strategies and rules relating to rewards and punishments. The amygdala has difficulty rapidly changing a positive or negative response that it has already learned. For example, if a monkey has learned that watermelon is good to eat, then is given watermelon laced with salt (making it unpalatable), its amygdala is slow to change its positive response to the watermelon. The monkey's amygdala is likely to continue fixating on a piece of watermelon, even though all the last several pieces have been salty. The orbitofrontal cortex, on the other hand, is comparatively quick to realize that watermelon is now not good eating. The amygdala's database of rewards and punishments seems to be relatively simpleminded and unsophisticated. It contains broad categories (all snakes are dangerous) rather than narrower categories based on more complex distinctions (only certain types of snakes, which can be identified by a close examination of their anatomy, are dangerous). The orbitofrontal cortex's role is more consistent with advanced cortical reasoning. Its cognitive maps contain sophisticated categories of emotional learning capable of being rapidly readjusted to changing circumstances. Once the amygdala has decided on the basis of a specific experience that a snake is dangerous, it tends to react to all snakes as dangerous. The orbitofrontal cortex can more easily create a cognitive map based on later sophisticated learning (such as reading about snakes), that distinguishes between dangerous and harmless snakes. And because of the intimate connections between the left orbitofrontal cortex, in particular, and the limbic system, the left orbitofrontal is better able to suppress the amygdala's outdated emotional reaction. Since it is part of the more complex structure of the neocortex, the orbitofrontal cortex can create an almost infinite number of flexible categories that embody finer and more subtle distinctions than the limbic system is capable of. The orbitofrontal cortex can use its sophisticated cognitive maps, along with those created by the rest of the prefrontal cortex, to project far into the future and the past.

There are basically three types of treatments for anxiety disorders: cognitive therapy, behavioral therapy, and biological therapy. Cognitive therapy involves trying to clear up a patient's rational misconceptions about his fears—for example, persuading him that garter snakes are harmless. But the results of cognitive therapy alone have been weak because most of these fear illnesses are controlled not by the rational fear system and advanced cortical reasoning but by the primitive fear system and primitive limbic reasoning, which is physiologically impervious to analytical categories beyond the middle level (snakes). In contrast, behavioral therapy has had some significant successes because through gradual exposure, usually guided by an experienced therapist, it deals directly with the primitive fear system. The behavioral therapist might treat a snake phobia by gradually introducing the person to a garter snake and showing his primitive fear system that, indeed, they are harmless. If the limbic fear is deep-seated, however, this can be a long, exhausting process. Limbic fears can be highly resistant to change. The degree of difficulty may depend on the temperament of the sufferer. Someone whose primary activation is in the right prefrontal cortex (a pessimistic, fearful person) may have trouble activating their left orbitofrontal cortex effectively, which is important for suppressing or extinguishing a fear. The behavioral therapist will often try to establish more positive thought patterns in the person that assist the left frontal lobe.

Biological therapy seeks to isolate the organic malfunctions in the brain that are responsible for anxiety disorders. For example, PET scans have revealed that a specific area of the limbic system—the right parahippocampal gyrus—has an abnormally high blood flow in victims of panic disorder. The right parahippocampal gyrus is intimately connected to the right orbitofrontal cortex.[13] The nature of this abnormality in the right hemisphere is more evidence that negative emotional states like panic and fear enter consciousness from the limbic system via the right orbitofrontal cortex. Biological therapy favors treating anxiety disorders with drugs and sometimes surgery. In patients with intractable, crippling anxiety disorders, the surgical severing of certain limbic circuits is sometimes used as the therapy of last resort. Although the patient is sometimes helped, psychosurgery is an inexact science.

There is also a problem with relying completely on drugs. If you take an antidepressant for snake phobia, your frontal lobes may be strengthened sufficiently to suppress your fear of snakes. But the fear is still there. When you stop taking the antidepressant, the fear comes back, perhaps stronger than ever because your frontal lobes aren't used to suppressing the fear without the help of the drug. But if you undergo behavior therapy, you're getting to the root of the problem by habituating the primitive fear system to snakes. Many therapists recommend that patients with severe anxiety disorders initially try antidepressants to break the hold of the illness temporarily, and then immediately begin behavior therapy with the aim of eventually weaning the patient off the drug. The alternative is to take the drug indefinitely. But antidepressants have significant side effects and some patients cannot tolerate them. Brain-imaging studies have compared obsessive-compulsive disorder patients who undergo drug therapy using fluoxetine (Prozac) with those treated with behavior therapy. The studies find that both groups show the same general improvements in brain functioning. Researchers have concluded that behavior therapy is just as effective as drug therapy in treating this painful illness.[14]

Over the last two decades there has been dramatic progress in improving the techniques of behavior therapy. "Under controlled conditions," writes Rachman, "it is now possible to produce substantial and lasting reductions of established fears, even life-long fears, within thirty minutes. It requires greater effort and far more time to reduce complex, intense fears such as agoraphobia, but even these respond reasonably well to training or treatment programs."[15]

The powerful technique that Rachman describes is called therapeutic modeling. In this approach, a therapist serves as a patient's model for normal behavior. Using a variety of techniques including rational explanation, visualization, and reward, the therapist will prepare the patient to approach the feared object or situation. The therapist will often explain that the fears the patient feels are not signals of real danger but only the malfunctioning of the fear systems, which are sending the wrong signals. The patient might use visualization to begin imagining an approach to the fearful situation. The idea is to develop the ability to visualize calmly, without activating a fear response. Once the patient feels more comfortable—the idea is to trigger the relaxation response as much as possible—the therapist will begin a process of controlled exposure to the fear. If the patient has a fear of being trapped in an elevator, the therapist and patient might go to a building that has elevators. The therapist will demonstrate the normal reaction to getting into an elevator and encourage the patient to copy this model of normal behavior. This process of gradual desensitization seeks to retrain the responses of the primitive fear system by repeated demonstration that the feared object or situation actually poses no threat. At each step of the patient's progress, the therapist might arrange for a reward—some item or activity that the patient enjoys, such as going to a movie or sporting event. The reward not only acts to reinforce normal behavior, it serves as a distraction from the fear. If the patient is thinking about the reward that will follow a successful therapy session, there is less focus on the fear. An important goal of therapy is to restore the patient's mental and behavioral flexibility, so that the patient no longer fixates on the fear. The goal of the therapy is for patients to completely habituate and carry on these activities on their own.[16]

With post-traumatic stress disorder the therapy is somewhat different. The person suffering from post-traumatic stress is usually reacting to a past event, not a current fear. The therapist, through extensive discussion with the patient, seeks to bring out these traumatic memories gradually so the patient can be exposed to them, understand his or her reaction to them, and habituate. Habituation will lead to acceptance of these memories and an ability to trigger the relaxation response. Patients with post-traumatic stress often suffer for years with hyperactive sympathetic nervous systems.

Obsessive-compulsive disorder is the most tenacious of the diseases of fear and the illness that causes the most suffering. This is because it usually combines intense obsessions and often exhausting compulsive behaviors with a sometimes broad array of phobias. These obsessions can dominate the patient's thoughts virtually around the clock, turning existence into a living hell. These obsessions are sometimes hidden because of the terrible fear they generate. The therapist tries to encourage patients to discuss the obsessions, and through this kind of exposure to reduce the fear. Some patients with obsessive-compulsive disorder are obsessed with knives, any kind of knives, because they have an overwhelming fear that they might use the knife to hurt someone. This is an example of the primitive fear system fixating on an irrational thought. Patients who have an obsession with violence are invariably the gentlest possible people. The reason why this obsession upsets them so much is that they abhor violence more than most people. This tends to be the pattern with all obsessions in this illness. The patient may have had an angry thought when someone cut him off on the highway, but instead of instantly suppressing it as a normal reaction to frustration, he might begin obsessively worrying about it. The obsessive worry can eventually become a full-fledged obsession. Patients always know their obsessions are irrational, but are unable to stop them. Because of neurotransmitter imbalances usually involving serotonin their frontal lobes have lost the power to inhibit stray or intrusive thoughts.

In severe cases of obsessive-compulsive disorder, the primitive fear system completely controls the patient's life in an endless succession of obsessive thoughts, compulsive rituals (often involving washing that is so frequent the patient's skin is raw), and phobias. These phobias can rapidly spread, crippling the patient's ability to function at all. A fear of knives can become a fear of kitchen knives, a fear of the kitchen, a fear of the entire house, a fear of stores that sell knives, and on and on. The illness can be so all-consuming that therapists often marvel at the unbelievable courage it takes for these patients to get through the day. Without treatment, a substantial number of obsessive-compulsives commit suicide. Yet all the while, obsessive-compulsive patients rationally understand that the torment they are going through is completely irrational. They are helpless because their rational fear system and conscious mind can't stop the thoughts and behaviors. Their primitive fear system dominates their lives. Many patients improve on antidepressant drugs. A persistent regimen of behavior therapy can also lead to substantial improvement.

Obsessive-compulsive disorder illustrates a critical point about dealing with fear. The primitive fear system is a form of awareness outside of consciousness. Consciousness itself and the rational fear system work together to create what we might call rational consciousness. The primitive fear system and rational consciousness compete for control of attention and behavior. In severe obsessive-compulsive disorder, the primitive fear system wins out completely. First, there is the creation of an irrational fear by the primitive fear system followed by an obsession with that fear as the primitive fear seizes control of the attention mechanism and fixates on the fear. What follows is compulsive behavior (sometimes based on primitive grooming rituals) in which the individual engages in painful rituals, such as excessive washing or cleaning, which ultimately may succeed in distracting the patient from the irrational fear and at least temporarily allowing them to shift their attention away from it. The compulsions are often painful and exhausting. Pain is sometimes the only way for individuals to distract themselves from the obsession. Patients have been known to slam drawers on their fingers and perform other forms of self-injury and self-mutilation to give themselves relief from the obsession. All the while their rational consciousness is working absolutely normally. Like the person with an intense phobia of snakes, they know perfectly well they are acting irrationally but have lost the power to control their attention, behavior, and their horrific fear response. They are completely helpless. In the worst cases, patients live their lives in the most extreme terror, on the verge of terror, or in extreme depression. They are often reclusive.

When people with a snake phobia see a garter snake they perceive it simultaneously through primitive awareness and rational consciousness. These two forms of awareness often perceive the snake in diametrically opposite ways. Primitive awareness sees it as a terrifying threat while rational consciousness sees it as harmless. The question then becomes which form of awareness will control attention and behavior. If primitive awareness is the victor, then the person's attention will be fixated on the snake and their behavior will shift to a primitive fight-or-flight response. That is when fear becomes a disease: when we lose the power to shift our attention to what we rationally believe is important and rationally control our behavior. Behavior therapy can restore this rational balance to the phobic. But whenever we deal with fear—other than the most instantaneous emergency—maintaining our rational control over attention and behavior is the critical goal.

Diseases of fear cost billions of dollars every year in medical expenses and lost wages. But the greatest price by far is in the unbearable suffering endured by the victims of these terrible illnesses and their families. Even the violent psychopath, so seemingly cold and unfeeling, may experience moments of ghastly remorse. Armchair detectives have never tired of continuing the search for the identity of Jack the Ripper. In recent years a man named Montague John Druitt has emerged as a prime suspect. Druitt, an unsuccessful barrister, came from a family that included several doctors. His office was near the sites of the murders. Pictures of him show not an ogre but an ordinary-looking young man. He fits the FBI profile of a serial killer: "a white male in his twenties or thirties who is reasonably attractive and commands average or above-average intelligence." A month after the murder of Mary Kelly, the last of the Ripper's victims, Druitt disappeared. Three weeks later his body was pulled from the Thames. He left no suicide note or other explanation. His coat pockets were filled with stones, perhaps a sign of the final struggle between man and monster.[17]

{ Chapter 10 }

The Paradox of Suicide

I f fear is such a potent emotion, why does suicide exist at all? The answer turns on the fact that human fear systems have a powerful ability to learn new behaviors, even behaviors that contradict the innate fear of death.

Since the evolutionary purpose of fear is to avoid pain, we should not be surprised that if a person experiences constant, intense pain, the fear of death begins to lose its sting, with death viewed as the only escape from pain. This occasionally happens when someone nears death after a lengthy, painful illness. It is also the reason people who experience intense, long-term, and apparently irreversible pain are sometimes more willing to consider suicide.

Yet there are people who consciously choose death though they are not in pain. This can be for many reasons. The young Japanese who volunteered to be kamikaze pilots in the last months of World War II— *kamikaze* means "divine wind"—believed they were protecting their homeland and the emperor as they flew their explosives-packed planes into American naval vessels.[1] We have seen a similar phenomenon in the wave of suicide bombers in the Middle East and elsewhere over the last thirty years. But there are also cases during wartime in which men volunteer for what are called suicide missions, knowing their chances of surviving are slim. John F. Kennedy's older brother, Joe, was killed on such a mission during World War II. He volunteered to pilot a plane full of explosives across the English Channel and aim it at a huge German gun emplacement. At the last minute, Joe Kennedy and his copilot were to bail out. For some unknown reason, the plane blew up in midair. In these instances, the rational fear system is forcibly able to suppress the fear of death using (in most people) the left orbitofrontal cortex. This ability to subdue the fear of death is usually reinforced by a sense of group solidarity or religious conviction. This spirit gives purpose to the death and, in the case of religion, often a promise of eternal life and happiness as a reward. Although we do not yet understand the mechanisms, group approval and encouragement seems to boost the natural opiate and nonopiate fear suppression systems controlled by the left frontal lobe. As long as death makes sense in the context of the group, the fear of death can sometimes be consciously suppressed, making even ridiculous-seeming suicides possible. Marshall Applewhite's claim that he and his followers by their deaths were moving into a realm that was beyond human and rendezvousing with a spaceship trailing the Hale-Bopp Comet made sense within the conditioning of the Heaven's Gate group and allowed thirty-nine men and women to suppress consciously their fear of death and commit mass suicide.

Fear is designed not only to warn against physical pain, but mental pain as well. And mental pain may also become so great that death seems welcome. Depression is a major source of mental pain, but other severe anxiety disorders like obsessive-compulsive disorder and post-traumatic stress syndrome can also cause it. The pain experienced after suffering a tremendous emotional loss, such as the loss of a spouse, can push some people into suicide. A powerful sense of helplessness and hopelessness can also be a major factor. Men are more vulnerable than women to these kinds of emotional losses.[2] Suicide involves turning the aggression unleashed by the fear response onto oneself. Instead of being afraid of death, the potential suicide becomes afraid of life and decides to flee in the only way possible: through death.

People are unique, and their reactions to severe stress are unique as well. During the bombing of London by the Nazis in World War II the suicide rate actually went down. There were reports that a substantial number of people who had been treated for anxiety disorders prior to the bombing improved because the uncertainty and excitement of the early war years distracted them from their illness. An astonishing external event gave their frontal lobes the push needed to shift their attention from their illness to other things.[3] In the entire realm of strategies for coping with fear and anxiety disorders, a paramount goal is to maintain or regain the conscious flexibility to shift one's attention freely. Much of what we mean by free will comes down to this ability to turn our attention wherever we consciously wish. Fear can destroy that ability and begin a cycle of self-destructive brooding that leads to suicide. Old traumas can lurk deep within our psyche, like time bombs, ready to go off at any moment and fixate us on some terrible source of fear or pain. Sometimes the resurfacing of these old wounds can be treated successfully; sometimes it can't.

Researchers on combat stress describe the case of one man, an Israeli, who had fought with distinction before and during the Yom Kippur War between Israel and the Arab states, which began in October 1973. During military confrontations in the years prior to this surprise attack on Israel, the man "had been decorated with one of the highest medals for rescuing soldiers from a burning tank." During the Yom Kippur War, "he was himself caught in a burning tank and suffered 40 percent burns and spent several months in the hospital." Although he was saved, he had watched a number of other men die in their tanks. After recovering, he finished his university education, married, and started a family. "He worked at various jobs, holding each for only a few years before quitting on account of small irritations that occur at every workplace." He had one minor episode of depression in the succeeding thirteen years, but was never diagnosed as suffering from post-traumatic stress disorder. "Neither his wife nor friends suspected that anything was seriously amiss."

He had one small ritual that seemed odd. "Every Friday evening, he would gather all the twigs and branches from his own and his neighbors' yards into a blazing bonfire." The fire became a kind of good-natured joke in his neighborhood "and his friends would even bring him cardboard and sticks to burn in his weekly bonfire." Then one day without telling anyone, he drove out to the dunes near the Tel Aviv airport, took out a can of gasoline, poured it over a patch of vegetation, and tied his own legs together. Then after "pouring gasoline on himself, he ignited both himself and the plants. Crawling onto the road like a flaming torch, he was spotted by some passersby and brought to the hospital." He lived for two days. During that time he talked about his experiences fighting in his tank among the Sinai dunes. As it turned out, pressures at work had triggered a severe depression which he hid from his family and friends. The depression engulfed him with the sense of helplessness that he experienced when he watched his comrades die in their burning tanks. "Here was a striving, idealistic young man who killed himself in a replica of his comrades' deaths in order to be at one with them in their final end."[4]

Try to recall vividly the experience in your life in which you were in the most physical pain. Now try to reexperience your greatest humiliation. Which seems clearer? For most people, painful emotional memories are much clearer than memories of physical pain. In fact, the brain seems to have a system for suppressing memories of intense physical pain—a system that is not well understood. People often verbally remember times that they were in great physical pain but generally cannot subjectively reexperience that pain. Yet the memory of even a minor humiliating incident decades before may still make you squirm and blush. The primitive fear system keeps emotional memories fresh so that our present and future behavior will be guided by them. But these memories can also be a constant source of mental anguish and depression.

Depression is the world's leading cause of suicide. In fact, surveys show that throughout the world, depression and anxiety disorders are the most crippling mental illnesses. No wonder that antidepressants like fluoxetine (sold under the brand name Prozac), which are used to treat both depression and anxiety disorders, constitute some of the most widely prescribed drugs in the world. No other species has the enormous breadth of fears of human beings, and no other species goes to such lengths to suppress them. Although men overwhelmingly dominate the categories of mental illness that involve aggression and violence, a World Health Organization study found that women, overall, have a rate of depression that is twice as high as men's. Suicide rates vary over time in particular cultures. During periods of rapid change and dislocation, the rate goes up, only to drift downward again during times of stability. Because of its huge population China now accounts for 40 percent of all the world's suicides. But China's suicide rate is about twice that of the United States, even though depression is five times less common in China than in the West. Some of these anomalies may be explained by reporting inconsistencies. Different cultures sometimes have a different willingness to discuss mental illness. Yet China does seem to have an unusually high rate of suicide among rural women. And there do seem to be major differences in the way mental illness is expressed in different cultures. "In the developed

Western world the symptoms of depression tend to be both psychological states—feelings of despair, sadness, belief that life is meaningless—and physical complaints," write Arthur Kleinman and Alex Cohen of the Harvard Medical School. "In general health care, patients highlight physical symptoms, whereas in psychiatric settings they emphasize psychological complaints. In non-Western societies and among traditionally oriented ethnic groups, there tends to be an emphasis primarily on bodily complaints (headaches, fatigue, dizziness, for example), and psychological symptoms are less frequent."[5]

Painful psychological symptoms are often deeply felt by artists and writers in the developed world. They suffer from higher rates of depression than the population as a whole. "The truth lay in this," said Leo Tolstoy, "that life had no meaning for me. Every day of life, every step in it, brought me nearer the edge of a precipice, whence I saw clearly the final ruin before me. To stop, to go back, were alike impossible; nor could I shut my eyes so as not to see the suffering that alone awaited me, the death of all in me, even to annihilation. Thus I, a healthy and happy man, was brought to feel that I could live no longer, that an irresistible force was dragging me down into the grave."[6] The poet Sylvia Plath made this entry in her diary while she was an undergraduate at Smith College: "I am afraid. I am not solid, but hollow. I feel behind my eyes a numb, paralyzed cavern, a pit of hell, a mimicking nothingness. . . . I look at the hell I am wallowing in, nerves paralyzed, action nullified—fear, envy, hate; all the corrosive emotions of insecurity biting away at my sensitive guts."[7] Tolstoy recovered from his bout with depression. Plath struggled with depression for years before committing suicide.

Since for most people the left frontal lobe is the center for conscious perception of positive emotions, depression can sometimes be triggered by an extremely low level of activity in that lobe.[8] More commonly, however, the depressed patient shows unusually low activity in both frontal lobes and many other areas of the brain as well. The mind no longer emotionally experiences the world around it or its own existence. The subjective feeling that this shutdown produces is one of intense mental agony. Depression is also accompanied by lower levels of activity in the immune system and hormone system. Arousal is so low in depressed patients that they cannot experience fear strongly enough (or any other emotion) to prevent them from killing themselves. Depressed individuals as well as those most likely to commit suicide often have unusually low levels of serotonin and other neurotransmitters in the prefrontal cortex.

In monkeys, low levels of serotonin in this area are associated with high levels of aggression and impulsiveness. In humans, the lower the level of serotonin the more lethal the suicide attempt. According to one investigator at Columbia University: "New research indicates that suicide is not a normal response to severe distress, but [is] the response of a person with a vulnerability to act on powerful feelings."[9] Suicide is the ultimate act of aggression against the self. Weakening the rational fear system centered in the prefrontal areas increases the likelihood that such aggressive impulses from the primitive fear system will be acted upon. The latest generation of antidepressants are effective in reversing depression in most patients. Their mode of action in the depressed person's brain is not completely clear, but they do tend to increase the amount of serotonin in the synapses between neurons and lengthen the time in which the serotonin is active. One problem is that antidepressants take several weeks to begin working. "Anyone close to a seriously depressed person knows that those two weeks can be a living hell," says neuroscientist Solomon Snyder. "The risk of suicide is particularly high during this lag period before a patient's mood improves."[10]

There are other treatments for depression as well. Lithium is used to treat manic depression, in which the patient's mood swings from the hyperactive manic state to deep depression. For extremely severe depression where there is an imminent risk of suicide, electroconvulsive therapy is also used. A short but powerful electrical current is passed between electrodes on the scalp. This produces a widespread brain seizure. This treatment is administered multiple times over several days. In about two-thirds of patients the convulsions cause the brain to return to normal and lift the depression. Developing treatments for depression is, in many ways, a matter of trial and error. Neuroscientists still don't know exactly why electroconvulsive therapy and lithium work. In one study, antidepressant drug therapy was compared with cognitive and behavior therapy, which in the case of depression is designed to reorient patients' thinking patterns aggressively and generate a hopeful, optimistic outlook. The drug therapy generally acted most quickly to clear up depression, but by the end of the sixteen-week trial the talk therapies were just as successful as drug therapy in eliminating depression. This study and many others that have looked at behavior therapy in anxiety disorders and depression show conclusively that what we say and do can reconfigure and rewire our brains just as surely as drugs can.[11]

The severely depressed patient, whose frontal lobes are barely active, experiences a deep sense of apathy. "I felt very still and very empty," wrote Sylvia Plath, "the way the eye of a tornado must feel, moving dully along in the middle of the surrounding hullabaloo."[12] When we lose our left prefrontal cortex, we lose an important center of what we call willpower—the conscious ability not only to shift our thoughts but shift our behavior. We can choose to do something or refuse to do it because of consequences that are far into the future. For example, even though we might want to sleep late one morning, we get up and go to work because in the long run that is the course of action that will best meet our career goals. People who are depressed often have difficulty getting out of bed for any reason. The motivational system centered in their frontal lobes is impaired. The left prefrontal cortex specializes in complex planning using its sophisticated model of the world—generated by all the senses and the emotional and cognitive memories of our entire life experience—to weigh the consequences of our actions and the many possible behaviors we might undertake prompted by our fears and desires.

Depression can insinuate itself into a person's life gradually. Negative thoughts begin to pop up more and more frequently until the mood of depression becomes entrenched. But where do they come from? Unexpected thoughts are not only a source of depression, they are the source of our creativity, in science as well as the arts. "The creative scientist has much in common with the artist and the poet," said physicist Leo Szilard. "Logical thinking and an analytical ability are necessary attributes to a scientist, but they are far from sufficient for creative work. Those insights in science that have led to a breakthrough were not logically derived from preexisting knowledge: The creative processes on which the progress of science is based operate on the level of the subconscious."[13] How does the brain produce the multitude of ideas that seem to flow beneath the conscious mind, undergo sophisticated rational and emotional processing, and then pop, sometimes full-blown, into consciousness? In people whose left hemisphere is dominant for language, this kind of holistic processing seems to take place mostly in the nonverbal right hemisphere and in the fleeting activation of ideas by the frontal lobes, an activation that is usually too brief to enable these ideas to flow back into consciousness. Words come sequentially, one at a time. But the right hemisphere tends to see things as a whole. When we listen to someone speak, the left hemisphere builds up the meaning of what they are saying one word at a time, but the right hemisphere grasps their emotional state as a whole, integrating simultaneously their tone of voice, facial expression, body language, and context.

Ideas that are simmering in the basically nonverbal right hemisphere might not be translated into the verbal, sequential left hemisphere until they have met certain emotional and rational criteria that have emerged through the interaction of the right hemisphere, the left hemisphere, and the outside world. This implies that there are two separate and parallel streams of thought in the human mind: a primarily verbal, sequential stream in the left hemisphere and a primarily nonverbal, holistic stream in the right hemisphere. There are images in the left hemisphere's stream of thought, but they appear sequentially, one after another, just as words do. This left hemisphere stream of thought, which is what we typically identify as the stream of consciousness, is capable of blocking out the stream from the right hemisphere unless the right hemisphere produces something that meets left hemisphere criteria. I would call the nonverbal holistic stream of thought in the right hemisphere the stream of subconsciousness.

Evidence for these dual streams of thought comes from what are called split-brain studies. Certain patients with severe epilepsy have operations cutting their corpus callosum, a bundle of fibers that is the primary communications channel between the two hemispheres. Cutting this band of fibers prevents the spreading of epileptic seizures from one hemisphere to the other. Normally the operation decreases the severity of the epilepsy without damaging intelligence. But these operations also give neuroscientists the opportunity to study each cerebral hemisphere independently. Since the eyes transmit information to the right and left hemispheres separately, scientists can create experimental arrangements in which they communicate with only one hemisphere. One problem with this research is that the right hemisphere has very limited language ability and thus cannot normally communicate with the outside world in words. But two neuroscientists, Michael Gazzaniga and Joseph LeDoux, who were among the pioneers of this kind of work, happened upon one young epileptic, Paul, whose left temporal lobe had been damaged when he was two. This stimulated his right hemisphere to compensate for the damage by developing verbal skills of its own. Gazzaniga and LeDoux felt they might be able to communicate directly with the right hemisphere. They had Paul sit at an apparatus that did not allow one hemisphere to know what the other was seeing. They would flash questions to both hemispheres at once, but the question that the left hemisphere saw would contain the word "blank" inserted in place of key words. The first question that the left hemisphere saw read: "Who *blank*?" But the right hemisphere saw a different question: "Who are you?" The researchers had Paul use his left hand (which is under control of the right hemisphere) to answer. The left hand spelled out, "Paul." "Overflowing with excitement, having just communicated on a personal level with a right hemisphere, we collected ourselves," wrote Gazzaniga and LeDoux, "and then initiated the next trial by saying, " 'Would you spell your favorite *blank*?' Then *'girl'* appeared in the left visual field. Out came the left hand again, and this time it spelled *'Liz,'* the name of his girlfriend at the time. . . . He spelled *'automobile race'* as the job he would pick. This is most interesting, because the left hemisphere frequently asserts that he wants to be a draftsman." Shortly after the test session, the researchers asked Paul what kind of job he would like to have "and the left hemisphere said, 'Oh, be a draftsman.' "[14]

Information gathered from many split-brain patients suggests, the two researchers said, "that there are multiple mental systems in the brain, each with the capacity to produce behavior, and each with its own impulses for action. . . ." They found that information recorded in the right hemisphere is not necessarily available to the left. "Could it be," asked Gazzaniga and LeDoux, "that in the developing organism a constellation of mental systems (emotional, motivational, perceptual, and so on) exists, each with its own values and response probabilities? Then, as maturation continues, the behaviors that these separate systems emit are monitored by the one system we come to use more and more, namely, the verbal, natural language system. Gradually, a concept of self-control develops so that the verbal self comes to know the impulses for action that arise from the other selves, and it either tries to inhibit these impulses or free them, as the case may be."[15]

Paul's desire to be a race car driver did not enter his verbal consciousness because it did not meet the criteria of the left hemisphere. The extent to which the stream of subconsciousness in the right hemisphere enters consciousness seems to depend, in part, on temperament. If our right prefrontal cortex is generally activated more strongly than the left, then more of the negative emotions that flow into the right prefrontal cortex are translated into words by the left and become part of our stream of consciousness. People who continually and heavily tap into these negative emotions tend to develop a pessimistic attitude about themselves and the world. But the degree to which these emotions enter consciousness in the right-prefrontal-activated temperament varies from individual to individual. Some people tend to be extremely pessimistic while others are only mildly so. People who activate the left prefrontal cortex more strongly tend to block out most of the negative emotions that flow through the right hemisphere's stream of subconsciousness. But, again, the degree of blocking varies. One individual may be almost impervious to these negative emotions and have a completely fearless and optimistic personality, while another may be aware of a substantial portion of these negative thoughts and be only tepidly optimistic. The rational fear system seems to work most effectively when it is aware of the fears and negative emotions of the right prefrontal cortex but not overwhelmed by them.

I believe the right hemisphere's stream of subconsciousness plays a critical role in our creative and emotional lives. Some people may have more routine access to this stream of thought and image and thus have a somewhat different experience of consciousness, with a larger nonverbal component. From the right hemisphere come the flashes of insight that allow us instantly to understand things as a whole. Have you ever been in an animated conversation with someone and realized you were expressing thoughts and insights that you weren't aware you had? At such times a flood of right hemisphere thoughts may be entering your left hemisphere where they are translated into words. Since the right frontal lobe is concerned with processing negative emotions from the primitive fear system, some of these thoughts may be the kind of pessimistic, fearful feelings that can begin an episode of depression in a susceptible individual. The real onset of the depression, however, may be a neurochemical change that begins lowering the activation of the left frontal lobe. The increasingly pessimistic cast of thought would be a reflection of that decrease in activity and the decreasing ability of the left frontal lobe to suppress it. When the left frontal lobe's activation is normal, it could use its opiate and nonopiate systems to block out negative emotions from the right while accepting the right hemisphere's insights that do not have this pessimistic character.

There may also be a third mechanism for generating ideas outside of verbal consciousness. This involves the fleeting activation of ideas and feelings by the frontal lobes in the areas farther back in the brain. If the activation were brief, these ideas would only be partially processed by the cortex (and would also be reacted to by the primitive fear system) but would not persist long enough to filter all the way back to the frontal lobes and into consciousness. Let's call this flashing of partially activated ideas the stream of preconsciousness. This is like flashing subliminal pictures on a screen too fast for consciousness to register. These briefly activated ideas and feelings would, at a minimum, have an effect on the emotional state of the mind. It may be that all our thoughts spring from a welter of briefly activated feelings and ideas—thousands of them every minute—some of which if they meet the shifting criteria of the limbic system, including the orbitofrontal cortices and perhaps other cortical structures, would have their patterns boosted so they would endure long enough to flow into the left frontal lobe. Often I will be aware that I have a fragmentary understanding of something, and then, during a conversation with someone, a much more complete understanding of the subject will flow into my mind. Since humans respond strongly to the presence and words of others, it may be that this conversation boosted my fragmentary understanding into a more persistent pattern that underwent more thorough processing, perhaps in the right hemisphere, and emerged as a coherent insight.

In summary, there appear to be three components of the complex mental life of humans: the primarily verbal and sequential stream of consciousness in the left hemisphere, the holistic, nonverbal stream of subconsciousness in the right hemisphere, and the subliminal, fragmentary stream of preconsciousness that flashes on and off in the portions of the neocortex behind the frontal lobes and is scanned by the primitive fear system of both hemispheres. These three streams of thought and feeling may comprise the experience of high-level consciousness generated by the primitive fear system (limbic system), the rational fear system (frontal lobes and particularly the prefrontal cortex), and the lateralized abilities of the two hemispheres.

The onset of depression is usually unpredictable. The complex nature of human thought and the human nervous system can combine to push an individual into depression when he least expects it. Depression drastically increases the subjective perception of mental pain, so much so that it can submerge the fear of death. A substantial majority of people with depressive illness have thoughts of suicide. Of the people who actually kill themselves, an estimated 60 to 80 percent suffer from depression. This is a particular problem with the elderly, who have the highest rates of depression. Although the elderly make up about 20 percent of the population, they account for approximately 40 percent of all suicides. As the average life span lengthens the risk of depression increases.

But there is the additional problem that arises because of medicine's improved ability to keep people alive—even some of those with terminal illnesses—for long periods of time. The physical pain of a severe illness can also lead to the disappearance of the fear of death and a desire to end one's life. Yet the disappearance of the fear of death does not necessarily mean the loss of the fear of the unknown, which death represents. Most people in severe physical pain continue to go on living as long as possible. Nevertheless, should competent terminally ill adults who are not depressed be allowed to choose to end their lives? If the decision is to die, should doctors or anyone else be allowed to assist the person in dying? This issue is being vigorously debated and raises society's fears about opening the door to euthanasia. Though more than half the states explicitly ban assisted suicide, the activities of right-to-die advocates like Jack Kevorkian have attracted a certain amount of support. Those who favor the right to die argue that an individual's choice in these matters should be protected by the Constitution's implicit right to privacy. Some right-to-die opponents oppose this on religious grounds. They argue that life is sacred and no one has a right to choose to end it. They also argue that a right to euthanasia might be abused: people who are extremely ill might be pressured to end their lives even if they didn't want to. The debate over the right to die, like the abortion debate, will probably linger for many years. It is one more difficult issue arising from the fantastically complex array of fears generated by the human brain.

{ Chapter 11 }

Fusing Mind and Body

Viewing the mind and body as separate and distinct is a serious error. All the evidence of modern neuroscience points to the mind as being produced by our wonderfully complex brain. As we have seen, if the brain is altered or damaged by drugs or injury, the entire personality can change. In disorders like episodic dyscontrol, damage to the limbic system, where the primitive fear system is centered, can turn people who are quiet, even fearful, into reckless, violent psychopaths.

Among the many reasons for using the conscious mind's rational fear system to control the stressful reactions of the unconscious limbic system is the effect on the immune system. Studies have shown that nerve endings from the brain make contact with many of the cells of the immune system. And there are a complex web of other connections between the brain and the immune system as well, some that we understand, many that we don't. Our emotional state influences the health of our immune system. Intense prolonged fear and anxiety depress the activity of the immune system; a happy, relaxed attitude rejuvenates it.

Which is worse for your health, physical or emotional pain? Surprisingly, mental pain can be just as dangerous as the physical pain of a serious illness or injury. This is because of the effect the brain has on the immune system. The study of how our emotions affect our health is a very young branch of medicine filled with questions and uncertainties. Nevertheless there have been a number of exciting breakthroughs in understanding brain-body mechanisms.

What are the most fearful and anguishing events in our lives? Studies agree that for children, the death of a parent is the cruelest emotional blow. For most adults, it is the death of the spouse. Men, in particular, are vulnerable to this kind of stress. Men who have lost a spouse generally show a dramatic decrease in their immune function for months following. Other events that most people fear include the death of a child or other close family member, a major negative change in health or behavior of a spouse, child, or close family member, separation or divorce, losing a job, and difficulties in the emotional and sexual relationships. Again, men tend to be more negatively affected than women. For example, men have a risk of suicide that is seven times greater than women after a calamitous event like the death of a spouse or the loss of a job.[1]

Although men are on average about 20 percent larger than women and have greater upper body strength, women generally seem to have more emotional toughness. This appears to translate into a healthier immune system and is part of the reason that women in developed countries outlive men by anywhere from five to ten years on the average. The cerebral hemispheres in the female brain tend to be less specialized than the male's and are better connected to each other. Females have a larger corpus callosum and a substantially larger anterior commissure—a bundle of nerve fibers that connect the amygdalae and other limbic structures in the two hemispheres.[2] Because of the greater flexibility in the wiring of their brains, women often recover more quickly and more fully from the effects of a stroke.

Besides the intrinsic trauma of the death of a spouse or other catastrophe, all these events have in common an increase in the sense of helplessness. Whether you lose a job or develop a serious illness, you tend to feel at the mercy of events that threaten to overwhelm you. This creates intense fears that have a negative effect on the immune system. Studies have placed groups of rats in enclosures that give them mild electrical shocks. One set of enclosures allows the rats to stop the shock by turning a wheel or pushing a lever. The other enclosures give the rats no control whatsoever. The results of such studies invariably show that the rats with no control suffer many more health problems. Other studies have compared people in high-powered, stressful jobs with lower ranking employees of similar age and health. These have found that despite the pressure of their jobs, top executives tend to have a significantly lower mortality rate than their subordinates. The most important variable between these two groups is the control they have over their environment. Executives tend to perceive themselves as in charge of their destiny, whereas employees usually feel much more at the mercy of decisions made by others. Greater control appears to mean a more robust immune system and greater protection against stress-related disorders like high blood pressure. But the sense of control must be subjectively perceived or there is no benefit. Executives who are objectively in positions of great power and control, but nevertheless perceive themselves to be at the mercy of events, perhaps because of their temperament, are just as vulnerable to stress as their lowest ranking employee.

If science has uncovered one important technique for managing fear and stress it is this: Try to avoid, whenever possible, circumstances in which you feel helpless and vulnerable. If this cannot be done, then, despite the circumstances, try to maintain a subjective attitude of optimism and reasonable control. A mail room employee obviously does not have much say about his working life. But that does not rule out a subjective perception of optimism and control. The employee can view his job as a stepping stone to a higher position; as a way to learn the organization from the bottom up; as the same job that many executives started in. The employee can take night courses, establish relationships within the company, or take other action that makes advancement more likely. If things don't work out, then the employee can self-confidently look for another job. But the moment a worker feels stuck or trapped, whether mail clerk or company president, a long-term fear response kicks in. Immune function begins to drop, the person becomes edgy, unhappy, and there may be a host of related problems: restless sleep, poor eating habits, strained relations with family and friends. A perception of control involves the freedom you feel to shift your attention and activity to those things you believe are important. The more you perceive that this freedom is constrained the more stress and fear you tend to feel, and the more negative effects there may be on your health and sense of well-being.

False or mindless optimism is not enough to actuate a positive immune response. The neocortex is very sensitive to context and nuance and, under normal circumstances, people are aware of whether the attitudes they project to the world are genuine or not. There are times, however, when a person can be confused about his or her feelings because of the complexity of the situation or conflicts among the stream of consciousness in the left frontal lobe, the stream of subconsciousness in the right frontal lobe, and the primitive emotional responses and urges of the limbic system. But there is usually no mistaking a genuine subjective sense of optimism and control. If someone is fired from every job, the bland expression of optimism and continued self-esteem may be a form of denial or unspoken panic. A person must consciously work to give optimism a concrete foundation, particularly if his or her temperament tends to be pessimistic.[3]

Researchers have shown in the laboratory how the brain can condition the immune response to specific circumstances, just as it can condition the fear response to the sight of a snake. This discovery was made accidentally a quarter of a century ago by psychologists Robert Ader and Nicholas Cohen. They performed a series of experiments in which rats were fed water sweetened with saccharin and then given an injection of the drug cyclophosphamide, which suppressed their immune systems, making them more likely to get sick. The rats learned to associate the sweetened water with feeling ill and stopped drinking the saccharin-laced water. Ader and Cohen then ended that portion of the experiment and the rats no longer received drug injections. Eventually, the rats lost their fear of water containing saccharin and they began to drink it again. About six weeks later, however, the psychologists noticed that an unusually high number of these rats began to die. Other rats who had not been involved in the earlier experiment with cyclophosphamide were also being fed water with saccharin, but their health was fine. After examining the sick and dying rats, Ader and Cohen realized that their immune response was being lowered by the saccharin-flavored water alone. Somehow their brains had learned during the earlier experience not only to generate a fear response when exposed to the sweetened water, but to generate a negative immune response as well. Although the rats had lost their fear response to the water, they had not yet lost their learned immune response.[4]

Let's say an emotionally sensitive girl was raised in a chaotic, abusive home where she learned to feel completely helpless and was always sick. If for some reason she visited that same house, now empty, as an adult, she might notice that she suddenly began to feel ill. Years before, her brain had learned to associate that fearsome household with a negative immune response. When she saw the house again years later, her brain subconsciously remembered that conditioned learning and depressed her immune system, making her feel sick. This reaction is not that unusual. People who are especially sensitive sometimes report that whenever they are under extreme stress they can feel themselves getting sick.

The limbic system is the part of the brain primarily responsible for learning fear responses. Where does immune learning take place? Evidence points to the hypothalamus, which is intimately wired to the limbic system, and damage to the hypothalamus has been shown to depress the immune response. Electrical stimulation of certain areas of the hypothalamus enhances the immune response. Remember that the hypothalamus controls the nearby pituitary gland, which is the brain's master gland. Studies have shown that the pituitary can increase or decrease the immune response, although the details of this process are not well understood.[5] All these interactions between brain systems, neurochemicals, and hormones are complex, but certain elements play leading roles. When the limbic system's primitive fear system detects a possible threat, it signals the locus ceruleus in the brain stem, the center of the brain's noradrenaline system. The locus ceruleus pumps noradrenaline to widespread areas of the brain, sharpening the senses so that the threat can be clearly detected. If the primitive fear system determines that the threat is real, then it signals the hypothalamus both directly and indirectly through the locus ceruleus, which is also wired to the hypothalamus. The hypothalamus, in turn, alerts the pituitary gland, which hangs by a stalk from the hypothalamus above the roof of the mouth. The pituitary gland secretes corticotropin-releasing factor (CRF), the master hormone that coordinates the fight-or-flight response. It is this hormone that activates the sympathetic nervous system and may depress the immune response. Once the threat has disappeared, the limbic system again signals the hypothalamus, which terminates the fear response and increases the immune response.[6] Through our experience with fear and stress, the brain learns when to turn the immune response up and down. This gives us a certain amount of direct control over our immune system. Many doctors have begun to realize that cultivating an optimistic outlook is just as important as maintaining a healthy diet and getting a moderate amount of exercise.

The fact that our state of mind can influence the state of our immune system helps explain one of the oddest phenomena of medicine: the placebo effect. Human fearfulness is so great that the mere expectation by a patient that a drug or other medical procedure will cure his or her illness often results in an improvement in health even if the drug ultimately turns out to be worthless. Placebos are inert medication with no active ingredients. Studies have shown that if a group of patients suffering from a wide variety of conditions are given placebos, and the patients believe the placebos are actual drugs, about a third of the patients will report that the placebo cured their ailment. This is true of many mental as well as physical illnesses.[7] And, in a sense, it did. In some cases, the placebo effect can be attributed to the self-limiting nature of the illness. Take the common cold, for example. If you have a cold and do nothing, the cold will go away by itself in a few days. But if you were taking a placebo, you might believe the placebo cured your cold. The placebo effect is also observed in cases that are not self-limiting. In these instances, a patient's positive expectations seem to turn up the immune system and allow the body to heal itself. Placebos have been given to patients who suffer from chronic pain and, again, a significant fraction of the patients report substantial improvement. Research has shown that this improvement is not imaginary. For when these patients are given drugs that block the effect of natural opiates (endorphins) in the body, the placebo effect usually disappears. Clearly the placebo has had the effect of turning on the chronic pain sufferer's own natural opiate system, which relieves the pain as well as or better than any external drug. The deployment of endorphins in the body is heavily influenced, like the immune system, by the limbic system and the hypothalamus.

The attitude of the doctor can have an important bearing on whether and to what extent the placebo effect is observed. "Physicians who can successfully elicit a placebo response tend to be optimistic and hopeful," writes Richard Restak, a physician himself. "In the face of uncertainty they emphasize affirmative emotions while encouraging confidence and expectations for recovery. Such physicians encourage their patients to develop a positive sense of themselves and their body, as well as to cultivate a trust in the body and its capacity for recovery."[8] The placebo effect is a secret that faith healers have known intuitively for centuries.

The testing for new prescription drugs has long taken account of the placebo effect. Drugs are usually tested in well-controlled double-blind studies in which some of the patients receive a placebo and the rest receive the actual drug, but neither the patients nor the researchers administering the test know until the test is over which patients received the actual drug and which the placebo. Any bias by the researchers is thereby eliminated and the placebo effect can be eliminated by comparing the outcomes of the group of patients who took the placebo with those who took the drug. If 30 percent of the patients taking the placebo show substantial improvement in their symptoms, and 30 percent of the patients taking the drug do also, then we can conclude that the drug performs no better than a sugar pill and is not effective. Only if, say, 60 percent of the patients taking the drug show improvement can we say that it is substantially more effective than the placebo.

When a prescription drug does survive this rigorous testing it is usually heavily promoted to doctors by its manufacturer. Particularly if the drug fulfills an unmet need in medicine, both the drug manufacturer and doctors have high hopes it will be just what their patients need. Occasionally such a drug does do exceptionally well the first few years it is on the market, sometimes better than we would have predicted based on the results of the rigorous tests. In this case we may have what I would call an enhanced placebo effect. Not only do the patients who take the drug fervently want it to succeed, so do the doctors who are prescribing it. Doctors have a strong professional, emotional, and economic interest in seeing that their patients improve. The doctor is usually far more enthusiastic about prescribing a drug that has been proven safe and effective than he would be if he were knowingly prescribing a sugar pill. This enthusiasm by the doctor may enhance the placebo effect in the patient. The drug may work more effectively than it did in the well-controlled studies because the combined enthusiasm of the doctor and patient give it a greater placebo effect. The patient's positive expectations, enhanced by his doctor's fervor, activate his immune system more strongly than was the case for patients in the study, and this enhances the new drug's effectiveness. Some medications like Prozac acquire the reputation of a wonder drug, which gives them a substantially enhanced placebo effect over and above their proven effectiveness. The danger, of course, is that in all this enthusiasm the drug will be overprescribed both because patients demand it and doctors are impressed by it. Every prescription drug has side effects, some extremely serious, and they should always be prescribed with the utmost care. A typical pattern for some new drugs is for there to be a burst of enthusiasm at the time the drug is first introduced and its enhanced placebo effect is at its peak, followed by a certain amount of disillusionment as the placebo effect begins to wear off, side effects are reported, and newer drugs enter the market. Among cynics in the medical profession there is a saying: Use new drugs quickly while they still work.

The placebo effect also illuminates a truth that perceptive physicians have known since ancient times: Laughter is excellent medicine. Three centuries ago a prominent English physician, Thomas Sydenham, wrote: "The arrival of a good clown exercises a more beneficial influence upon the health of a town than twenty asses laden with drugs."[9] As we discussed in Chapter 8, laughter appears to trigger the relaxation response in our autonomic nervous system. There is a sudden dissipation of fear and our parasympathetic nervous system is more strongly activated than the fight-or-flight-oriented sympathetic nervous system. Researchers have found that nerves from the sympathetic and parasympathetic nervous systems terminate at key centers of the immune system.[10] When we relax and laugh, the immune system can directly register the change. A prolonged state of humor-induced relaxation undoubtedly enhances the immune response, as do virtually all stress-relieving activities.

"One of the common characteristics of serious illness is panic," observed writer and editor Norman Cousins. "Medical science has been able to identify the negative effects of such emotions. . . . It is essential to control the panic. Many physicians make a special effort to encourage their patients' will to live and, indeed, the full range of the positive emotions. For the best way to deal with the panic is to replace it. It is in this context that laughter—and the positive emotions in general—perform a useful function. By changing the mood of the patient the physician is able to set an auspicious stage for treatment. It is useful, I believe, to reach beyond laughter to all of the positive emotions—hope, faith, love, will to live, purpose, and confidence."[11]

The placebo effect has one other important benefit. It shifts a feeling of helplessness to one of control. This occurs whenever a sympathetic doctor assures us that he will find a way to help. By going to the doctor we have acted to take control of our illness and that can boost both our attitude and our immune system. Even when the illness would not necessarily respond strictly to the immune system, this is important. For instance, the placebo effect is highly important in treating many mental illnesses. If the therapist persuades the patient that he can get well, the patient tends to make the maximum effort and the outcome of treatment is often much better.

There is one final mystery. Why does prolonged fear depress the immune system? Wouldn't it be better if the immune response were enhanced so we would have a better chance of surviving a fearful environment? This is particularly puzzling since, among other things, the decline in immune response slows wound healing and increases the possibility of infection. Scientists do not yet know the answer to this difficult question. They theorize that shutting down the immune response is like shutting down the digestive system, which also occurs during the fear response—both these actions may conserve energy that can be channeled into more immediate fight-or-flight needs.[12] But another theory postulates that this decline in immune response may be nature's way of thinning a population when it gets too dense for the environment to support. The maximum decline in the immune response occurs during long-term stress. One important source of this stress for animals is an increase in population density. If rats are crowded into a cage, their fertility decreases as well as their immune response. In the wild, significant numbers of rats and other mammals are sometimes observed dying off suddenly when population densities are great. Studies of these dead animals reveal severely weakened immune systems. Humans may have inherited a similar response to long-term stress from our early mammalian ancestors. If this theory proves true it clearly has important health implications both for the rapidly growing worldwide human population and the pattern of crowding into urban areas that began with the rise of civilization.

Over the last ten thousand years, the human population has exploded from around 10 million to almost 6 billion today. Given the potential effects of overcrowding on the human immune system, the population explosion could lead to further AIDS-like epidemics as other viruses emerge from the tropical rain forests and elsewhere into the crowded urban centers. If the human species is to survive in these large populations, it is essential for us to learn much more about the relationship between fear and the immune system.

The entire population issue centers on questions involving human sexual behavior. Yet this is a painful subject for our species. Of all the social mammals, we are the only species that mates overwhelmingly in private. Our sexual habits and intense sexual fears make issues surrounding reproduction—birth control, abortion, promiscuity, and so forth—particularly difficult. How did humans evolve such unusual sexual behavior? When private copulation does occur in other social animals, it is often due to fear. A typical dominant male gorilla, for example, has a harem of three to six females and copulates openly with receptive females. But occasionally females will try to sneak away from the watchful dominant male to have sex with a lesser male. This is done in private because if they are caught by the dominant male there will often be a bloody fight between the two males.

There are many theories that try to explain the unprecedented human pattern of private lovemaking. One of the most common is that private sexual activity promotes social cooperation. If humans copulated publicly, this would increase the interest of other males and females in having sex, and social cooperation would be more difficult. But with few exceptions, public sexual activity is the pattern with the common and pygmy chimpanzees. Why wouldn't it work for us? Why do we require so much more social cooperation than our cousins the chimps? Scientists have no firm answers. One possibility rests on the unusual vulnerability of human beings. Despite their sometimes comical appearance, chimpanzees are skillful survivors. Their social organization is sufficiently advanced to spot predators and they have retained their extraordinary tree-climbing skill, an ability that humans have largely lost. Few predators can successfully chase a chimpanzee through the trees. As relatively clumsy tree climbers, humans are basically stuck on the ground, easy prey for most large predators unless the band of humans is well organized and armed with protective tools like spears, axes, and fire. Early humans may have developed the pattern of having sex at night after the band had found a safe hiding place, so that sexual activity would not distract from the close social cooperation needed to find food and defend themselves during the day. But if this was so, why couldn't that nightly sexual activity be more open and even promiscuous?

The answer may lie with the extraordinary helplessness of the human infant. Given that helplessness on the savanna of Africa, it would take both the male and female, working closely together for a number of years, to feed, protect, and teach a child the skills necessary to survive. As Jared Diamond points out, private exclusive sexual activity powerfully cements the bond between male and female as a parental and economic unit.[13] Fears surrounding sexual performance and sexual attractiveness might have arisen because inadequate sexual performance or attractiveness by either male or female would tend to diminish the ability to create and maintain this bond. There may be other evolutionary sources for the multitude of human fears that surround sexual activity. For the early human male to spend years of his short life helping to raise a child, he would have to have some assurance that the child was truly his genetic offspring. This might be the source of a common fear that falls under the category of jealousy (male version). An unfaithful female would cause a male to run the risk of raising other men's children, leaving no genetic offspring of his own.

For early human females, on the other hand, sexual activity might be viewed fearfully because pregnancy and childbirth among humans, unlike chimpanzees and other apes, is risky, painful, and—prior to modern medical advances—sometimes fatal to the mother. Under these circumstances, females would not take sexual activity lightly. A female on the savanna would have a strong incentive to mate with a male that she believed would work closely with her in raising the dependent infant. A strong fear of abandonment might develop in females, because to be abandoned by the male in this hostile setting would be an almost certain death sentence for the infant and perhaps for the mother herself. Thus the prospect of her mate being lured away by another female would be a perpetual source of fear and the root of female jealousy. Infidelity by either partner might also be a source of fear for males and females equally because it would increase the likelihood of contracting sexual diseases that might then be passed on to the other partner. Even today, sexual jealousy is one of the leading causes of murder among both men and women.

Our fearful nature adds an unusual dimension to aggression in human society: it can make us extremely brave and extremely violent. The exploits of Randy "Duke" Cunningham, who served as an extraordinary Navy fighter pilot, illustrate the depth of this bravery.[14] Cunningham as a young pilot in Vietnam faced almost impossible odds in a dogfight for which he was nominated for the Congressional Medal of Honor. He was flying his F-4 Phantom with five others from his squadron when they were ambushed by twenty-two North Vietnamese MIG fighters. He saw his executive officer with three MIGs on his tail. He was momentarily overcome with fear, he told me. "My mind went into slow motion, I don't know for how long. It was if it was trying to take me out of this predicament. Then, suddenly, I snapped back into real time. I tried to think of every reason in the world to cut and run. But in the end I just couldn't."

Cunningham shot down three MIGs in ferocious dogfights. His total of five kills that day made him the Navy's first air ace of the Vietnam War.

The tremendous fear we feel when faced with violence and the prospect of death makes eliminating that fear all the more pressing. If you kill an enemy, you permanently eliminate his ability to cause you future fear or pain. People frequently perceive this sharp reduction in fear as pleasurable, which is why nations so often celebrate their victories in war, even though each victory represents the slaughter of countless other human beings. Similarly, supporters of the death penalty often celebrate the

execution of a notorious murderer. Yet human fear is exceptionally volatile. Even the death of a rival may not be enough to quell it. We have
touched on the concept of fear contagion, as when panic rapidly spreads
among a group of people. This might be called subject contagion—the
number of people subject to the fear increases swiftly. But there is another
form of fear contagion. Let's call it object contagion. This is when the
object of our fear—people, animals, or events—spreads rapidly. Our
primitive fear system naturally lumps the things around us into simplistic
categories. One snake becomes all snakes. With our large brain's capacity
for creating these broad categories, we have a tendency to experience
enormously rapid and widespread object contagion. If a large category
of persons is the object of fear and hatred (the Jews and Gypsies to Hitler,
for example) then there may be an attempt to destroy that entire category.
In the case of a violent act against another person, the fear of retaliation
takes hold. Since the other person is part of a larger group (family,
community, even nation), there is a tendency for the fear to spread to
the entire category of people who may seek to retaliate. Thus human
violence can escalate to holocaust proportions.

From earliest recorded times to the ethnic cleansing in the former
Yugoslavia, the frequent episodes of genocide and attempted genocide
that mar human history are not solely the result of willfulness and malevo-
lence, but an outgrowth of the way irrational fear is embedded in the
human nervous system. Both the primitive fear system and rational consciousness contain a model of the world. Within the primitive fear system's
model our basic fears and desires are expressed as middle-level categories.
This is a world of simplified cues and stereotypes that the primitive
system continually uses to monitor the world around us for potential
danger. This early warning system operates in the fraction of a second
prior to conscious awareness and can be critically important in a life-or-
death situation. In contrast, rational consciousness can recognize the
unique qualities of a person, object, or event. Consciousness contains a
model whose potential for detail is unlimited because the time it can take
for reflection is unlimited. Nevertheless, consciousness is perfectly capable
of hasty generalization, misplaced causality, and other types of fallacious
and superficial reasoning. It just commits these fallacies more slowly than
the primitive fear system. If you tell someone with a severe snake phobia
that there is a snake sitting in a cage in the next room, it will be difficult
for him to think about anything else. Even though the snake poses no
real threat and he knows it, his primitive fear system forces him to focus

his attention on the snake and the fear it represents. There is a constant competition in all of us between primitive awareness and rational consciousness for control of attention and behavior. We are always struggling to find the balance between gut instinct and rational analysis. In a panic, the primitive fear system can seize total control, blocking out the rational fear system and our conscious model of the world and forcing us to react in a primitive fight-or-flight mode. Demagogic leaders like Adolf Hitler seek to connect with the primitive awareness of their followers, appealing to primitive stereotypes and simplistic hopes and fears. When leaders like this are successful in capturing the public imagination, they are capable of releasing primitive fear and anger in deadly, irrational torrents.

Demagogues appeal to prejudice, and prejudice is a product of the primitive fear system, which easily creates primitive stereotypes of people along racial, ethnic, or religious lines. Prejudice involves judging someone solely as a member of a superficial category rather than as a unique individual. These stereotypes can be positive or negative. When they are negative they resemble a phobia—a phobia involving human beings instead of snakes or spiders. If a person has absorbed these negative stereotypes, then they are as difficult to eradicate as any phobia since they manifest themselves preconsciously and can take on the full force of the primitive fear system's life-or-death orientation. Prejudiced attitudes among groups of people are often denied but can usually be detected if there is a hesitance about intermarriage. The prejudiced reaction to a person as a member of a stereotyped class intrudes before the person's unique qualities can be consciously assessed. People with and without these stereotypes can see the same situation in a completely different way. An outsider going to Northern Ireland, for example, sees the inhabitants not first as Catholics or Protestants but as individuals. The depth of the hatred and mistrust between these two groups can seem totally bewildering. The primitive fear systems of infants and toddlers are not sufficiently developed to absorb these fairly abstract primitive stereotypes about other people, and very young children of different racial, ethnic, and religious groups play together spontaneously, if allowed to do so, no matter what the attitudes of their parents. But older children raised in a prejudiced environment seem to absorb these stereotypes readily. Racial prejudice and other forms of irrational prejudice by one group of human beings against another should be classified among the most persistent and dangerous diseases of fear.

{ Chapter 12 }

Conscious Mastery

There is growing evidence that consciousness itself may have developed as an evolutionary response to the problem of fear. The neocortex—the folded outer layer of the brain essential to consciousness and self-awareness—evolved from the emotional centers of the limbic system. The rational fear system developed within the neocortex.

This rational system gives us a highly flexible way to program our fears that is far more sophisticated than the fight-or-flight reaction of the primitive fear system. If scientists announce this week that cranberries cause cancer, we stop buying them. If next week, they admit they made a mistake, we start buying them again. Thanks to the rational system, our fears can be exceptionally pliant—a unique attribute of human nature. Yet rational fear system's struggle to master the primitive fear system consciously never ends. We rationally know that we are far safer riding in a commercial airliner than driving on the freeway. But we may nevertheless feel queasy when we look down at the ground far below. What if something did happen?

At 11:10 A.M. on November 23, 1996, Franklin P. Huddle and his wife Chanya were relaxing in the cabin of an Ethiopian Airlines Boeing 767. They were on the second leg of a trip that would take them from

Bombay, India, where fifty-three-year-old Franklin was U.S. consul general, to a safari in Kenya. They never made the safari. About twenty minutes after Flight 961 left Addis Ababa, Ethiopia, a voice in broken English came over the intercom. It said something about a hijacking and opposition. There was confusion among the passengers. It took them a while to realize that the plane had been hijacked by three men whose motives were never clear. Two of the three hijackers walked into the business-class cabin. They were slender, one well-dressed and the other tough looking. They carried a small ax and an object they said was a bomb.

"The mood in the cabin was a sort of fixed nervousness. I felt a mixture of anger and frustration that we couldn't challenge these guys," said Franklin. "For the next few hours we didn't know where we were. . . . I tried to get passengers next to us to look out the window. I wanted intelligence! But they kept reading their newspapers. People were jittery. They did not want to irritate the hijackers."

Unknown to the passengers, the hijackers had ordered the plane's captain to head for Australia, ignoring his pleas to refuel the aircraft. There was a state of confusion in the cockpit because it was so hard to communicate with the hijackers.

Chanya, forty-three, a former psychiatric nurse and a native of Thailand, was optimistic: "I wasn't nervous at all—in a kidnapping like this, usually you don't die. I thought the military or someone would save us, like in the movies."

After almost four hours of silence, the intercom crackled to life. The captain announced that the hijackers had refused his request to refuel and one engine had already shut down. He ordered the cabin crew to prepare for a crash landing. Franklin, an experienced pilot of small planes, immediately knew the terrible danger they were facing. Chanya tried to remain calm: "I said, 'Don't worry, we will be on CNN.' And Franklin said, 'This is no joke—we're dying,' " Franklin said.

"There was a fair amount of panic now," Franklin recalled. "Some people were crying. But we stayed calm and took charge. Chanya was amazing. Several people owe her their lives, because she helped them keep calm and find their life vests. We could hear people in tourist class inflating their vests—pop, pop, pop. After the crash, their section turned upside down, and they were trapped under the fuselage by the air in their jackets. We told people near us not to inflate theirs prematurely, and to sit down."

"I asked my husband to get his extra glasses, and I put them and his passport in a plastic bag in his pocket," Chanya said. "And I asked him to give me one hundred dollars—I wanted to have money when we landed."

"In the last two minutes, I was really focused and much less nervous," Franklin said.

Chanya recalled that Franklin "looked at me and said, 'I love you.' I said, 'No, don't say that, we will not die.' "

The giant aircraft eased down onto the water about five hundred yards off Great Comoro Island in the Indian Ocean. There were several resorts nearby and the tourists watched in disbelief as the plane skimmed the water. One person videotaped the entire crash.

"I intentionally relaxed at the moment of impact," Franklin said. "At first it was gentle; the second bounce was like a sixty-miles-an-hour collision. Then there was a tremendous tumbling." The plane began cartwheeling and breaking apart. "Water gushed in," said Chanya, "and I closed my eyes. Somehow I came to the surface. I opened my eyes and saw Franklin, and he said, 'We're alive.' "

"The seats were like inner tubes," Franklin said, "they floated to the surface. We went from sitting upright in the plane to sitting upright in the water."

Bodies were drifting around them, as were windsurfers from the nearby resorts. People at the resorts rushed out to help, and the Huddles were pulled into a rubber dinghy. Franklin's left foot was sliced open and his right hand was injured. Chanya suffered only minor cuts. "It wasn't so bad—we are lucky, and we feel sorry for the poor people that died," Chanya said.

Of the 175 people on board, only 50 survived, including two of the hijackers. It was the second-deadliest hijacking in aviation history.[1]

Franklin and Chanya Huddle's behavior was an extraordinary example of maintaining conscious mastery in the most impossible of situations. Let me summarize the structure of fear that has emerged in the last eleven chapters and use this structure to analyze the Huddles' experience.

We have identified three fear systems—primitive, rational, and conscious—that play different roles in the creation, control, and experience of fear. The primitive system, centered in the limbic system, serves as an alarm. It scans all external and internal stimuli, generating a continual preconscious emotional response. The rational fear system, centered in the frontal lobes, uses advanced cortical reasoning to divide reality into categories and determine cause-and-effect relationships. It uses the results of this analysis along with the entire life experience to plan, predict, and generate scenarios for the present, past, and future. Under the direction of consciousness, the rational fear system selectively inhibits or releases the primitive fear system. Consciousness, which seems to involve the entire neocortex and other parts of the brain as well, is the center of self-awareness and decision making. It balances the other components of the mind, especially the primitive and rational fear systems, and the right and left cerebral hemispheres.

As soon as the Huddles registered the word "hijacking," they were fixated on finding out what was going on. Franklin kept trying to obtain more information, but the other passengers had difficulty cooperating with him. Their tendency was to freeze. In times of danger, when there is no immediate avenue of escape, the primitive fear system tries to shut off any unnecessary movement, reasoning that if you stay still you might not be noticed.

Primitive limbic reasoning is shaped by its origin as part of the ancient alarm system. It operates under the severe time constraints of preconscious processing, which must identify a threat and estimate the potential danger in about a tenth of a second. It can only classify objects, events, and phenomena into middle-level categories. Although the limitations of primitive limbic reasoning are understandable, given the constraints, they often seem irrational to the neocortex (we are consciously embarrassed by our phobias) and result in the twin logical fallacies of hasty generalization and misplaced causality. The shortcoming of primitive reasoning can lead to the creation of phobias and other damaging and dangerous prejudices, and to a simplistic view of the world as made up of simple categories evoking primal emotions. If the primitive fear system generates a preconscious emotional reaction that passes a certain threshold, which varies depending on the context and the individual temperament, then a major fight-or-flight response can be triggered.

The primitive fight-or-flight response plays out in two basic ways. One response is fear-flight-panic, the other is fear-fight-anger. Alarm calls can quickly activate the primitive fear systems of individuals and deactivate the frontal lobes because the brain interprets alarm calls as signaling a threat to survival, which takes precedence over all other thoughts and behaviors. Depending on the context, the alarm call can lead to fear-flight-panic response and a mass panic or to the fear-fight-anger response and mob behavior.

Franklin's first reaction was anger. If a substantial number of the other passengers had had a similar reaction, it is possible they might have tried to jump the hijackers. But the threat of a bomb seemed to push most of the passengers that Franklin observed into the panic response. Chanya, in an amazing display of self-control, remained calm, and experienced neither panic nor anger.

The degree of perceived helplessness or control over a fearsome situation determines the degree of fear, the likelihood of panic, and the potential for anger or violence. An optimistic attitude tends to help preserve mental and behavioral flexibility and a sense of control. Helpless terror is the most dreaded type of fear. Controlled fear is more palatable and is even sought out by some in the form of action movies, roller coaster rides, extreme sports, and other thrilling experiences.

The sense of helplessness on Flight 961 increased dramatically when the captain announced that he was out of fuel and would have to crash-land the plane in the ocean. Panic quickly spread and there were signs of confusion and disorientation among some of the passengers.

The primitive fear system is primarily responsible for habituation and sensitization, which are basically subconscious processes. Phobias, including prepared fears, are a form of sensitization. Unusually intense sensitization along with specific malfunctions in the fear systems can lead to post-traumatic stress disorder, obsessive-compulsive disorder, and other anxiety disorders. The rational fear system is sensitized primarily with noradrenaline and can aid in habituation through cognitive processes. Consciousness can also aid in habituation through the exercise of will and the inhibition through the frontal lobes of the primitive fear system.

Fear and pain seem to be the foundation of most, if not all, emotions, with desire and pleasure being experienced as variations in the levels of fear and pain. Natural opiates like endorphins as well as neurochemicals like dopamine are a primary natural method for reducing fear and pain and producing a sense of pleasure and well-being. A reduction in fear is perceived as pleasurable, while an increase in fear is perceived as painful. Humor and laughter are produced by a sudden activation of the relaxation response in the parasympathetic nervous system. Fear leads one to avoid an object or situation because of its likelihood for increasing pain, while desire leads one to seek out an object or situation because of its likelihood for reducing fear and pain. The dynamic balance between the sympathetic and parasympathetic nervous systems, which reflect the activity of the limbic system and neocortex, helps determine the body's current emotional state.

When the plane began to prepare for the crash, the Huddles refused to give in to helplessness. They used all their knowledge and experience in making plans to survive. By taking responsibility for nearby passengers they helped limit the contagious spread of panic and ensure that their rational fear systems stayed in control. The neurochemicals generated by the primitive fear system gave them unusual focus. Chanya repeatedly used humor to try to relax the situation and maintain her optimism. By staying clearheaded and aware, the Huddles were able to avoid fatal mistakes like prematurely inflating life jackets and helped others do the same.

The frontal lobes are asymmetrical, with the right cerebral hemisphere in most people specializing in the conscious perception of negative emotions coming from the limbic system and the left cerebral hemisphere specializing in the perception of positive emotions that are produced by suppressing the fear and pain of the limbic system. This is part of the general asymmetry observed in the split-brain phenomenon. Limbic emotions are produced preconsciously but are also experienced consciously (though nonverbally) through the right hemisphere, and particularly through the right prefrontal cortex and the orbitofrontal cortex. Consistently greater activity in the left hemisphere, particularly the left prefrontal cortex, indicates an optimistic personality. Consistently greater activity in the right hemisphere, particularly the right prefrontal cortex, indicates a pessimistic personality.

The normal mind experiences mental pain as well as physical pain, and fears both. Mental pain or anxiety is produced by the generation of scenarios by the frontal lobes through the rational fear system. Mental pain is also produced by loss of valued people or things whose presence tended to reduce fear and pain. Mental pain is an important source of empathy because out of the experience of suffering the mind can create a scenario in which it is intuiting the mental or physical pain of others.

As the plane nosed down toward the water, Chanya continued to focus on planning for survival, refusing to give in to despair. She made sure her husband had his extra pair of glasses and that she had some money in case they were separated. She kept reminding her husband that they were going to live, even refusing to say a final good-bye. Franklin consciously tried to relax as the plane hit the water. By activating his parasympathetic nervous system he was ensuring that he wouldn't be overwhelmed by fear, and would thus have the maximum flexibility of thought and behavior to deal with whatever might happen. They were lucky, but their calm, controlled response to the crisis ensured that they had the maximum chance of survival.

The Huddles' heroic behavior during this crisis represents the three fear systems operating at their best. The couple used the concentration and focus of the alerting mechanism of the primitive fear system but still were able to maintain conscious mastery and control. But the fear systems are also capable of producing the worst possible behavior. Take prejudice and racism, for example. Here, conscious mastery is lost and primitive limbic reasoning lumps individual human beings into amorphous categories based on race, religion, ethnicity, or some other general classification. These categories become the object of fear, mistrust, and hatred. Prejudice is a kind of phobia about other groups of human beings, and many of the same behavioral techniques used to treat phobias can be used to lessen prejudice.

The orbitofrontal cortex is the primary structure responsible for the modification, suppression, and extinction of primitive fears and the primitive fear response. The brain remains plastic and can be rewired throughout adulthood, though sometimes with difficulty. There are different strategies for behavior therapy, all designed to lead to habituation.

Mental disorders limit our free will. There are some conditions in which conscious control is extremely difficult without a long-term, sustained effort (episodic dyscontrol, severe phobias, obsessive-compulsive disorder, panic disorder), some conditions in which conscious control is possible but arduous (moderate phobias, mass panic), and some conditions in which control should consistently be maintained (mild fears).

The brain has evolved a complex set of systems in dynamic balance to give our bodies and minds the flexibility to react to any given situation. These systems are in dynamic tension and often conflict with each other and include the sympathetic nervous system and parasympathetic nervous system, fear-pain and desire-pleasure, the right cerebral hemisphere and the left cerebral hemisphere, the rational fear system and the primitive fear system, habituation and sensitization.

We can illustrate the difficulty of eradicating prejudice by returning again to the snake phobia, which is a paradigm for primitive system processing and reasoning. The primitive fear system only understands two propositions: all snakes are harmless and all snakes are dangerous. It is incapable of understanding the more sophisticated proposition that some snakes are harmless and others are dangerous. The first thing to do in treating anxiety disorders like phobias is to reinforce the logical understanding of the rational fear system. If a person consciously and mistakenly believes that all snakes, indeed, are dangerous then this error is reinforcing the primitive fear system and must be corrected. The next step uses a series of techniques including exposure, visualization, and modeling, to reinforce the primitive proposition that all snakes are harmless. This is a nonverbal, preconscious understanding that the primitive fear system learns only by experience. We call it desensitization.

But since the proposition that all snakes are harmless is false, if the desensitized patient does have a subsequent fear experience with a dangerous snake, the entire phobia may be resurrected. That is the frustration of dealing with the primitive fear system. The only two propositions it understands—all snakes are dangerous and all snakes are harmless—are both false. Yet this is the only logic we can use if we have any hope of desensitizing the primitive fear system when a powerful fear is involved. The sole alternative is for the rational fear system to suppress completely the primitive fear system's response, and that can be difficult or impossible. Since we are dealing with a false proposition (all snakes are harmless) then just one negative experience will shift the primitive fear system into the other false proposition (all snakes are dangerous) and the phobic behavior.

We also see this kind of primitive limbic reasoning at work in racial and ethnic prejudice. In the case of the Croats and the Serbs, for example, if one Croat happens to be a psychopath who tortures and kills Serbs, there will be a strong tendency for Serbs who have been raised with a preconscious prejudice to conclude from this one incident: "See, all Croats are evil." The Nazis explicitly played on primitive limbic reasoning not only by classifying their enemies as vermin and snakes but also by trumpeting individual wrongdoers who happened to belong to these classes, while of course ignoring "Aryan" criminals. The Soviet and Chinese Communists did the same thing with kulaks, bourgeois counterrevolutionaries, capitalist roaders, and other so-called class enemies. Like phobias, prejudice can easily return if it is not rooted out over time. The hope is that future generations won't have these preconscious prejudices at all and we will not see the world through prejudiced eyes, just as most outsiders who go to Northern Ireland don't see the distinctions between Catholics and Protestants. They do not have the preconscious prejudices of those who are raised in an atmosphere charged with ethnic tension.[2]

Mental illness is a source of another persistent prejudice. People have experience with physical pain, and they empathize with the burn victim or other injured person who has to go through terrible suffering to recover—and they view such a person as immensely courageous. But they may have never experienced the tremendous mental pain that accompanies a brain disease like depression or panic disorder. They often have trouble empathizing and think the person is weak, when in reality fighting a malfunctioning brain twenty-four hours a day, seven days a week takes the kind of courage most people cannot imagine.

It is interesting to compare the perception of mental disability to physical disability. For example, when actor Christopher Reeve had his riding accident and became paralyzed, people viewed him as heroic and his wife as courageous for sticking with him. If a spouse leaves an injured mate under such circumstances, the individual is often criticized. If the spouse leaves because coping with the injury is too stressful, people will say that this is the kind of stress one has a moral and ethical duty to bear, that it boosts your appreciation of life, and makes you stronger. But if Reeve had had a mental illness (a brain disease instead of a spinal injury), the perception of many people would have been exactly the opposite. He would have been viewed as weak and pitiful. Some people would have felt sorry for his wife for having to put up with him. Many of us do not appreciate the simplest and most important things in life, particularly having a healthy brain that does not generate painful, irrational fears that cripple our thoughts and behaviors.[3]

It has often been observed that no sane man would willingly go to war. Yet millions of men and women have willingly fought and died for ideals they believed in. How can that be? It is certainly true that if guided only by the primitive fear system—with its innate fear of death and its tendency to panic and run at the first sign of danger—no one would go to war. Clearly consciousness and the rational fear system can, with patience and persistence, be trained to overcome the primitive system's aversion to risk.

Yet we ignore at our peril the evolutionary wisdom embodied in the brain's primitive system. We can use the rational fear system to instill an attitude of courage and self-sacrifice sufficiently strong to overcome the innate fear of death. But we should do so cautiously and selectively. The risk represented by war is worth taking in only the most compelling cases. Suppressing our natural fear of death can lead not only to courageous soldiers, but fanatical terrorists and suicide bombers.

Humans, particularly males, have evolved not only with prepared fears but with what might be called prepared violence. Although as in all matters of the brain, individuals vary, it is generally true that males can be quickly desensitized to violence and motivated to act aggressively on behalf of themselves and others.[4] This is the trait we rely on to transform millions of civilians into soldiers quickly in times of national crisis like World War II. Soldiers can be resensitized to violence, however, as the millions of returning veterans who adjusted normally to civilian society have demonstrated. This prepared violence evolved as part of the fight response to the fear reaction. Evolution allows an individual to be tuned to his environment, so if sustained aggressive action is necessary to ensure the survival of himself and the group he belongs to, he will be ready to respond appropriately.

"It's hard to imagine how we, and other nice ordinary people that we know, could bring ourselves to look helpless people in the face while killing them," writes physiologist Jared Diamond, recalling his experiences doing fieldwork in New Guinea. "I came closest to being able to imagine it when a friend whom I had long known told me of a genocidal massacre at which he had been a killer. Kariniga is a gentle Tudawhe tribesman who worked with me in New Guinea. We shared life-threatening situations, fears, and triumphs, and I like and admire him. One evening after I had known Kariniga for five years, he told me of an episode from his youth. There had been a long history of conflict between the Tudawhes and a neighboring village of Daribi tribesmen. Tudawhes and Daribis seem quite similar to me, but Kariniga had come to view Daribis as inexpressibly vile. In a series of ambushes the Daribis finally succeeded in picking off many Tudawhes, including Kariniga's father, until the surviving Tudawhes became desperate. All the remaining Tudawhe men surrounded the Daribi village at night and set fire to the huts at dawn. As the sleepy Daribis stumbled down the steps of the burning huts, they were speared. Some Daribis succeeded in escaping to hide in the forest, where Tudawhes tracked down and killed most of them during the following weeks. But the establishment of Australian government control ended the hunt before Kariniga could catch his father's killer. Since that evening, I've often found myself shuddering as I recalled details of it—the glow in Kariniga's eyes as he told me of the dawn massacre; those intensely satisfying moments when he finally drove his spear into some of his people's murderers; and his tears of rage and frustration at the escape of his father's killer, whom he still hoped to kill someday with poison.

That evening, I thought I understood how at least one nice person had brought himself to kill. The potential for genocide that circumstances thrust on Kariniga lies within all of us.''[5]

Given this prepared capacity for violence in human nature, a society should be wary of creating an environment, especially for children and adolescents, that inadvertently turns them into soldiers. This may explain at least part of what is happening on the streets. An atmosphere that glorifies violence, aggression, and guns and carves up territory so that the clearest possible distinction can be made between "us" and "them" is extremely explosive. The FBI estimated in 1997 that there are around half a million people, from children to adults, who belong to approximately eight thousand gangs in the United States. We tend to view gang members as aberrant. But if these same young men were in uniform killing the enemies of their country we would be applauding them. There is no excuse, of course, for random, wanton violence. But as a society we should not only be careful to avoid creating conditions that aggravate this tendency to violence, we should be doing a better job of thinking of social conditions that suppress it. The coarsening of society represents the increasing ascendance of primitive limbic reasoning—with its primal emotional responses and simplistic categories—over advanced neocortical reasoning, which thrives on deliberation, nuance, complexity, and extended conscious reflection.

Hollywood has found that mass audiences prefer happy endings. There may be lots of violence and killing in between, but if the ending isn't happy, the film has a better than average chance of failing at the box office. Serious films that play the art houses usually have a darker tone and are more complex. Think of a film like Federico Fellini's *La Strada*, in which the heroine dies miserable and the antihero—a brutish, inarticulate circus strongman—pathetically perseveres in his chosen profession. Why are artists drawn to the dark side of human nature? One possible explanation for this tendency is that artists are often introverts, and introverts, neuroscience is discovering, seem to activate their right frontal cortex more strongly than the left. It is the right frontal lobe through which the negative forces of the limbic system—the fear, the violence, the primal desires—flow into consciousness. In a sense, this is where many artists live and this is the territory they want to explore. Introverts are more sensitive to themselves and other people. And the emotions they feel in their right frontal lobe are often painful. This helps explain the unusually high incidence among artists and writers of depression, alcoholism (alcohol is often used to combat depression), and other mood disorders. Artists delve into the nonverbal, spatial, holistic realm of the right hemisphere, but that also happens to be where these negative emotions lurk. This accident of brain asymmetry tends to push many artists toward the dark side.[6]

Introverts are in the minority and their sensibilities can sometimes offend the majority. What is it that makes people happy? In recent years psychologists have turned more attention to this issue, discovering that human beings are, by and large, happier than one might think after watching the evening news. In surveys, only about one in ten report that they are unhappy. The majority say they are reasonably happy while almost a third report they are very happy. This correlates remarkably well with studies of frontal lobe activation among adults. Only 10 to 15 percent of adults strongly activate the right frontal lobe and are classified as inhibited, pessimistic, and introverts. Between 30 and 35 percent strongly activate the left frontal lobe and are classified as optimistic extroverts. The rest mainly activate the left frontal lobe but not as strongly as the most extroverted adults. This rough breakdown on happiness holds across racial, gender, and even economic classifications. The superrich are not that much happier than the average American.

What are the qualities that make people very happy? "In study after study, four traits characterize happy people," say psychologists David G. Myers and Ed Diener. "First, especially in individualistic Western cultures, they like themselves. They have high self-esteem and usually believe themselves to be more ethical, more intelligent, less prejudiced, better able to get along with others, and healthier than the average person. . . . Second, happy people typically feel personal control. Those with little or no control over their lives—such as prisoners, nursing home patients, severely impoverished groups or individuals, and citizens of totalitarian regimes—suffer lower morale and worse health. Third, happy people are usually optimistic. Fourth, most happy people are extroverted. Although one might expect that introverts would live more happily in the serenity of their less stressed lives, extroverts are happier—whether alone or with others."[7]

Helplessness is the enemy of happiness and the ally of fear. A vital element of feeling happy is having a sense of control, of being free to shift your attention to the things that are important to you and mold your behavior accordingly. People burdened by irrational fears don't have that luxury because of the idiosyncrasies of the brain's fear circuits. For example, most of us feel confident—too often overconfident—about driving a car because we have a sense of control. Yet there are people who have a phobic reaction to driving. These people obsess about their helplessness to control the actions of other drivers. They are overwhelmed by the fear that the drivers around them will suddenly take some reckless action that will cause a horrible accident. While perfectly comfortable on lightly traveled roads, they are terrified at the thought of driving on a busy freeway.

This irrational sense of helplessness can take many forms. Take the case of a middle-aged man who had an intense fear of heights. It was impossible for him to climb even two flights of stairs in a building without being overcome with terror. His fear became so crippling that even seeing a tall building became intolerable because he would imagine the horror of being on top of it. Yet this same man was a private pilot who thought nothing of flying his plane ten thousand feet into the air. Actually, it is not unusual for people with a fear of heights to have no particular fear of flying.

To our primitive fear system, something is present on top of a building that isn't present in the cockpit or cabin of an airplane. Some primitive cue for the fear of heights is missing in a plane. Perhaps what is missing is the sense that we can fall out of the plane, the way we sense we can fall off a cliff or a building. The fear of flying is quite real for many people but it seems to center around a lack of control or claustrophobia rather than a fear of heights. When you are in a plane, you normally don't have the sense that you might fall out of it, though you may fear that the plane itself will fall. This seems to make a crucial difference to the primitive fear system, which signals a fear of heights whenever you have a sense that you might fall (a fear that evolved early in human evolution) but not when you sense that the structure you are traveling in might fall (something that would have been beyond the experience of early humans). This quirk in the primitive fear system is a reminder that our primitive awareness constantly searches the shifting landscape of our experience not just for the dangers of today but for dangers that were present one hundred thousand to one hundred fifty thousand years ago when *Homo sapiens* evolved with a limbic system whose architecture remains basically the same today.

Science believes that a hundred thousand years ago humans lived in small, tightly knit bands resembling the hunter-gatherer societies that persisted into the twentieth century in remote parts of the world. Social cooperation was essential because the unaided individual was generally too weak to survive for long in such a harsh environment. The complete helplessness of human infants also made cooperation imperative. The dependence of early humans on each other, starting in infancy, generated a fear of separation that continues to be a fundamental part of the human psyche. The ultimate form of separation is the death of another human being, particularly a friend or loved one. This may explain why our grief, which flows from the limbic system, is often so overwhelming and inconsolable. Friends and loved ones were the people who helped early humans survive.

There would undoubtedly have been fighting among the different bands of early humans living near each other as they competed for scarce resources, just as today we see such fighting among rival bands of chimpanzees. This hostility carries over in our tendency to be fearful and suspicious of outsiders.

Fighting would have occured not just between bands of humans but within the separate groups themselves. Just as there is infighting and jockeying for power in social groups today, we assume there was similar infighting within the bands of early humans. This infighting would have been deadly serious, particularly for the losers. Any lowering of social status or weakening of ties to the group could be fatal both physically and genetically, resulting in less food, less protection, less access to mates, and even being killed or banished. This is another dimension of the fear of separation that manifests itself today in our sometimes intense fear of the disapproval of others and in the various social phobias.

The fear of public speaking is the most common of the social phobias. Nearly half of people who admit to having phobias say that their worst fear is of public speaking. We tend to feel safer as part of a crowd of observers. If we are suddenly called upon to speak, the feeling of fright can be overwhelming, leading in some people to uncontrollable trembling caused by an extreme tensing of the muscles in preparation for the fight-or-flight response. Why should anyone who has to deliver an innocuous speech to a local civic group feel such a terrible case of stage fright? It seems ridiculous. But again we must look back to early humans for the answer. Anyone who stood out in a band of early humans was subject to sanctions that could mean life or death. Speaking in front of a group carried the greatest danger. With so many watching, the consequences of a mistake or bad impression were multiplied. Humans are extremely fearful and potentially violent. Any person who stands out can become a target of this violence. This is as true today as it was a hundred thousand years ago—remember John F. Kennedy, Martin Luther King, Jr., Robert Kennedy, Malcolm X, the Stalinist purges, the Cultural Revolution in China, and the killing fields of Cambodia under the Khmer Rouge.

The case of Mohandas Gandhi is a poignant example. Trained as a lawyer, Gandhi became so overwhelmed by fear during his first appearance in court in India in 1889 that he was unable to speak. In the humiliating aftermath, he accepted a position as counsel for a Muslim business in South Africa. There he was subjected to a brutal regime of racial discrimination against nonwhites. He was repeatedly manhandled and beaten for trying to assert his rights as a British subject. When he boarded the first-class section on a train, for example, he was physically ejected. Outraged, Gandhi overcame his fear of public speaking and founded a South African civil rights movement. Returning to India, he became the leader of nonviolent resistance to British rule and the internationally revered father of Indian independence. His outspoken opposition to the violence between Hindus and Muslims that was tearing British India apart angered fanatics on both sides. On January 13, 1948, while going to prayer, he was shot to death by a Hindu extremist.

When our primitive fear system detects a situation that involves helplessness, heights, public speaking, spiders, snakes, or the other prepared fears, it has a tendency to interpret them as life-or-death situations, just as if we were living a hundred thousand years ago. This quality of the primitive fear system gives us an explanation of why the strength of our emotional reactions is sometimes so out of proportion to the reality of a situation. We have within our limbic system remnants of a primitive awareness that evolved in much earlier humans for whom a small accident, injury, or mistake could mean swift and terrible death. This primitive awareness has significant drawbacks, but important advantages as well. It gives us the rapid ability to duck, jump, freeze, fight, or flee in a dangerous situation. And it can lead us instinctively and courageously to fight to save our lives and the lives of others. Our rational consciousness, though far more sophisticated, is nevertheless capable of making calculated decisions that are heartless and cruel. The Nazis rationally, coldly, and efficiently planned and carried out the slaughter of six million Jews. Nevertheless rational consciousness has allowed us to probe and analyze our fear responses, distinguishing between the various types of fear and developing ways to control our fears. This is the source of conscious mastery.

In coping with fear, we must first distinguish between rational fears and primitive fears. Rational fears can be countered by knowledge. We can measure, for instance, whether the El Niño warming of the Pacific Ocean exists in any given year. If it does not exist, then we needn't fear the pattern of extreme weather conditions El Niño sometimes causes. Fear, in fact, can aid in the accumulation of knowledge that we use to explain and counter threats that we foresee. The fear reaction, if it does not slide into blind panic, can promote intense concentration, increased energy, and powerful motivation. Fear focuses our attention on the problem and makes it easier to ignore distractions. You'll remember in Chapter 6 how Abraham Pais, while hiding from the Nazis, experienced an amazing improvement in his concentration when working on physics. "I would get up, exercise, have breakfast, then sit down at my little worktable and, presto, thoughts emerged totally unforced, by themselves, you might say," he said. The noradrenaline and other neurochemicals that flood into our frontal lobes during a crisis not only increase our alertness but prod our memory as consciousness searches through our past experiences for guidance. If the fear is sudden and shocking enough, we may experience this deluge of memories as our life flashing before our eyes. Because of the effects of fear on the human mind, the pace of innovation can increase dramatically during wartime, as each side works feverishly to find ways to defeat the other. World War II and the succeeding Cold War period were times of exceptionally rapid scientific and technological progress, as enormous amounts of money and effort were poured into research and development in the name of national defense, producing everything from jet aircraft to computers. But knowledge not only reduces our fear by increasing our control of the world around us through technology, it also increases our fear by identifying and creating new threats, such as nuclear weapons and other means of mass destruction.

One other important reason that knowledge increases more rapidly during a crisis is that fear can allow us to work together more efficiently. When panic occurs, fear causes the rapid distintegration of order. But fear can cause the spontaneous creation of order and cooperation when it takes the form of the fight rather than the flight response. Fear is a powerful promoter of spontaneous cooperation. Political leaders have long known that the quickest way to national unity is the threat of outside attack. Any kind of widespread fear can cause spontaneous cooperation. This is particularly true when there is a compelling alarm call designed to stimulate the fight response. The modern consumerism movement began when Ralph Nader tapped into widespread fears about shoddy and dangerous products beginning with his 1965 book *Unsafe at any Speed: The Designed-in Dangers of the American Automobile.* I interviewed Nader as a college journalist in 1970 and was impressed by his intense and outspoken anger. Rachel Carson struck a similar chord with the public in her 1962 book *Silent Spring,* which focused on the dangers of pesticides like DDT and helped transform the older conservationist movement into more militant environmentalism. Martin Luther King, Jr., tapped into the widespread fear and resentment over segregation among African-Americans to help create the civil rights movement. The fear of a generation of students facing the prospect of fighting a poorly understood war in Southeast Asia flared into the antiwar movement of the 1960s. Protest movements that arose in the former Soviet-dominated Eastern bloc, such as Solidarity in Poland, were partly responses to the fear of continued totalitarian rule. Wherever there is widespread fear among human beings, our fear circuitry makes it relatively easy for spontaneous movements to arise.

Primitive fears cannot be curbed by knowledge alone, however. No matter how many times you rationally explain to someone with a severe snake phobia that most snakes are harmless, they will still react fearfully to any snake. Reeducating the primitive fear system requires the repetitive techniques of behavior therapy, in which the patient is gradually exposed to the object of the fear with the aid of a therapist. In extreme cases, medications can also be used that affect the neurochemistry of the brain and allow the patient to more easily suppress irrational fears. Therapists are beginning to successfully apply new computer-aided techniques such as virtual reality in treating certain types of phobias. A patient with a fear of heights, for example, might wear virtual reality headgear that projects a realistic computer-generated image that gives him the impression of standing on the edge of a cliff. By experiencing this sense of heights in a safe, controlled setting, the patient will gradually habituate and become less fearful in real situations that once triggered anxiety.

Evidence also suggests that the fearfulness of children is strongly influenced by the attitudes of their parents. Harvard psychologist Jerome Kagan studied the children of mothers with severe phobias and anxiety disorders and noted that they tended to be much more fearful than normal. Other studies have noted that during a crisis, like the bombing of London by the Nazis, the calmness or fearfulness of children was closely related to the reaction of their parents.[8] Studies also indicate that young children with a stronger than normal tendency to be fearful seem better able to control their fear if their parents actively and firmly monitor their behavior and encourage them to be bolder. The underlying mechanism is not yet known. It may be that limits on behavior condition the limbic system to be less reactive, or build stronger ties between the frontal lobes and limbic system, allowing the rational fear system to more easily suppress the primitive fear system.[9]

The purpose of all techniques used in coping with fear is to control attention and behavior. If we become obsessed with a fear, as someone with claustrophobia becomes obsessed if they have to enter an elevator, then our free will is crippled. The goal is to maintain the mind's flexibility to focus attention on rationally solving problems in the face of the primitive fear system's attempt to seize control of attention and fixate on the primitive fight-or-flight response. This was what Chanya and Franklin Huddle were able to do during the hijacking of Flight 961. It allowed them to survive. The primitive fear of death dramatically increased their alertness and motivation, but did not overwhelm their rational consciousness. This is the difference between constructive and destructive fear. Our minds must always strike a balance between primitive fear and rational fear suppression. A certain amount of fear suppression allows us to maintain our optimism in the face of stress. But if we are too successful in shifting attention away from the source of fear—the problem of denial—we can ignore dangers and become overconfident.

The nature of the attention mechanism in the brain is still not well understood. It seems to involve areas of the frontal and parietal lobes, thalamus, and the limbic system. There may be at least two centers of attention, one controlled by the rational fear system and the other by primitive awareness. They seem to compete for the control of behavior. Let's say that on your way to work you were stopped for speeding. When you arrive at the office you immediately focus on the work at hand and seem to behave perfectly rationally. But in the back of your mind you are still brooding about the speeding ticket. Some slight annoyance can abruptly bring the upset over this event to the foreground of your mind. As a result, you snap at a colleague, for no good reason as far as he can see. Here, the rational attention system is trying to focus on your work while the primitive system continues to obsess about the fear and embarrassment caused by the traffic ticket.

Fear threads its way through human nature in extremely complex ways. It limits our ability to fulfill our potential by preventing us from doing things we might otherwise wish to do, such as speaking out in our own behalf. But fear also pressures us into accomplishing things we might otherwise not accomplish. The fear of criminal punishment and the disapproval of others are important elements in creating a civil society. The psychopath has no such fears. But these kinds of fears can also lead to oppression. Like fear, courage is a complex quality. For the soldier in battle, it means resisting the impulse to flee and, instead, fighting. The greater the risk of death, the more courage is required to suppress the primitive impulse to flee. Courage may also mean resisting the impulse to both fight and flee, as with those like Gandhi and Martin Luther King, Jr., who advocated nonviolence and passive resistance.

Courage suggests another fear, one that may be unique to our intensely self-aware species: the fear of self. Within the human brain, rational consciousness continually struggles with the primitive fear system for control of behavior. Rationally, we can never be completely certain about how we will behave, particularly in an extreme situation. Celebrated Navy fighter pilot Randy "Duke" Cunningham normally exudes supreme confidence. "I never went into the air thinking I would lose," he said. While flying his F-4 Phantom in Vietnam he wore a solid-black flight suit that made him stand out from the other American fliers. It was his way of using fear to intimidate enemy MIG pilots. "I wanted them to know who I was," he said, "and know that if they tangled with me they were going to die." Yet on the night before his first combat, he was so overcome with anxiety he couldn't sleep. He went out on the deck of the aircraft carrier and stared at the black water. "I kept thinking to myself, would I fight or would I run." The next morning he discovered that most of the other pilots had spent a similarly sleepless night. This battle for self-control between rational consciousness and primitive awareness, which contains our primal fears and desires, occurs in all of us. It is a moment-to-moment nightmare for those fighting alcoholism, drug addiction, and mental illness.

One way to cope with fear is by trying to tinker with our brains. Humans have always done this in a crude way by using drugs like alcohol, opium, and opium-derivatives such as heroin. But we have become much more sophisticated with the development of antianxiety medications like Valium and antidepressants like Prozac. Now, there is the possibility of using genetic engineering to manipulate the genetic components of fear, including memory. But all this raises many complex questions. In post-traumatic stress disorder, for example, some people who have survived major traumas like the brutality of combat or the horror of terrorism will be plagued for years by gruesome and violent memories in the form of flashbacks and nightmares. They are unable to get over their fear. New research on the nature of memory has discovered that long-term memories seem to be stored only if certain genes are turned on. If these genes are not activated, the memories are lost. This raises the possibility that we may one day have a morning-after pill for trauma victims that would, essentially, erase traumatic memories by preventing the brain from storing them in long-term memory. We are only beginning to grapple with the perplexing ethical questions raised by such a prospect. What about trauma victims who are witnesses to a crime? Witnesses to history? Don't we learn important lessons from surviving a traumatic event?

Despite the many dangers of the limbic system, we should think carefully about engineering primitive fear out of the human psyche. It is the primitive fear system that allows most of us to cope with the death sentence we live under in the form of our mortality. On a primitive level, we habituate to the idea of death. Our primitive awareness reasons that since I have never died, I never will. Although rationally we know this is false, it provides a certain basic level of emotional comfort. Our primitive fear system stereotypes death as something that happens to other people. It facilitates hope and optimism by allowing us to live the bulk of our lives relatively untroubled by the certainty of our own death. It is the source of our primitive vitality.

Yet primitive fear is a tremendously volatile emotion that can cause sudden and dangerous flare-ups of unrest and violence: spontaneous mobs, financial panics, warfare among nations. The concentration of fear that developed in the Cold War has produced a situation that still threatens the destruction of human civilization: nuclear war. Although the United States and Russia have announced with great fanfare that their nuclear missiles no longer target each other, it takes only a few keystrokes on a computer keyboard to reprogram the missiles to their old targets. And the danger of an accidental firing of nuclear missiles seems to be growing. With Russia's huge defense cutbacks and economic disarray, its missile forces are not being well-maintained and its system for warning of sneak attacks has become far less reliable because of lack of maintenance and the loss of key radar sites due to the breakup of the Soviet Union. This has led to an unstable situation in which an inappropriate fear response could spark a worldwide calamity.

Both the United States and Russian missile forces are capable of being launched in minutes, just as at the height of the Cold War. If faced with a sudden perception of danger in the form of an apparent attack, we still run the risk of fear fueled by incomplete or erroneous information overwhelming rational judgment. Once these missiles are launched they cannot be recalled, retargeted, or detonated in mid-flight. And it takes a surprisingly long time to exchange information on the so-called "hotline" between Washington and Moscow, even assuming that under conditions of extreme fear one side would believe the others' protestations of innocence.

In January 1995, for example, Norway launched a scientific rocket to study the earth's upper atmosphere. The Norwegians had notified Russia well in advance of the launching, but somehow the notification was lost in the bureaucracy. Russian early-warning radar spotted the missile and interpreted it as a possible opening salvo of an attack by a U.S. Trident submarine on Moscow. Russia's top military authorities notified President Boris Yeltsin that, if this was indeed an attack, he had ten minutes to decide whether to order a counterattack before Moscow would be destroyed. Sources in the intelligence community say that it took the Russians almost eight minutes of that time to decide that the rocket was indeed a harmless scientific experiment. Clearly, cultivating trust between nations is critical to reducing risks like this in the future. Constructive fear of accidental war may help the United States and Russia find ways, as some are advocating, to take their nuclear forces off this hair-trigger.

Basic research on the brain and the nature of fear clearly enhances our ability to survive, and must be a priority as we approach the new millennium. Our growing understanding of the brain's fear circuitry gives us the tools to intelligently manage our fears. Whether we will use those tools wisely is another question. We must constantly strive to find the right balance between the conscious and the subconscious, the rational and the irrational, the fear of death and the willingness to sacrifice.

We now better understand the wave of pleasure a teenage gang member feels after escaping unharmed from a shoot-out. But how to wean the teenager off violence remains a difficult problem. As Winston Churchill observed: "Nothing in life is so exhilarating as to be shot at without result."

Fear evolved as an early warning system for pain and death. This warning system has spurred us to move beyond much of the pain early humans took for granted. Our fear of death has goaded us into creating advanced technological societies that are healthier and more complex than early humans would have dreamed possible. Instead of living only into our twenties and thirties as they did, we can expect to live into our eighties, nineties, or even longer. Yet our global civilization has also created new threats to our survival that are fueled by our fearful nature: genocide, nuclear war, environmental catastrophe.

Now that we are moving beyond pain, should we think about moving beyond fear? In one sense, yes. We have the tools to transcend the destructive, irrational fears generated by the primitive fear system. But fear—and the satisfaction we experience in overcoming it—is also a constructive force. It helps give us our drive, dynamism, maturity, and depth. If we lived only for pleasure, we as a species might lapse into a contented, stultifying stagnation. To maintain our uniqueness we must retain our zest for challenging and overcoming fear itself.

{ Notes }

1 WHAT IS FEAR?

1. Charles Darwin, *The Expression of Emotions in Man and Animals* (New York: St. Martin's Press, 1979), pp. 308, 362. The text is based on the 1872 edition.
2. Joseph E. LeDoux, "Emotion, Memory and the Brain," *Scientific American* 270, 6 (June 1994), p. 56.
3. Antonio R. Damasio, *Descartes' Error* (New York: Grosset/Putnam, 1994), pp. 191–92, 195.
4. Darwin, *The Expression of Emotions in Man and Animals*, pp. 102, 291–92.
5. Chuck Yeager and Leo Janos, *Yeager: An Autobiography* (New York: Bantam Books, 1985), p. 67.
6. Ibid., p. 151.
7. Ibid., pp. 68–69.
8. S. J. Rachman, *Fear and Courage*, 2d ed. (New York: W. H. Freeman, 1990), p. 19.
9. John P. Wilson, Zev Harel, and Boaz Kahana, eds., *Human Adaptation to Extreme Stress* (New York: Plenum, 1988), p. 67.

2 THE SCIENCE OF FEAR

1. P. Rogers, "Men at Peace," *People* (Dec. 16, 1996), p. 46. *See also* Paul Reed, *Kontum Diary* (Arlington, Texas: Summit, 1996).

2. Michael Davis, "The Role of the Amygdala in Conditioned Fear," in John P. Aggleton, ed., *The Amygdala* (New York: Wiley-Liss, 1992), p. 284.

3. Jerome Kagan, *Galen's Prophecy* (New York: Basic Books, 1994), pp. 54–56, 105.

4. I interviewed Joseph LeDoux on January 28, 1998. *See also* Eric Halgren, "Emotional Neurophysiology of the Amygdala within the Context of Human Cognition," in Aggleton, ed., *The Amygdala*, p. 212. LeDoux discusses his research on the thalamus-amygdala circuit in Joseph LeDoux, *The Emotional Brain* (New York: Simon & Schuster, 1996), pp. 156–65.

5. Richard M. Restak, *The Modular Brain* (New York: Macmillan, 1994), pp. 147–48.

6. Ibid., p. 80.

7. Beata Jablonska, Malgorzata Kossut, and Jolanta Skangiel-Kramska, "Transient Increases of AMPA and NMDA Receptor Binding in the Barrel Cortex of Mice after Tactile Stimulation," *Neurobiology of Learning and Memory* 60 (1996), pp. 36–43.

8. Tim Beardsley, "Memories Are Made of . . ." *Scientific American* 276, 3 (March 1997), pp. 32–33.

9. Roberto Galvez, Michael H. Mesches, and James L. McGaugh, "Norepinephrine Release in the Amygdala in Response to Footshock Stimulation," *Neurobiology of Learning and Memory* 66 (1996), pp. 253–57.

10. Quoted in Jane Dodd and Vincent F. Castellucci, "Smell and Taste: The Chemical Senses," in Eric R. Kandel, James H. Schwartz, and Thomas M. Jessell, eds., *Principles of Neural Science*, 3d ed. (New York: Elsevier, 1991), p. 512.

11. Hadley Cantril, *The Invasion from Mars: A Study in the Psychology of Panic* (New York: Harper, 1966), pp. 4–5. This study of the famous Mercury Theater broadcast was originally published in 1940. Howard Koch's script for the broadcast, from which the following excerpts are taken, is on pp. 4–43.

12. Ibid., p. 190.

13. Ibid., pp. 123–24, 94.

14. Ibid., p. 51.

15. Ibid., p. 171.

16. Ibid., p. 142.

17. Rachman, *Fear and Courage*, 2d ed., p. 62.

18. P. A. Russell, "Fear-Evoking Stimuli," in W. Sluckin, ed., *Fear in Animals and Man* (New York: Van Nostrand Reinhold, 1979), p. 88.

3 MIND READING

1. Richard Restak, *The Brain* (New York: Bantam, 1984), p. 140.
2. Kagan, *Galen's Prophecy*, p. 291.
3. Richard Restak, *Brainscapes* (New York: Hyperion, 1995), p. 19.
4. Restak, *The Modular Brain*, p. 141.
5. Restak, *Brainscapes*, pp. 19–20.
6. Bernard T. Donovan, *Hormones and Human Behavior* (Cambridge: Cambridge University Press, 1985), pp. 166–67.
7. Andrew Mayes, "The Physiology of Fear and Anxiety," in Sluckin, ed., *Fear in Animals and Man*, p. 36.
8. Donovan, *Hormones and Human Behavior*, pp. 152, 166–67. *See also* S. Clare Stanford, "Monoamines in Response and Adaptation to Stress," in S. Clare Stanford and Peter Salmon, eds., *Stress: From Synapse to Syndrome* (San Diego: Harcourt Brace, 1993), pp. 283–85.
9. Richard Restak, *The Mind* (New York: Bantam, 1988), p. 285.
10. Restak, *The Brain*, p. 140.
11. V. H. Mark, F. R. Ervin, and W. H. Sweet, "Deep Temporal Lobe Stimulation in Man," in B. E. Eleftheriou, ed., *The Neurobiology of the Amygdala* (New York: Plenum, 1972), pp. 485–507. Mark's discussion of his research is from Restak, *The Mind*, p. 278–82.
12. Restak, *The Modular Brain*, p. 150.
13. Restak, *The Mind*, p. 284.
14. Daniel Goleman, *Emotional Intelligence* (New York: Bantam, 1995), p. 314.
15. Marcus E. Raichle, "Visualizing the Mind," *Scientific American* 270, 4 (April 1994), pp. 58–64. John C. Mazziotta, "Mapping Mental Illness," *Archives of General Psychiatry* 53 (July 1996), pp. 574–76. Restak, *Brainscapes*, pp. 80–90.
16. Halgren, "Emotional Neurophysiology of the Amygdala within the Context of Human Cognition," in Aggleton, ed., *The Amygdala*, pp. 196–99. William H. Calvin and George A. Ojemann, *Conversations with Neil's Brain* (New York: Addison-Wesley, 1994), pp.

75–76. George Ojemann, "Brain Mechanisms for Consciousness and Conscious Experience," *Canadian Psychology* 27 (1986), pp. 158–68.

17. Restak, *The Brain*, p. 305.

18. A. Ohman, "Fear and Anxiety as Emotional Phenomena," in M. Lewis and J. Haviland, eds., *Handbook of Emotions* (New York: Guilford, 1993), pp. 511–36.

4 WHY ARE WE AFRAID?

1. Damasio, *Descartes' Error*, p. 291. *See also* Thomas M. Jessell and Dennis D. Kelly, "Pain and Analgesia," in Kandel, et al., *Principles of Neural Science*, pp. 385–99.

2. Damasio, *Descartes' Error*, p. 265.

3. James L. Gould and Carol Grant Gould, *The Animal Mind* (New York: Scientific American Library, 1994), pp. 135–40.

4. Tim Jeal, *Livingstone* (New York: Putnam, 1973), pp. 58–59. David Livingstone is quoted in Jessell and Kelly, "Pain and Analgesia," in Kandel, et al., *Principles of Neural Science*, p. 398.

5. Rachman, *Fear and Courage*, 2d ed., p. 74. *See also* A. T. Carr, "The Psychopathology of Fear," in Sluckin, ed., *Fear in Animals and Man*, p. 216.

6. Rachman, *Fear and Courage*, 2d ed., p. 151.

7. Ibid., p. 74.

8. Ibid., pp. 352, 390.

9. Ibid., pp. 198, 204–5.

10. Richard Leakey, *The Origin of Humankind* (New York: Basic Books, 1994), pp. 13–16. *See also* Roger Lewin, *The Origin of Modern Humans* (New York: Scientific American Library, 1993), pp. 11–12.

11. Phillip V. Tobias, "The Brain of the First Hominids," in Jean-Pierre Changeux and Jean Chavaillon, eds., *Origins of the Human Brain* (New York: Oxford University Press, 1995), pp. 67–69.

12. Jared Diamond, *The Third Chimpanzee* (New York: HarperCollins, 1992), pp. 291–92.

13. Ibid., pp. 42–51. *See also* Leakey, *The Origin of Humankind*, pp. 54–55.

14. Lewin, *The Origin of Modern Humans*, pp. xi–xii.

15. Ian Tattersall, "Out of Africa Again . . . and Again?" *Scientific American* 276, 4 (April 1997), pp. 60–67.
16. Ibid., pp. 66–7.
17. Bernard Vandermeersch, "The First Modern Men," in Changeux and Chavaillon, eds., *Origins of the Human Brain*, pp. 3–10.
18. Tobias, "The Brain of the First Hominids," in Changeux and Chavaillon, eds., *Origins of the Human Brain*, pp. 61–83.
19. Lewin, *The Origin of Modern Humans*, p. 30. *See also* Leakey, *The Origin of Humankind*, p. 82.
20. William H. Calvin, "The Emergence of Intelligence," *Scientific American* 271, 4 (October 1994), pp. 101–7. *See also* William H. Calvin, *The River that Flows Uphill* (New York: Macmillan, 1986), pp. 309–12, 340–49.
21. Rachman, *Fear and Courage*, 2d ed., p. 191.
22. S. J. Rachman, *Fear and Courage* (New York: W. H. Freeman, 1978), p. 141.
23. Ibid., p. 85.
24. Rachman, *Fear and Courage*, 2d ed., p. 91.
25. Diamond, *The Third Chimpanzee*, pp. 223–25, 298.
26. Rachman, *Fear and Courage*, 2d ed., p. 93.
27. Michael Allaby, *Fire: The Vital Source of Energy* (New York: Facts on File, 1993), pp. 119–22.
28. Leslie Sue Lieberman, "Biocultural Consequences of Animals Versus Plants as Sources of Fat, Proteins, and Other Nutrients," in Marvin Harris and Eric B. Ross, eds., *Food and Evolution* (Philadelphia: Temple University Press, 1987), pp. 249–50.

5 CHILDREN AND FEAR

1. Dennis D. Kelly, "Disorders of Sleep and Consciousness," in Kandel, et al., *Principles of Neural Science*, p. 812.
2. Calvin, *The River that Flows Uphill*, p. 372.
3. Leakey, *The Origin of Humankind*, pp. 44–45. Calvin, *The River that Flows Uphill*, p. 297–98. Diamond, *The Third Chimpanzee*, p. 69.
4. Michael Gazzinaga and Joseph E. LeDoux, *The Integrated Mind* (New York: Plenum Press, 1978), pp. 158–59.
5. Rush W. Dozier, Jr., *Codes of Evolution* (New York: Crown, 1992), pp. 1–31.

6. Antonio R. Damasio and Hanna Damasio, "Cortical Systems for Retrieval of Concrete Knowledge: The Convergence Zone Framework," in Christof Koch and Joel L. Davis, eds., *Large-scale Neuronal Theories of the Brain* (Cambridge, Mass: MIT Press, 1994), pp. 63–64, 67.

7. Rhawn Joseph, *The Naked Neuron* (New York: Plenum, 1993), p. 10.

8. LeDoux, "Emotion, Memory and the Brain," *Scientific American*, p. 56.

9. Mayes, "The Physiology of Fear and Anxiety," in Sluckin, ed., *Fear in Animals and Man*, p. 33.

10. Donovan, *Hormones and Human Behavior*, pp. 175–76.

11. Gould and Gould, *The Animal Mind*, pp. 198–99.

12. Richard Mayeux and Eric Kandel, "Disorders of Language: The Aphasias," in Kandel, et al., *Principles of Neural Science*, p. 842.

13. Kagan, *Galen's Prophecy*, pp. 261–65.

14. Peter K. Smith, "The Ontogeny of Fear in Children," in Sluckin, ed., *Fear in Animals and Man*, pp. 164–98. Kagan, *Galen's Prophecy*, pp. 180–82.

15. Martin Tropp, *Images of Fear* (Jefferson, N.C.: McFarland, 1990), p. 4.

6 FEAR OF THE UNKNOWN

1. Sherwin B. Nuland, *How We Die: Reflections on Life's Final Chapter* (New York: Knopf, 1994).

2. Quoted in Irving Kupfermann, "Hypothalamus and Limbic System: Peptidergic Neurons, Homeostasis, and Emotional Behavior," in Kandel, et al., *Principles of Neural Science*, p. 735.

3. Béla Bohus and Jaap M. Koolhaas, "Stress and the Cardiovascular System: Central and Peripheral Physiological Mechanisms," in Stanford and Salmon, eds., *Stress: From Synapse to Syndrome*, pp. 81–84, 93.

4. Solomon H. Snyder, *Drugs and the Brain* (New York: Scientific American, 1986), pp. 190–93.

5. Abraham Pais, *A Tale of Two Continents: A Physicist's Life in a Turbulent World* (Princeton, N. J.: Princeton University Press,

1997). *See also* Abraham Pais, "Physics in Hiding," *Discover* 18, 4 (April 1997), pp. 68–75.

6. D. W. Cooke, R. L. Hodes, and P. J. Lang, "Preparedness and Phobia," *Journal of Abnormal Psychology* 95 (1986), pp. 195–207.

7. Mayes, "The Physiology of Fear and Anxiety," in Sluckin, ed., *Fear in Animals and Man*, p. 41. *See also* Larry Cahill, Bruce Prins, Michael Weber, and James L. McGaugh, "B-Adrenergic Activation and Memory for Emotional Events," *Nature* 371 (October 20, 1994), pp. 702–4.

8. Joseph, *The Naked Neuron*, pp. 79–80, 83–86, 88–90. Halgren, "Emotional Neurophysiology of the Amygdala within the Context of Human Cognition," in Aggleton, ed., *The Amygdala*, p. 208.

9. Goleman, *Emotional Intelligence*, pp. 90–95.

10. C. E. Osgood, "Studies on the Generality of Affective Meaning Systems," *American Psychologist* 17 (1962), pp. 10–28. Kagan, *Galen's Prophecy*, p. 57.

7 FROM ANXIETY TO TERROR

1. Niccolò Machiavelli, *The Prince*, Quentin Skinner and Russell Price, eds. (Cambridge: Cambridge University Press, 1988), p. 59. Machiavelli wrote this work in 1513.

2. Restak, *The Brain*, p. 26.

3. Machiavelli, *The Prince*, p. 59.

4. Gould and Gould, *The Animal Mind*, pp. 60–61. *See also* Russell, "Fear-Evoking Stimuli," in Sluckin, ed., *Fear in Animals and Man*, pp. 95–96, 153.

5. Gregg D. Jacobs and David Snyder, "Frontal Brain Asymmetry Predicts Affective Style in Men," *Behavioral Neuroscience* 110, 1 (1996), pp. 3–6.

6. Restak, *The Brain*, p. 138.

7. Damasio, *Descartes' Error*, pp. 1–51.

8. Raymond P. Kesner, "Learning and Memory in Rats with an Emphasis on the Role of the Amygdala," in Aggleton, ed., *The Amygdala*, p. 393.

9. Damasio, *Descartes' Error*, pp. 76–77.

10. Machiavelli, *The Prince*, p. 62.

8 THE PLEASURE OF FEAR

1. Leslie L. Iverson, "How Does Morphine Work?," *Nature* 383 (October 31, 1996), pp. 759–60.
2. Solomon H. Snyder, *Brainstorming* (Cambridge, Mass.: Harvard University Press, 1989), pp. 27–35, 65–66.
3. Ibid., p. 126.
4. Ibid., p. 142. *See also* Restak, *The Modular Brain*, p. 142.
5. Restak, *The Mind*, p. 110.
6. Quoted in Jessell and Kelly, "Pain and Analgesia," in Kandel, et al., *Principles of Neural Science*, p. 398.
7. Quoted in Restak, *The Mind*, p. 110.
8. Kagan, *Galen's Prophecy*, pp. 288–89.
9. Gould and Gould, *The Animal Mind*, pp. 1–2.
10. Daniel S. McGehee and Lorna W. Role, "Memories of Nicotine," *Nature* 383 (October 24, 1996), pp. 670–71. Richard Gray, Arun S. Rajan, Kristofer A. Radcliffe, Masuhide Yakehiro, and John A. Dani, "Hippocampal Synaptic Transmission Enhanced by Low Concentrations of Nicotine," *Nature* 383 (October 24, 1996), pp. 713–16.
11. Paul Rozin, "Psychobiological Perspectives on Food Preferences and Avoidances," in Harris and Ross, eds., *Food and Evolution*, pp. 189–91.
12. Pais, "Physics in Hiding," *Discover*, p. 68.
13. I interviewed James Cameron on February 3, 1998.
14. Tropp, *Images of Fear*, p. 219.
15. John Krakauer, *Into Thin Air: A Personal Account of the Mount Everest Disaster* (New York: Villard, 1997).

9 DISEASES OF FEAR

1. Kagan, *Galen's Prophecy*, pp. 235–36, 261–64.
2. Ibid., p. 53.
3. Restak, *The Mind*, p. 310.
4. Tropp, *Images of Fear*, pp. 114, 116.
5. Ibid., p. 113.
6. Ibid., p. 130.
7. Damasio, *Descartes' Error*, pp. 209, 211. *See also* A. R. Damasio,

D. Tranel, and H. Damasio, "Somatic Markers and the Guidance of Behavior: Theory and Preliminary Testing," in H. S. Levin, H. M. Eisenberg, and A. L. Benton, eds., *Frontal Lobe Function and Dysfunction* (New York: Oxford University Press, 1991), pp. 217–29.

8. Damasio, *Descartes' Error*, p. 208.
9. Restak, *The Mind*, pp. 308–9.
10. Eric Hollander, Concetta M. DeCaria, Anca Nitescu, Robert Gully, et al., "Serotonergic Function in Obsessive-Compulsive Disorder," in *Archives of General Psychiatry* 49 (January 1992), pp. 21–28.
11. Lewis R. Baxter, Jr., Michael E. Phelps, John C. Mazziotta, Barry H. Guze, Jeffrey M. Schwartz, and Carl E. Selin, "Local Cerebral Glucose Metabolic Rates in Obsessive-Compulsive Disorder," in *Archives of General Psychiatry* 44 (March 1987), pp. 211–18.
12. Raymond P. Kessner, "Learning and Memory in Rats with an Emphasis on the Role of the Amygdala," in Aggleton, ed., *The Amygdala*, pp. 380–81.
13. Eric R. Kandel, "Brain and Behavior," in Kandel, et al., *Principles of Neural Science*, pp. 14–15.
14. Lewis R. Baxter, Jr., Jeffrey M. Schwartz, Kenneth S. Bergman, Martin P. Szuba, et al., "Caudate Glucose Metabolic Rate Changes with Both Drug and Behavior Therapy for Obsessive-Compulsive Disorder," in *Archives of General Psychiatry* 49 (September 1992), pp. 681–94.
15. Rachman, *Fear and Courage*, 2d ed., p. 1.
16. Ibid., pp. 209–25.
17. Restak, *The Mind*, p. 308. Tropp, *Images of Fear*, p. 132. *See also* Daniel Farson, *Jack the Ripper* (London: Michael Smith, 1972).

10 THE PARADOX OF SUICIDE

1. Rachman, *Fear and Courage*, p. 147.
2. Joseph, *The Naked Neuron*, pp. 87–88.
3. Rachman, *Fear and Courage*, 2d ed., pp. 20–25.
4. Zahava Solomon, *Combat Stress Reaction* (New York: Plenum, 1993).
5. Arthur Kleinman and Alex Cohen, "Psychiatry's Global Challenge," *Scientific American* 276, 3 (March 1997), p. 88.

6. Quoted in Snyder, *Drugs and the Brain*, p. 92.
7. Quoted in Kagan, *Galen's Prophecy*, p. 288.
8. Erin D. Bigler, Ronald A. Yeo, and Eric Turkheimer, "Neuropsychological Functioning and Brain Imaging: Concluding Remarks and Synthesis," in Erin D. Bigler, Ronald A. Yeo, and Eric Turkheimer, eds., *Neuropsychological Function and Brain Imaging* (New York: Plenum, 1989), p. 343.
9. Kristin Leutwyler, "Suicide Prevention," *Scientific American* 276, 3 (March 1997), pp. 18–20.
10. Snyder, *Brainstorming*, p. 184.
11. Restak, *The Mind*, p. 191.
12. Quoted in Snyder, *Drugs and the Brain*, p. 93.
13. Damasio, *Descartes' Error*, p. 189.
14. Gazzinaga and LeDoux, *The Integrated Mind*, p. 143.
15. Ibid., p. 150.

11 FUSING MIND AND BODY

1. Joseph, *The Naked Neuron*, p. 88.
2. Ibid., p. 297.
3. Goleman, *Emotional Intelligence*, pp. 87–90.
4. Restak, *The Mind*, p. 191. *See also* Robert Ader, et al., *Psychoneuroimmunology*, 2d ed. (San Diego: Academic Press, 1990).
5. Donovan, *Hormones and Human Behavior*, p. 22.
6. Paul Glue, David Nutt, and Nick Coupland, "Stress and Psychiatric Disorder: Reconciling Social and Biological Approaches," in Stanford and Salmon, eds., *Stress: From Synapse to Syndrome*, pp. 63–64.
7. Restak, *The Mind*, pp. 160–61.
8. Ibid., p. 162.
9. Quoted in Restak, *The Mind*, p. 159.
10. Goleman, *Emotional Intelligence*, p. 167.
11. Quoted in Restak, *The Mind*, p. 159.
12. Mayes, "The Physiology of Fear and Anxiety," in Sluckin, ed., *Fear in Animals and Man*, pp. 34–35.
13. Diamond, *The Third Chimpanzee*, pp. 67, 71, 79–84, 95–99. *See also* Jared Diamond, *Why Sex Is Fun: The Evolution of Human Sexuality* (New York: Basic Books, 1997).

14. I interviewed Randy "Duke" Cunningham about his Vietnam experiences on January 28, 1998. Cunningham is now a member of Congress from Southern California, representing the northern section of San Diego County.

12 CONSCIOUS MASTERY

1. "Beating the Odds," *People* (Dec. 16, 1996), pp. 127–28.
2. Restak, *The Modular Brain*, p. 148.
3. Rachman, *Fear and Courage*, p. 245.
4. Joseph, *The Naked Neuron*, pp. 125–26.
5. Diamond, *The Third Chimpanzee*, pp. 307–8.
6. Restak, *The Modular Brain*, p. 171.
7. David G. Myers and Ed Diener, "The Pursuit of Happiness," *Scientific American* 274, 5 (May 1996), pp. 70–72.
8. Kagan, *Galen's Prophecy*, p. 356. Rachman, *Fear and Courage*, 2d ed., pp. 158, 186, 218–19, 230.
9. Kagan, *Galen's Prophecy*, pp. 204–7, 251–52.

{ Bibliography }

Ader, Robert, et al. *Psychoneuroimmunology.* 2d ed. San Diego: Academic Press, 1990.

Aggleton, John P., ed. *The Amygdala.* New York: Wiley-Liss, 1992.

Allaby, Michael. *Fire: The Vital Source of Energy.* New York: Facts on File, 1993.

Bigler, Erin D., Ronald A. Yeo, and Eric Turkheimer, eds. *Neuropsychological Function and Brain Imaging.* New York: Plenum, 1989.

Bryceson, Dave. *The Titanic Disaster: As Reported in the British National Press from April to July 1912.* New York: W. W. Norton, 1997.

Calvin, William H. *The Cerebral Code.* Cambridge, Mass.: MIT Press, 1996.

———. *The River that Flows Uphill.* New York: Macmillan, 1986.

Calvin, William H., and George A. Ojemann. *Conversations with Neil's Brain.* New York: Addison-Wesley, 1994.

Cantril, Hadley. *The Invasion from Mars: A Study in the Psychology of Panic.* New York: Harper, 1966.

Carson, Rachel. *Silent Spring.* Boston: Houghton Mifflin, 1962.

Changeux, Jean-Pierre. *Neuronal Man.* New York: Oxford University Press, 1986.

Changeux, Jean-Pierre, and Jean Chavaillon, eds. *Origins of the Human Brain.* New York: Oxford University Press, 1995.

Churchland, Patricia Smith. *Neurophilosophy.* Cambridge, Mass.: MIT Press, 1986.

Coles, Robert. *Children of Crisis.* Boston: Little, Brown, 1967.

Damasio, Antonio R. *Descartes' Error.* New York: Grosset/Putnam, 1994.

Darwin, Charles. *The Descent of Man.* London: Murray, 1871.

——. *On the Origin of Species by Means of Natural Selection.* London: Murray, 1859.

——. *The Expression of Emotions in Man and Animals.* New York: St. Martin's Press, 1979. The text is based on the 1872 edition.

Dawkins, Richard. *The Blind Watchmaker.* New York: W. W. Norton, 1987.

——. *The Selfish Gene.* New York: Oxford University Press, 1976.

De Becker, Gavin. *The Gift of Fear.* Boston: Little, Brown, 1997.

Dennett, Daniel C. *Consciousness Explained.* Boston: Little, Brown, 1991.

Diamond, Jared. *The Third Chimpanzee.* New York: HarperCollins, 1992.

——. *Why is Sex Fun: The Evolution of Human Sexuality.* New York: Basic Books, 1997.

Donovan, Bernard T. *Hormones and Human Behavior.* Cambridge: Cambridge University Press, 1985.

Dozier, Rush W., Jr. *Codes of Evolution.* New York: Crown, 1992.

Farson, Daniel. *Jack the Ripper.* London: Michael Smith, 1972.

Fritz, Charles E., and J. H. Mathewson. *Convergence Behavior in Disasters.* Washington, D.C.: National Academy of Sciences, 1957.

Gazzinaga, Michael S., and Joseph E. LeDoux. *The Integrated Mind.* New York: Plenum Press, 1978.

Goleman, Daniel. *Emotional Intelligence.* New York: Bantam, 1995.

Gould, James L., and Carol Grant Gould. *The Animal Mind.* New York: Scientific American, 1994.

Harris, Marvin, and Eric B. Ross, eds. *Food and Evolution.* Philadelphia: Temple University Press, 1987.

Harth, Erich. *The Creative Loop.* New York: Addison-Wesley, 1994.

Jamison, Kay Redfield. *Touched With Fire: Manic-depressive Illness and the Artistic Temperament.* New York: Free Press, 1993.

Jeal, Tim. *Livingstone.* New York: Putnam, 1973.

Johnson, George. *In the Palaces of Memory.* New York: Knopf, 1991.

Johnson-Laird, Philip N. *The Computer and the Mind.* Cambridge, Mass.: Harvard University Press, 1988.

Joseph, Rhawn. *The Naked Neuron.* New York: Plenum, 1993.

Kagan, Jerome. *Galen's Prophecy.* New York: BasicBooks, 1994.

Kalivas, Peter W., and Charles D. Barnes, eds. *Limbic Motor Circuits and Neuropsychiatry.* Boca Raton, Fla.: CRC Press, 1993.

Kandel, Eric R., ed. *Molecular Neurobiology in Neurology and Psychiatry.* New York: Raven Press, 1987.

Kandel, Eric R., James H. Schwartz, and Thomas M. Jessell, eds. *Principles of Neural Science.* 3d ed. New York: Elsevier, 1991.

Koch, Christof, and Joel L. Davis, eds. *Large-Scale Neuronal Theories of the Brain.* Cambridge, Mass.: MIT Press, 1994.

Krakauer, Jon. *Into Thin Air: A Personal Account of the Mount Everest Disaster.* New York: Villard, 1997.

Kulka, Richard A., William E. Schlenger, John A. Fairbank, Richard L. Hough, B. Kathleen Jordan, Charles Marmar, and Daniel S. Weiss. *Trauma and the Vietnam War Generation.* New York: Brunner/Mazel, 1990.

Leakey, Richard. *The Origin of Humankind.* New York: Basic Books, 1994.

LeDoux, Joseph. *The Emotional Brain.* New York: Simon & Schuster, 1996.

Levin, H. S., H. M. Eisenberg, and A. L. Benton, eds. *Frontal Lobe Function and Dysfunction.* New York: Oxford University Press, 1991.

Lewin, Roger. *The Origin of Modern Humans.* New York: Scientific American, 1993.

Llinás, Rodolfo R., ed. *The Biology of the Brain.* New York: W. H. Freeman, 1989.

———. *The Workings of the Brain.* New York: W. H. Freeman, 1990.

Lyons, John W. *Fire.* New York: Scientific American, 1985.

Machiavelli, Niccolò. *The Prince.* Quentin Skinner and Russell Price, eds. Cambridge: Cambridge University Press, 1988.

Mayr, Ernst. *The Growth of Biological Thought.* Cambridge, Mass: Harvard University Press, 1982.

McGaugh, James L., Federico Bermúdez-Rattoni, and Roberto A. Prado-Alcalá, eds. *Plasticity in the Central Nervous System.* Mahwah, N.J.: Lawrence Erlbaum, 1995.

McNamara, Robert S. with Brian VanDemark. *In Retrospect: The Tragedies and Lessons of Vietnam.* New York: Times Books, 1995.

McNeill, William H. *Plagues and People.* New York: Doubleday, 1976.

———. *The Rise of the West.* Chicago: University of Chicago Press, 1963.

Nader, Ralph. *Unsafe at any Speed: The Designed-in Dangers of the American Automobile.* New York: Grossman, 1965.

Nuland, Sherwin B. *How We Die: Reflections on Life's Final Chapter.* New York: Knopf, 1994.

Pais, Abraham. *A Tale of Two Continents: A Physicist's Life in a Turbulent World.* Princeton, N. J.: Princeton University Press, 1997.

Passingham, R. E. *The Frontal Lobes and Voluntary Action.* Oxford: Oxford University Press, 1993.

Pechura, Constance M., and Joseph B. Martin, eds. *Mapping the Brain and Its Functions.* Washington, D. C.: National Academy Press, 1991.

Rachman, S. J. *Fear and Courage.* San Francisco: W. H. Freeman, 1978.

———. *Fear and Courage.* 2d ed. New York: W. H. Freeman, 1990.

Reed, Paul. *Kontum Diary.* Arlington, Texas: Summit, 1996.

Restak, Richard M. *The Brain.* New York: Bantam, 1984.

———. *Brainscapes.* New York: Hyperion, 1995.

———. *The Mind.* New York: Bantam, 1988.

———. *The Modular Brain.* New York: Macmillan, 1994.

Rodgers, R. J., and S. J. Cooper. *Endorphins, Opiates and Behavioural Processes.* Chichester, U.K.: John Wiley, 1988.

Shepherd, Gordon M., ed. *The Synaptic Organization of the Brain.* 3d ed. New York: Oxford University Press, 1990.

Sluckin, W. *Fear in Animals and Man.* New York: Van Nostrand Reinhold, 1979.

Snyder, Solomon H. *Brainstorming.* Cambridge, Mass.: Harvard University Press, 1989.

———. *Drugs and the Brain.* New York: Scientific American, 1986.

Solomon, Zahava. *Combat Stress Reaction.* New York: Plenum, 1993.

Stanford, S. Clare, and Peter Salmon. *Stress: From Synapse to Syndrome.* San Diego: Academic Press, 1993.

Tropp, Martin. *Images of Fear.* Jefferson, N. C.: McFarland, 1990.

Trotti, John. *Phantom over Vietnam.* Novato, Cal.: Presidio Press, 1984.

Warburton, David M. *Brain, Behavior and Drugs.* New York: John Wiley, 1975.

Watkins, J. C., and G. L. Collinridge, eds. *The NMDA Receptor.* New York: Oxford University Press, 1989.

Wilson, John P., Zev Harel, and Boaz Kahana. *Human Adaptation to Extreme Stress.* New York: Plenum, 1988.

Wolfenstein, Martha. *Disaster: A Psychological Essay.* Glencoe, Ill.: The Free Press, 1957.

Yeager, Chuck, and Leo Janos. *Yeager: An Autobiography.* New York: Bantam, 1985.

{ Index }

accidents. *See* automobile accidents
acetylcholine, 34, 132, 164, 168
Acheulean tools, 93, 98
action films, 169-170
action potentials, 48
addiction
    to pleasure of fear, 172
    theories of, 162, 163
Ader, Robert, 210
adrenal glands, 34, 44
adrenaline, 34, 45
    experiment with, 122-123
    increased physical strength from, 67
    linked to anxiety and panic, 63
advanced cortical reasoning, 106-107,
        126, 152, 158
    detailed categorizing in, 116-118,
        122
Africa
    evolution of walking apes in, 86-87,
        89-93, 95, 96
    humans' migration out of, 93-95, 99
    new Paleolithic technology in, 99
African-Americans, nonviolent
        resistance by, 153, 237
Agee, James, 111

aggression. *See* anger
agoraphobia, 83, 102-103, 190
agriculture, cooking and rise of, 109
AIDS, fear of, 130, 149
airplanes
    bombing by, 23-24
    dogfights by, 19, 22, 217
    fear of crashes in, 18-21
    hijacking of, 221-226
    pilots' attitude in disasters of, 19-20
    test-flying of, 20, 22-23
alarm calls
    by animals, 56
    as method of communication, 148
    of protest movements, 236-237
    as signaling threat to survival, 152,
        224
alcohol
    fear reduced by, 165
    recklessness and violence from, 68
Alien series, 170
Allen, Woody, 154
American Revolution, 150
AMPA receptors, 49
Amsterdam (Netherlands), Pais in
        hiding in, 134-138